# LYRICS OF MY LIFE

## BEN MARNEY

# LYRICS OF MY LIFE

## AUTOBIOGRAPHICAL SHORT STORIES

Written by
Ben Marney
Copyright © 2017 by Ben Marney
Published by Ben Marney Books
**ISBN:** 9781521430866
www.benmarneybooks.com

# DEDICATION

*For Mom, Dad, Ron, John Sivil, Sam and Elaine
and of course, Dana*

# AUTHOR'S NOTE

I am not a star, not a celebrity and certainly not famous. So why would I spend the uncountable, lonely hours it took to write this autobiography?

Honestly, I did it for two reasons. Number one, because my friends who know me well have been asking me to write it for years.

Number two, because I must admit, my life has been an amazing and interesting journey, with so many ups and downs it sounds more like fiction than truth.

When I was 15, I actually hit that grand slam at the bottom of the ninth with the bases loaded, when we were down by three and the count was 2 strikes and three balls. In my 20's and 30's, with my beautiful wife Dana by my side, we performed in or traveled through all 50 of the United States. After that, we traveled and performed literally around the world...

We've walked the tiny winding streets of Zanzibar off the east coast of Africa; jogged the snow packed streets of Juneau, Alaska; ran through the back alleys of Hong Kong, China; and whisked through the crowded streets of Cochin, India in the back of a three-wheeled scooter taxi on the way to see a twenty-five hundred year old Buddhist temple.

We've ridden a train through the beautiful countryside of Sri Lanka and rode on the back of an elephant in Candidasa; scuba dived an ancient sunken ship off the island of Bali; bought hand painted silk art on the streets of Bombay, India and strolled along the breathtakingly beautiful beaches of the Seychelle Islands that some believe was the Garden Of Eden.

We've stood in the center of Tiananmen Square and walked the ancient paths through the Forbidden City in Beijing, China.

Also, we've traded tequila shots with Hank Williams Jr. in the back of his million-dollar tour bus, got a contact high in Willie's, smoked cigars in Waylon's and actually lent my Cadillac for two days to Kenny Rogers.

We have performed my original songs to crowds of hundreds, to crowds of thousands, and even over thirty thousand once, backed up by the Jackson Symphony Orchestra.

And most importantly, we are personal friends of Mickey Mouse.


Hopefully, we're not done yet...

# PROLOGUE

Until I was nine years old I was convinced that I was adopted. This was a result of my older brother Ronald Dean (from age 5) constantly pointing out the reasons why, along with the terrifying caveat of, "Benny, If you keep screwing up, Dad will just take you back to the orphanage where he found you."

OK, I'll admit I wasn't the crispiest chip in the bag back then, but Ron did have a strong argument.

I had white hair until I was about 8 years old. Not blonde, but white. My dad's nickname for me back then was Cotton. I had (and still do) have blue eyes and a light complexion.

My mother was part Cherokee Indian and had black hair, dark brown eyes and an olive complexion. In her younger pictures she looks like an Indian squaw. My father had dark brown eyes, dark brown hair and always appeared to be dark complected. My brother Ron took after my mother; black hair, dark brown eyes and olive skin.

"Just look in the mirror," Ron would say, "you don't even look like us." He was right, so I swallowed it hook, line and sinker for years.

But what I didn't realize was that my father wasn't dark complected; he worked in the sun most of the time and was always tan. Also, my mother's mother, Nova (whose hair was prematurely gray ) used to have light brown (almost blonde) hair, was like complected and had blue eyes. You don't notice those sort of things when you're a little kid.

One day when I was 9, I did something pretty bad, I don't remember what it was now, but my dad overheard my brother telling me the orphan story again and finally set me straight... and my brother had trouble sitting down for about a week after that.

That experience was one of my first lessons in life I've never forgotten. Of course, I was skeptical of anything my brother told me after that, but the biggest thing I learned was to figure things out for myself, not to get brainwashed and simply go along with popular opinion, but to instead look at all the facts before I made up my mind.

That's why I've always turned left when everybody was going right, or right when they went left, and why I took a different path to walk down with my life.

That path wasn't always clear. Many times I've had to climb over rocks and boulders and pull the fallen trees out of my way to get where I was going, but as a result, I've lived a life most folks only dream about.

Along this crook-ed fork in the road I chose for my life, I survived by remembering and relying on the lessons I learned (usually the hard way) as I stumbled along.


THIS BOOK IS a collection of short stories of some of those hard learned lessons.

# LYRIC OF MY LIFE

## AUTOBIOGRAPHICAL SHORT STORIES

# 1

# CHILI CHEESEBURGERS

**M**y father taught high school auto mechanics for 30 years. On the days my old clunker of a car wouldn't start, which was often, I'd catch a ride to school with him. On one of those days, for some reason, school had let out early (at noon) and on the ride home, Dad told me he had to drive to Baytown to cash a check, so I rode there with him.

To make extra money on the side, my father was what he called a horse trader. He didn't actually trade horses, but my old man was a master at wheeling and dealing. He would buy anything; old cars, boats, watches, diamond rings, shotguns, RV's, deer rifles... nothing was off limits. He was always saying that everything he owned was for sale except for his wife and kids, but he would be open to renting out his kids if the price was right. Through all of his wheeling and dealing somehow he always made a profit. It was amazing to watch him negotiate these deals and he loved doing it.

One of my most prized possessions is one of his old business cards. On the front under his name and phone number it says, "We buy junk!" On the back it says, "Fine merchandise for sale!"

We were driving to Baytown that day to cash a check he'd gotten on one of his "horse trades." He didn't say it, but I figured he was driving all that way so he could get the cash in his pocket before the person who had bought some of his "fine merchandise" had the chance to change their minds and stopped payment on the check.

My father was the most honest man I've ever known, except when it came to a trade. Half the fun he had with all this horse trading was as he put it, "Taking someone's britches off." He had a regular group of guys he dealt with all the time he called his "trading buddies" and they were constantly trying to get the better of each other.

At the time, we lived in North Shore Texas, a small suburb of Houston. Baytown was only about 20 miles east, but with all the traffic it took us 45 minutes to make it to the bank.

At the drive up window, the young teller took the check and came back with the cash in a small envelope. Dad stuffed it in his pocket and drove off. It was now about 2:30pm and the Houston traffic was beginning to back up. We'd been driving for about 40 minutes, only a few miles away from our exit, when the traffic suddenly came to a complete stop. A wreck, construction or whatever had blocked the highway. It was something that happened all the time on the Houston freeways that you had to get used to, so my father just put his truck in park and took the time to count the money in the envelope.

"Shit!" He said when he finished his count.

"She short change you?" I asked.

He shook his head and said, "No, she gave me too much."

When the traffic began to move he took the next exit and turned around. An hour later we parked in front of the bank and walked inside.

It took him a minute to find the young teller who had made the mistake. He walked up to her window and said, "Young lady, I think you made a mistake when you cashed my check. You gave me 47.50."

She smiled and said, "Oh I'm sorry, did I miscount? How much was the check for?"

I'll never, for as long as I live, forget what he said next.

"It was for 46.50, you gave me a dollar too much."

I couldn't believe that he'd fought that bumper to bumper traffic for almost an hour driving back to that bank, just to give her back one dollar.

That was my father. He'd take your britches completely off in a horse trade, making you drop the price to practically nothing, but if you gave him 10 cents too much, he'd drive a hundred miles to give it back to you.

Dad believed that whatever money you had, if you worked for it fair and square, you could keep it, but if it wasn't yours, no matter how you got it, you had to give it back. Like I said, he was the most honest man I've ever met.

Dad used to take his pocket change and drop it into a red canvas bank sack every night before he went to bed. I'd seen him do it a thousand times. After a while that sack would get almost full.

When I was a teenager, I was a hungry kid and ate like a horse. I never missed breakfast, lunch or dinner and snacked all day in between. As crazy as it sounds, most nights my best friend John Sivil would be at our house at dinner time and would eat with us, then we'd go over to his house and I'd eat dinner again, with him and his family.

John and I were eating machines, but both of us were athletes with super charged metabolisms and no matter how much we ate, we never gained a pound.

One day, John and I were walking home from school and saw a big sign on the Mr. Hamburger marquee that said "chili cheeseburger just 26 cents."

We dug in our pockets but came up 15 cents short. Then I remembered my dad's change sack and figured he'd never miss 15 cents.

I can't tell you how much I loved and still love chili cheeseburgers. I love them almost as much as I like chocolate. Well, almost.

So, for almost 2 months, I would sneak into dad's room and get 52 cents out of his change sack, stop by Mr. Hamburger's after school and chow down on my two chili cheeseburgers. Oh yes... life was good in those days.

I was lying on my bed practicing my guitar when I heard my father say, "Ronald Dean, have you gotten some of my change out of this sack?"

Ron was working as a soda jerk at the local drug store at that time and said, "No dad, I have my own money."

"Dorothy Lee," he yelled. "You been dipping into my change?"

She walked into the bedroom and said, "No, is some missing?"

Dad walked into my bedroom and asked, "Benny Max, have you been getting money out of this sack?"

In a million years I wouldn't have thought that he had actually counted all that change. Through the process of elimination, dad knew he'd come down to the only possible suspect... me.

Trying my best to look innocent, I looked up at him and said, "No dad, it wasn't me."

He frowned, then stood there looking at me for a long time.

"Benny Max," he said, "there are two kinds of people I hate in this world, a thief and a liar. You just proved to me that you are both. You are no son of mine." Then he walked out.

For almost three weeks, he wouldn't even look at me. When he saw me coming down the hall, he would turn and walk the other way. He never spoke a word and it was killing me. I felt ashamed of myself for what I'd done, lower than a snake in the grass, but couldn't figure out anyway to make up for it.

This went on for almost a month. Then one day my father walked into my room and sat on the edge of my bed.

He stared at me with this very disappointed look on his face. "I guess this must be my fault. I've tried my best to teach you right from wrong, but somehow I failed, and I wanted to tell you that I'm sorry I did such a bad job as a father."

To be honest, every day for the last month I'd been expecting a visit like this, but thought it would be for a spanking. It was rare for my father to spank me, but he believed in corporal punishment and knew how to use his belt when it was necessary. But he was there not to spank me, but to apologize for not being a good father.

If I could have crawled under a rock I would have, because I felt about that small. I was the thief and liar, but he was taking all the blame for it. At that moment, I would have given anything if he would have just spanked me, grounded me or taken away my guitar for what I'd done... Anything else, but look at me with all that disappointment in his eyes. I just wanted to die.

"Son, there's just nothing worse than being a thief and a liar," He said. "All a man really has in his life is his integrity. If you don't have that, you have nothing. If you don't earn it, it's not yours, and nothing good will ever come from it. And no matter how hard it may be, or what may come from it, you must always tell the truth. Always, with no exceptions, you have to tell the truth about anything you've done. Do you understand how important that is?"

I was crying. "Yes sir. I'm so sorry."

Then he smiled and said, "Benny, you're gonna make a lot of mistakes in your life. That's how you learn. I've made a million of them. But when you do make a mistake, no matter how bad you may have messed up, always hold up your hand high and say I did that." Then he hugged me and told me that I was forgiven. I wanted to jump up and dance.

On his way out, he turned back around and asked, "What did you spend all that money on?"

I looked up at him and said, "Chili cheeseburgers."

I've never forgotten that lesson and have never stolen anything else. And sometimes to my own detriment, I always tell the truth.

MY FATHER TOLD this story and laughed about it for years. What can I say... I was hungry.

# 2

# 9.9 BAREFOOT ON THE GRASS

I've always been a bit too serious, cautious and reserved; never the life of the party. My whole life I've envied those who could go a little crazy and just have a blast. I have a friend, Steve Knight, who has always been that way and has some of the funniest stories you'll ever hear. Like the time he had a bit too much to drink in Jackson, Mississippi and somehow woke up (actually sobered up) the next day and found himself in New York City. In his drunken state he had driven to the airport, walked up to the gate and said, "When's your next flight and where's it going."

My wife Dana and I were the on air television hosts of the United Cerebral Palsy Telethon in Jackson, Mississippi for 5 years. During the show, many local community leaders would come on as guest to show their support. When we would break and switch back to the National Broadcast, I had the chance to have coffee and get to know some of those important people.

I need to preface this by telling you that a few months earlier I'd had my 30th birthday and it had been quite the event. In those days I owned the hottest nightclub in the State called, Marney's and held my birthday party on stage celebrating with 500 of my fans and closest friends. It was one of the rare times of my life that I was actually trying to not be so serious and have fun.

The party had started early. I'd rented three limousines, filled them full of my friends, including my older brother Ron and we had driven around all day drinking (Yep, I was actually drinking Champagne that day) and having fun doing silly things like riding go carts, electronic bulls and raising a little hell.

Riding in the limousine with me was one of my dearest friends, Herman Fillingane. He was a Jackson police officer; a great cop, highly decorated, but at the same time one of those people I envy who is completely nuts.

That year at the telethon one of my guests was the Jackson Chief of Police. On the network break we grabbed some coffee and sat down together in the studio.

"We have a mutual friend," I told him.

"Really?," He said. "Whose that?"

"Herman Fillingane, he's one of your officers," I said.

The Chief thought for a moment, then his expression changed with recognition.

He started smiling and said, "It was 'YOUR' birthday."

"What?" I said confused.

He began to chuckle and said, "I'm in my office and get a call from an irate citizen telling me something she'd seen. It sounded unbelievable so I tracked down the officer involved and called him in to explain it to me. I was furious. Did you really do a donut in a parking lot in a marked police car dressed in a cowboy hat, with your shirt unbuttoned holding a bottle of Jack Daniels in your hand?"

He looked at me still laughing, "He was in some deep shit, but do you know what he said to me?"

Knowing Herman like I did, there was no telling what he said, "I have no idea. What'd he say?"

The Chief smiled and said, "Now understand this guy was standing there on the carpet talking to his boss. Herman did you do this?" I asked him.

"Yes sir I think I did 'three' donuts." He said.

"Why in the hell would you do that?"

The Chief looked at me and laughed. "That idiot looked me in the eye and said... 'because it was Ben's Birthday!'"

We laughed for a long time, then he said, "If he wasn't such a great officer I would have fired him on the spot, but how do you stay mad at someone like that?"

The point of the story is... even at my own birthday party, Herman had more fun than me.

I've had many years to contemplate why I've never been able to just let lose and be nuts. I'm pretty sure it comes from my childhood.

My brother Ron was five and a half years older in age, but in intellect it was more like 20. In reality, I grew up with two male parenting influences; my father and my brother.

Ron was a brilliant guy. His IQ was off the charts and as a result he became very rich and successful in his life, but like me, somewhere along the way he became too serious, especially when he was a teenager. All he cared about was making good grades, being in the honor society and graduating at the top of his class. He was always reading something. Seriously that's all he ever did.

I was the exact opposite. When I was a kid, I hated reading and could care less about my grades. As long as I passed I was happy, and that drove Ron crazy.

From about 5 years old he would force me to read and started teaching me math. I hated it, but he was bigger than me and easily angered. If I acted up, he would grab me and give me a frog on my arm. If you aren't familiar with frogging that's when you punch someone on their arm so hard a knot rises up. It hurts like hell.

All Ron's extra tutoring apparently sunk in somehow, because when I started the 5th grade the teacher gave me a test and soon I was moved up a grade. So, although his teaching techniques came with frogs, it was effective.

When he wasn't making me study, the one thing he just couldn't stand was when I acted like a little kid. Unfortunately, I "was" a little kid, so I acted that way a lot.

When I did my inevitable little kid thing, he would calmly give me a warning to cut it out, but of course, that just made me do it more. Usually after two, maybe three of his warnings he would drop his book and lunge at me. I eventually got wise to him and would jump out of his reach and take off running. He had amazing endurance and always wore me down, catching me down the block and passing out his dreaded frogs.

Through the years, dodging my mother's spatulas, brooms or anything else she could find to swing at me, and running for my life from my enraged brother, I developed super quick reflexes and speed.

Having that ability led me to learn one of the most important lessons of my life.

When I was 12 years old, Ron asked me what time I ran the 100 yard dash in.

"Oh, I don't know. I think maybe 11.7 or something," I answered.

"What?" He said stunned, "I can run an 11 flat and I can't catch you anymore. You can run that fast backwards."

"I out run everyone else," I said.

His face turned red––it did that a lot when he was talking to me in those days. "Benny, outrunning everybody else is not the point. If you'd just, for once in your life actually apply yourself and give 100% there's no telling how fast you could run it!"

I just shrugged, "All the coaches seem to think I'm fast enough."

By that time, Ron had figured me out pretty well and knew I was motivated by money; always mowing people's grass and washing cars to earn money for new guitar equipment and my beloved chili cheese-burgers.

The next day, Ron walked into my room and bounced something off my head. It was a stack of one dollar bills.

"What's that for?" I asked.

He smiled and said, "That's yours, but you'll have to earn it first."

"Doing what?"

"Doing something you've never done in your life; actually applying yourself and giving 100% on something. That's 50 crisp new one dollar bills. All you have to do is, sometime this year, bring me a letter from your coach that says you ran 100 yards under 10 and a half seconds, and it's all yours."

The next day I handed him a letter that said I'd ran a 9.9 bare-footed on the grass from a standing start. For the rest of the year I was in chili cheeseburger heaven.

I was only in the 8th grade, but after that I started competing in the 9th grade track meets and beat them all. I eventually broke all our high school records when I ran a 9.6 at a regional meet. That day I met the track coach from Rice University who told me if I just didn't get any slower I could get a full ride track scholarship at Rice.

But my true epiphany of realizing the benefits of giving 100 percent came when we moved to Huntsville, Texas so my father could take some college courses for his teaching degree.

My football coaches at Galena Park dropped by our house and tearfully handed me a letter the day before we moved. They made me promise I wouldn't read it and told me to give it to the head coach in Huntsville when I got there.

I'd honestly forgotten about the letter until I'd already signed up for the team and had been issued my equipment. Galena Park was a large 4A school with a good sports budget. Huntsville was a much smaller, poorer school, so I wasn't used to being issued old ragged equipment, but I didn't complain and put it on.

On my way to the practice field I remembered the letter and handed it to the coach and ran out. A few minutes later they yelled at me and took me back inside and issued me some brand new equipment.

When I had changed and ran back out to the field, they lined us all up on the goal line and told us they were going to clock us running the length of the field. I ran a 10 flat in full pads and had smoked them all by 20 yards. Four days later we played our first game against Conroe, and playing in my new first string running back position, I ran 5 touchdowns.

Although I'd just moved there, the next week everyone seemed to know my name. Suddenly I was Mr. Popular and I was soon elected Vice President of our class.

Ever since then, I have become absolutely obsessed to give my all; 100% to anything I did.

Although my wife tells me that sometimes I get a bit too obsessed with it, but putting 100% of my heart and soul into my projects has proven to be a winning combination for me.

There is no doubt in my mind it all started with my brother's insistence to apply myself...


AND THAT 9.9 HUNDRED, barefoot on the grass.

# 3

# BLACK AND GOLD REVIEW

A s I write this book, in between chapters, I am rehearsing for my next music gig. My wife and I are the entertainment for a Christmas party for the doctors and staff of the Florida Hospital--Something we've done for years.

Earlier this year, Dana and I traveled over 50,000 air miles performing our show on cruise ships literally around the world. From Shanghai, China, to Cape Town, South Africa. This will mark the 44th year Dana and I have performed together. It will also mark the 52nd year I've been a musician and singer. When I think about that, it seems impossible, because wasn't it just a few years ago that I learned how to play the guitar and formed my first band?

Both of my grandfathers died before I was 6 years old, so I don't have many memories of them. The only vivid memory I have of my father's father, Benjamin Franklin Marney (I was named after him), is one of me sitting on his lap, with him bouncing me on his knee to music. I can still remember the song. It was called "Shake Rattle and Roll." I can remember looking up at him watching him sing along to the song.

Although he was only in his mid 50's at this time he had mysteriously lost his eyesight. Dad said the doctors back then had no real idea why, but he was blind and had on a pair of dark sunglasses, looking a little like Ray Charles. I think I was about 4 or 5, but can still see and hear him rocking back and forth singing and saying, "Shake Rattle and Roll. Come on, sing with me Benny, I love this song!."

I sadly have no memory of my mother's father Jessie, but understand he was quite a fiddle player. Back in those days, especially in West Texas, most people lived on farms and ranches. For entertainment, they would pick someone's house and actually take all the furniture out of the living room and my mother, father and grandfather Jessie would provide the music for the dance. My mother sang and played guitar and mandolin. My father played guitar, mandolin and fiddle. My grandfather Jessie only played the fiddle, but from what I've heard from my aunts and uncles, he was a great musician.

When I got old enough to travel on my own (about 12), my parents would ship me off to West Texas for a few weeks in the summers to visit my Grandmothers. When I stayed with my father's mother, Alice Cornelia Marney, she always made me one of her famous chocolate cakes and each night she would sit on her hand made padded pickle barrel cover, behind her old upright grand piano and sing and play for me. She only knew Christian hymns and couldn't sing very well, but seemed to love playing and singing them for me. Every time I hear the Bill Withers song, "Grandma's Hands" I am always taken back to those nights, watching her old arthritic, wrinkled hands moving across those keys.

I am old enough to have lived through segregation. Galena Park was located along the Houston ship channel. Our house was only about two miles from it. In those days no one had ever heard the word's environmental protection and the ship channel was full of nasty gunky crap. We used to think it was fun to see how far we could chuck rocks into it. It was easy to see who won the contest, because the rocks didn't sink, they just plopped on top of the gunk. To keep the shipping lanes clear, they pumped that nasty gunk into a landfill located between Galena Park and Fidelity Mainor, the segregated black community. This landfill was about 400 yards wide and ran north for about 15 miles to Jacinto City.

When it was first pumped in, it was just a soft mud consistency, but after a few months, it would harden enough to actually walk on. However, it had some areas that never really solidified, so you had to be very careful or you'd get stuck and possibly brake through and get sucked under. Kind of like quick sand in all the Tarzan movies. Now understand this is not scientific, geological fact, but when you're 8 years old and your best friend, John Sivil tells you this, well then you know it had to be true. We spent many hours exploring that dangerous quicksand filled terrain. I did lose a shoe one time, but somehow always avoided the dreaded quicksand. This landfill was probably toxic, radio active or even worse, but it was our favorite playground.

One Saturday evening in the summer (it was daylight savings time, so it was still light outside), right in the middle of one of our safaris on the hunt for zebras, lions or tigers, I heard music, so I followed the sound. It was coming from a small white church on the edge of the landfill where Fidelity Mainor began.

I'd never heard music like it before, so John and I sat down and listened. It was a black church and we could see the parishioners through the windows. Everyone inside was dancing and singing, rocking out to the lord.

John thought it was funny, but that music stirred something inside me. Almost every Saturday night after that, I walked across the landfill to that church, laid in the grass and listened to the music. I did it for years.

I guess someone had seen me there, because one night the preacher, dressed in this purple and gold robe came outside and invited me in. When we walked in everyone started clapping and hugging me.

Until we moved from Galena Park, when I was 13, Every Saturday night I was usually there, dancing and singing along and it's where my love for gospel music comes from.

My father told me that when I was only 5 I picked up his guitar and apparently knew how to hold it and picked out a tune on the strings. So, I guess I could say I've been playing guitar since I was 5 years old, but I actually didn't know how to play until I was about twelve.

I can't explain why I did it this way, but it's all true. My mother was a cosmetologist and had a beauty shop in our garage. We had one of those large TV, stereo, record player cabinets in our living room. When my father was at work and my mother was fixing hair in her shop, I would put on my "Learn to play guitar with the Ventures" album and crank up the volume. Then (and this is the part, I can't explain) would go back to my bedroom, close the door and practice, listening to the instructions from the blaring stereo through the walls.

Every hour or so my mother would come in the house and scream at me at the top of her lungs to turn down the music, and then she would walk into the living room and turn it down. When she'd leave, I'd turn it up again and resume my practice behind the closed door in my room. Why I just didn't take my guitar into the living room and practice is one of the mysteries of my life. The only thing I can think of is that I was too shy to let anyone know what I was doing. After a lot of practice and screaming fits from my mother, I eventually got the hang of it and didn't need the Ventures' help anymore. So, in secret I practiced and practiced and got pretty good.

One day at school a friend of mine brought his new guitar. It was just laying in the case, so I picked it up and started playing it.

When he realized I could play, he said, "We ought to start a band." So we did.

It's been too many years to remember all of their names, but my friend with the guitar was Randy Walters and the drummer was Edward Serenil. We had a bass player and a keyboard player too. I played rhythm guitar and sang lead. The name of the band was "Poverty's Children," which wasn't too far from the truth.

The year we formed the band was also my first year to sing in the school choir and where I found out I could sing. Our choir director's name was M.J. Stockton and I credit him for my entire music career. He used to walk up and down the risers as he directed us, occasionally stopping in front of a student to listen. It used to make me real nervous when he would stop and listen to me, but one day after choir practice he asked me to stay late so he could talk to me.

"Benny, I've been listening to you," he said."And you can sing."

It was one of those, "awww shucks" moments, and I didn't know what to say.

"I'm serious Benny, you have a really nice voice. Would you mind if I gave you some solos in our performances?"

I'm sure Mr. Stockton didn't realize it then, but his words to a shy, very unconfident kid, turned out to be golden. He was the first person to ever tell me that I could sing, and the confidence he gave me that day was the first brick in the foundation of my musical career.

A few months later sitting around the dinner table I said, "My band is playing in the Black and Gold Review Friday and I'd like all you to come."

It was the biggest show our school produced each year and was called that because Black and Gold were our school colors.

My brother Ron busted out laughing, "You are going to be in the Black and Gold Review? Doing what, raising up the curtain?"

"It's not just me, it's my band." I said.

My dad held up his hand, "Wait. What band? What are you talking about?"

"My band, Poverty's Children." I said.

"What do you do in this band?" My mother asked.

Shyly I said, "Play guitar and sing."

My father almost did a spit take, "You play guitar? When did you learn to play a guitar? How did you learn that?"

When Friday night came and my parents and brother (sitting in the second row) heard me play and sing for the first time they almost fainted. My tender hearted father instantly started crying, my mother just sat there with her mouth open and my brother started yelling!

Poverty's Children - That's me in the middle!

The next week my father traded for my first real electric guitar; a black Les Paul Custom. He only had about $100.00 in it. At that time, I only weighed about 130 lbs soaking wet and that Les Paul felt like it weighed 50, so I asked dad to trade it for a lighter one.

I still have that much lighter Epiphone hollow body guitar in my safe, but will always regret getting dad to trade away that 1952 Les Paul. It actually only weighed about 9 lbs and today would be worth about $75,000.

After I moved away to Huntsville, Poverty's Children lasted a few more months, but eventually the guys stopped playing. I hooked up with some new musicians in Huntsville and started my next band named "The Chevells" and played at most of the high school dances, even at my senior prom.

After graduation, I stopped playing and married my high school sweetheart, (stupid, stupid, stupid) went to work and tried to go to college.

You'll hear more about my marriage to my "High School Sweet-heart" in another story, but for now let's just say that didn't work out so good.

Working full time and going to college didn't work out either. I wasn't making enough money to pay our bills and my college tuition.

So I quit college and somehow landed a job as a state-wide Rep for a trade school called *Career Enterprise*. I was only 18 and the youngest State Rep in the country. Of course, my territory was Texas. Every Monday morning I would get on a plane and fly to some city in Texas and walk into the school unannounced and flash my credentials. The schools taught IBM keypunch. That was how all data was entered into computers back then and it was a desirable occupation.

The schools were overseen by the "Director" which was a fancy name for salesmen. The classes were all taught by experienced Keypunch operators, so that part of the school was never my concern when I got there.

My job (and I absolutely hated it) was to check the books. The deal was that the company ran a lot of advertising in the local papers that boasted JOBS JOBS JOBS! The receptionist's job was to take the calls and convince the usual desperate and out of work callers to come in and talk to the "Director." The Director's job was to convince the people who actually bought the receptionist's song and dance, that indeed there were lots of JOBS JOBS JOBS that he could help them get, however they needed to sign up to the school first to receive the training needed to land the gig.

It wasn't a complete scam, there actually was a need for keypunch operators, but most of the people who signed up would never master the technique to do it. Because it was a cash business, with most of the students paying weekly, it was fraught with misappropriation of funds by the Directors. All that cash was just too tempting for some of them.

That part of my job was actually pretty simple. All I had to do was talk to the instructors and count the students and then compare it to the weekly income. It was just simple math, but it was amazing how many Directors I caught with their fingers in the cookie jar. If I found any discrepancies, my job was to fire the Director and the receptionist on the spot (they always seemed to be in cahoots) and then hire a new Director and receptionist. Next, I was expected to have a good week of new student sales acting as the stand-in Director. Can you see why I hated this job?

It was an 8 to 5 operation, so every night after my work at the school, I went back to my hotel alone. Those nights alone were the worst. I didn't drink, but would usually wind up in the hotel bars listening to the bands. Most of them were really bad.

After doing this horrible job for almost a year, traveling week after week, staying in hotel after hotel and listening to all those bands, the idea of quitting my job, putting together a new band and working in some of those same hotels started sounding pretty damn good.

However, when I brought up this idea to my now married to me high school sweetheart, she wasn't exactly over the moon with that concept. She'd never liked me playing in a band in high school and would give me hell if any girl even smiled at me when I was on stage playing. I won't even mention how upset she was when I told her my band had been hired to play for our senior prom. That was not one of our better nights.

So, I tucked away my idea of starting up a new band and trudged along firing and hiring sticky fingered Directors for another 6 months.

By this time my brother Ron had hit several home runs with his commercial real estate business and was rolling in cash. Although most of his money was reinvested in large plots of land and other real estate holdings, one of his friends talked him into investing in the movie business. His first investment was to finance a University of Texas student film, but he did it as more of a donation, rather than an investment, but actually made his money back and a small profit. The producer of that student film was Toby Hooper who later became famous with his movie "Texas Chain Saw Massacre." Ron's second, and last movie investment was in a major motion picture called The Wind Splitter. It was filmed in Columbus, Texas and I actually had a small part in that film. It wasn't a major hit, but I think Ron made most of his money back.

For the wrap party, Ron asked me to bring my guitar and sing the Wind Splitter's title song called "The Road Home" for the guests and cast. The music producer for The Wind Splitter was Jackie Mills. He was a big time Hollywood music producer with a client list including

David Cassidy, a TV star on a show called "The Partridge Family" and a big teen idol at that time.

After I sang the title song for the cast, Ron told me that Jackie Mills wanted to meet me, so he took me to him and introduced me.

After he shook my hand he said, "To be honest with you Ben, when Ron told me his little brother was going to sing that song, I figured you were going to suck, but I wanted to tell you that I was pleasantly surprised. You sing great."

It was one of those Ahh Shucks moments. "Thanks," I said, "That means a lot coming from you."

"I'm serious," He said, "You did a great job on that song. So, do you normally do a solo act or do you have a band?"

I smiled and said, "Actually, I don't sing professionally, I just did this tonight as a favor for Ron.

Jackie wrinkled his brow and looked over at my brother, "Why isn't this kid singing?"

Ron held up his hands and shrugged his shoulders, but before he said anything I answered for him, "I used to sing in a band in high school, but I got married and had to get a real job."

Jackie took a piece of paper and wrote in large letters SHOW BUSINESS, then he underlined BUSINESS three times and handed it to me.

"Memorize this Ben and never forget what it means. You are one of the lucky ones, you've got real talent. You don't need a real job, you should easily be able to make a living playing that guitar and singing. But promise me, you'll always remember that there's no show, without the business. You've got the talent, so you don't have to worry about the show side, but your real job, is to learn and understand how show business really works."

For almost an hour, Jackie talked about the business of show business, and he told me a lot of things I didn't know.

The most important thing I learned was that you didn't have to become a big star to make a living, there were a lot of levels that I could actually achieve as long as I was smart, thinking with my head and not my ego.

I think Ron was as impressed as I was with everything Jackie told me, and I couldn't wait to tell Gail all about it, but when I tried, she didn't want to hear it. She just rolled her eyes and walked away.

My assignment for the week was in Lubbock. As you read more stories in this book you'll discover that the city of Lubbock has played a major part in my life.

When I arrived at the school and the receptionist opened the director's door, I was taken-a-back. The man sitting behind the desk could have been my father's twin. He was about the same age and build, with the same silver hair. The second the receptionist told him who I was, he immediately broke down and started crying. His daughter was in the hospital and he'd borrowed some money out of the till to help pay the hospital bill.

"I swear I'll pay it back, just please don't fire me." He pleaded to me. "I can't lose my job, I really need the money."

When I called my supervisor, he was heartless. "Did he take money?"

"Yes, but..." I tried to say.

"There's no buts. Fire his ass." He said coldly. I did my job that week, but turned in my resignation that Saturday.

The next week I dropped by my brother Ron's office and told him my story about having to fire a man who reminded me of our father.

"So now what are you going to do?" He asked.

"I'd love to take Jackie Mill's advice, put a band together and try singing again," I said, "but I sold all my equipment to pay some bills. To be perfectly honest, I have no idea what I'm going to do next."

Ron reached into his desk, pulled out his check book, signed a blank check and handed it to me. "Go buy what you need, but buy the best equipment they have. If you're going to do this little brother, then don't do it half assed."

I was 19 at that time. And thinking back, I'm not sure if I ever paid him back for what he did that day, but with that equipment I put together a new band and started a music career that's lasted 47 years.

AND IT ALL started with my first performance at the Black and Gold Review.

# 4

# OUT BY THURSDAY

My father had to drop out of school when he was 12 years old to earn money to help support his family, working as a farm laborer in the cotton fields around Lubbock, Texas. His father, Benjamin Franklin Marney (Frank), was a disabled veteran and wasn't capable of doing hard labor. In World War I, Frank had fallen off the back of a supply truck and destroyed his right hip. As a result, his right leg was about 3 inches shorter and he walked with a severe limp.

This doesn't really have anything to do with this story, but since I'm talking about Frank I found it interesting to learn that his mother, my great grandmother was paraplegic. I've never been able to find out if she was born that way or it was as a result of an accident, but I understand that apparently, it didn't slow her down much. Supposedly she did all her housework and cooking, walking on her hands, dragging her legs behind... Somehow, this amazing woman successfully raised 5 children. That's astounding to me.

In 1942 when my father was 14, he met my mother hoeing cotton in one of those West Texas fields; she was 15 at that time. A year later they ran off and got married. That marriage lasted 69 years.

They settled in a tiny town 33 miles East of Lubbock called Ralls, and 9 months later my mother gave birth to my brother Ron. My dad had a good sense of humor and always said, "Yep, we got hitched and Ron was born 9 months and 10 minutes later, and I was damn proud of those 10 minutes."

I will talk much more about my father in another story, but wanted to explain a little about where he came from. To say they were poor would be an understatement. To raise his new family, dad knew he had to learn a trade. Although at that time he had no real formal education, he was a very smart guy. Somehow, self taught, he learned how to repair automobile motors and also became an expert working on diesel engines. All of the farms in that area used diesel engines to pump water to their crops and soon, when dad was only 16, he became the go-to guy to contact when they went down.

By the time I was born, Dad had evolved into a master mechanic and was the number one guy at the Ralls Ford dealership. When I was 3 and Ron was 9, dad began to recognize Ron's intellect. He knew Ron and I would never get the kind of education we deserved in that small town, so he packed us up and moved to Houston.

In Galena Park, working full time, my father passed his G.E. D. (high school equivalency) and going to night classes three nights a week for years, he eventually earned a Bachelor of Arts college degree in Education.

Although my father always thought of himself as just a dumb old country boy, he was a lot more than that. He was a very humble man, soft spoken with unbelievable patience. He had a great sense of observation and had the most common sense of anyone I've ever met in my life.

As you can probably tell, I was a big fan of my father, we were always very close, but I will tell you he wasn't perfect. He had demons in his life, like all of us do, that he fought off and on until he was in his late 50's, but that's another story I'll talk about later.

My wife Dana and I never had any children and when we would get together with our friends and hear about their trials and tribulations they were having raising their kids, we normally would just sit quietly and let them vent. Because I had no real experience in raising children I always tried my best to keep my mouth shut. All I knew about it was how I was raised.

I **DO** realize it was a different time back then, but from listening to my friends complaining about their kids all those years, it has become apparent to me that kids are kids and unless they learn somehow not to do something, they'll try to do the same things my friends and I tried to do all those years ago.

A lot of folks from my generation believe that the problem with today's kids is the lack of discipline that we got from corporal punishment. Personally I think the pendulum has swung a bit too far when a parent faces jail time just for spanking their child. Somehow that's now considered child abuse, but I believe there's a difference between a necessary swat on the butt to accentuate a lesson and actually beating a child.

However, I have to say the fear of my father's rare use of his belt was not how I learned my lessons in life. The truth is I got a lot more of that sort of thing from my vice-principles and coaches at school than I ever got at home. Those were normally the result of me being a smart ass and unfortunately, all those pops with those boards didn't solve that problem, just ask my wife.

So no, the cognitive cerebral hemisphere in my brain was not connected to my ass. I learned the lessons in my life another way and they were very effective.

Due to some health problems my father had to quit working as a line mechanic and took a job teaching high school auto shop. Doing this, he took a large drop in pay, but gained long term benefits like a pension and health insurance. Somehow through all of that I never wanted for anything. My mother took me shopping every new school year and bought me new supplies, new shoes and clothes. And remember how hungry I was? Somehow we always had a full pantry of food. And when I was old enough to drive, my father bought me a car.

I realize now they had to be barely scraping by, but at the time I had no idea of the incredible sacrifices they were making for that to

happen. Somehow I always had lunch money, new clean clothes, baseball gloves, even gasoline for my old car.

The facts are that when I was in high school I lived a privileged
life. I was making pretty good money playing gigs with my band on
the weekends, but I never had to spend any of my own money on the
things that were sustaining my lifestyle, like food, clothes or gasoline,
so I had no idea of how tough the real world could be. I didn't realize
it then, but I was spoiled rotten.

The only time my father asked me to spend some of my money
was in the middle of my senior year.

One Saturday my father asked me, "Benny, do you have any money
saved up?"

"Yeah, a little, why?"

"How much you got?" he said not answering my question.

Reluctantly I said, "About $400.00"

"Let me have it," he said holding out his hand.

I wasn't happy about it, but I figured it must have been important,
so I gave it to him and didn't ask again what he needed it for.

"My car is acting up," he told me, "so I'm going to drive yours. I'll
be back later." He said, then drove off with my wheels.

He was gone all day and I was pretty pissed off about being
stranded there without my car.

He finally showed up about 7:00 pm. When he walked into the
house he threw me my keys, but they were different.

"These aren't mine," I said.

"Sure they are," He said grinning, "go look outside."

Parked in the driveway was a glistening, baby blue 1963 Thunder-
bird. In shock I looked back at my dad standing in the door way, "Is
this mine?"

My mother had joined him in the doorway, "Are you just going to
stand there?" she said, "Why don't you go take it for a spin."

Somehow my old man had taken my $400.00, some of his trading
material and a little of his cash and bought me that beautiful car. Like
I said... spoiled rotten.

That's the way it had been my entire life up until then. My parents lived like paupers, so I could live like a king.

It was about this time my brother's wisdom profoundly affected my life again. Ron was married with kids of his own by then and apparently, my father had expressed some concern to him about my naïveté of the way the real world was. He knew he'd spoiled me and was worried about how I would be able to survive as an adult. So, the two of them concocted a plan.

Because I was put up a grade I was only 17 when I graduated high school. I was the second, after my brother, to graduate from high school in our entire extended family.

After the ceremony and allowing me to celebrate through the weekend, that Monday morning my dad asked me if he could talk to me privately for a second.

We sat next to each other in the living room, "Benny, I want to tell you how proud you have made me by doing so well in school and graduating with honors. As you know, I had to drop out of school and go to work. And I'm real sorry I haven't made enough money in my life to pay for you to go to college, but you are very bright and I know you're gonna do well with your life."

Then he lit up a cigarette and leaned back on the couch, "You are a grown man now and I hope I've taught you well. I have tried my very best for you. When I was your age I was working full time, married and raising your brother. I'm glad your mom and I have been able to get you this far, and because we have, we believe you're going to have a much easier life than we've had. I want you to know that your mother and I will always be here for you, but I need you out of the house by Thursday."

I started laughing, thinking he was just messing with me.

"I'm serious Benny, it's time for you to get out on your own and make a life for yourself."

Suddenly I realized that he wasn't joking, "What? You want me to move out? Where am I supposed to go?" I asked.

Dad raised up his arms and said, "I'm not sure, that's up to you, but you need to figure it out pretty soon. Your mother has always wanted a sewing room and I've got a carpenter coming over Thursday morning to help me start working on it."

In a state of shock I murmured, "A sewing room... Thursday?"

He stood up and said, "Yep, she's always wanted one of those. But remember, we'll always be here if you need us." Then he walked out, leaving me there mumbling to myself.

My brother Ron had become very successful selling cookware door to door and for months had been dropping hints for me to give it a try when I finished school. He wanted me to recruit some of my friends to do it too, move back to Houston and sell the cookware working out of his office.

In a panic, I called four of my best friends and convinced them to move to Houston with me, share an apartment and sell pots and pans for the Summer.

So, for the next three months I sold cookware and lived in a two bedroom apartment with four other guys.

So far I haven't mentioned that I am the definition of Obsessive Compulsive and also a clean nut. Growing up, my room did not resemble a normal teenager's dwelling. My clothes were always neatly hung in the closet, the bed was always made and every inch inside my room was spotless, squeaky clean. That was all my mother's doing.

When my father was 35 we thought he'd had a heart attack, but later found out it wasn't that serious, but for several months he couldn't work. It was a tough time for us. To survive, we all had to chip in. My mother had to work full time in her beauty shop fixing hair to support the family. My brother got a job to help out and I became the cook and house cleaning slave.

Once a week, usually on Saturday, my mother used to put on a white glove and do a clean inspection. If the house wasn't spotless, rather than getting to go play with my friends, I had to clean it all over again. I soon became an expert at how to deep clean and even when dad got better and mom took back over, I continued to clean my room that way.

For a clean freak with O. C. D., living in that small apartment with four complete slobs, was an experience I wouldn't wish on my worst enemy.

I shared one of the two bedrooms with my friend Jeff Slater. Trust me, it wasn't hard to tell which side of the room was mine. When we moved in, like a normal human being, I bought some sheets, pillows, a blanket, a bedspread and towels.

Jeff didn't have sheets, pillows or a towel, just an old bedspread his mother had given him. Every morning he would fall out of bed dragging his bedspread behind him, get in the shower and then use the bedspread to dry off. For three months he never washed it, just hung it over the closet door to dry before he used it again to sleep with that night.

Rather than take the trash out to the dumpsters, one of my brilliant roommates decided it would be a lot easier to drag a 55 gallon barrel up the stairs and put it in the coat closet. Apparently, he hadn't calculated how he was going to empty that full barrel, because when it finally filled up, they just started piling the trash sacks on top, all the way to the ceiling.

The kitchen was filthy, always full of dirty pots and dishes. For about a month I'd tried to keep up with it, but finally gave up and started leaving threatening notes stuck to the dirty dishes. CLEAN UP THIS SHIT! But by that time I was pretty sure they were so dumb they couldn't read either.

About a week before my first semester of college began I came home to find my father standing in the kitchen of the apartment.

"Hey dad, what are you doing here?" I asked.

He grinned at me and said, "I bet this is driving you crazy." Pointing at the full sink of dirty dishes.

"Open the door next to you," I said, "That's what's killing me."

When he opened the door and the stench of the garbage hit him, he started coughing and laughing at the same time.

"I need to ask you something." He said.

"Sure, ask me anything." I said.

"Do you know what a loaf of bread costs?"

""Yes sir."

"What about a gallon of milk or a gallon of gas?"

I told him the prices and he smiled.

"So, do you think you understand what a hard earned dollar is worth."

I smiled, "Absolutely."

"Ok, here's the deal. You can come back home and live with us for this first semester. After that, depending on how you do, we'll talk again."

Thirty minutes later I was out of that pig sty and on my way to my parent's house. I actually beat my father home.

I found out later that he'd been keeping close tabs on me through my brother and had wanted to come rescue me earlier, but Ron had convinced him to let me live through it the full summer.

I've never forgotten that lesson and have tried my best not to take anything I have for granted again. And, that lesson is why I've earned the knickname "tight wad" from my wife.

The further you read in this book, I'm sure you'll agree with me when I say, I am convinced that all of my brain cells didn't connect until I was about 30 years old. After all I'd gone through that long hot summer, believe it or not, I didn't take advantage of my parents free room and board to go to college. Instead, I made the brilliant decision to throw that all away and get married to my high school sweetheart that December.

STUPID STUPID STUPID!

# 5

# I'LL BUY A CORVETTE

Because I skipped the fifth grade, I only went to Texas public schools for 11 years. Nine of those years were in Galena Park and two were in Huntsville, but the Huntsville years were not back to back. Strange I know. As I mentioned earlier, my freshman year of high school we moved to Huntsville so my father could take some classes for his teaching degree. We were only there one year. The second year I was in Huntsville was my senior year. The reason for that move was because of love.

Although this story is not really about my Dad, that move is just another amazing testimony of what kind of father he was.

I met Gail Nightmare (note: I've been advised not to use her real name, because she might sue me!) in Galena Park when I was about nine years old in the fourth grade. Trust me, it was not love at first sight, in fact I couldn't stand her. She was one of those real short girls (never did grow past 4 foot 11), cute I guess for a fourth grader, but she was a serious know it all, and bossy as hell. It wasn't just me, actually none of the kids liked her, so when she moved away the following year, it didn't bother anybody, good riddance...

Her father was a Galena Park police officer and had been offered a position in Huntsville working for the Texas Department of Corrections. So, when we moved to Huntsville my Freshman year, Doug and Cookie, Gail's parent's invited us over for dinner the day we arrived.

Knowing that Gail was going to be there I tried my best to convince my parents to let me buy a hamburger for dinner and just hang out in my new room, but they wouldn't have it, so very reluctantly I went with them.

They were all standing on the front porch waving at us when we arrived. For a second I thought it was Gail's older sister Sharon standing there waving, but when Sharon appeared in the doorway I realize it was her. I hadn't seen Gail since the fourth grade and although she had only grown an inch or two in height, she had grown in other areas substantially. The gangly skinny little girl I'd known in elementary school had been replaced with a fully developed young woman. When our eyes met, she gave me a big smile and I began to think that perhaps this night wasn't going to be that bad after all.

Throughout dinner, Gail kept staring at me, but was quiet and didn't say much. When we finished, we all moved to the living room and Gail and I sat next to each other on the couch. I hadn't realized it before, but apparently my parents had been friends with Doug and Cookie for years and for about an hour we sat there listening to the old folks reminisce about the good old days in Galena Park. Actually, Mom and Dad were only 35 and 36 at that time, but Gail and I were only 14 and listening to them got real boring real quick, so we excused ourselves and moved to the front porch.

"Do you have a girlfriend?" She asked boldly.

At that moment I thought I did, "Yes, her name is Linda."

"That's too bad," She said with a luring smile.

Linda Tice and I had been boyfriend and girlfriend since the six grade and she was the only reason I regretted moving away from Galena Park. She was my first love, but only four weeks later, broke my heart when she told me on the phone that because I'd moved away we had to break up. I learned later it was her parents that had made her do it, but it still hurt.

My grieving over Linda didn't last long. I was doing good in Huntsville High by then, and because of my instant celebrity as a football star, I'd met a lot of other girls and had my eye on a few.

I was extremely shy in those days and it took me a few weeks to build up enough courage to ask one of those girls out.

When I finally asked Leigh Brooks she said, "What about Gail? Aren't you guys together?"

"What? Gail Nightmare?" I said shocked.

"Yes, Gail is telling everyone at school that you're her new boyfriend."

Knowing what I know now, I realize that hearing that from Leigh should've sent up a red flag, and I should have run the other way, but I was only 14 and when it came to girls, my driveway didn't quite reach the road. I was dumb as a brick. Rather than getting mad at her, I drove to her house after football practice and asked her about it.

Looking up at me, batting her long eyelashes at me she asked, "Are you saying that you don't want to be my boyfriend?" Then she stood on her tip toes and gave me a French Kiss. It was my first...

What can I say, that was that, and for the next year thinking with my little head only, I was her boyfriend and she was my girlfriend.

A few months later, we went all the way and had sex for the first time. I was so naïve, Gail actually had to show me where everything was, and seemed to know what to do. Another red flag I didn't see or understand the significance of. For the rest of that year, Gail and I were inseparable, and spent many evenings in the woods watching the submarine races.

The term "love is blind" fit me like a glove in those days because the little girl in the fourth grade I couldn't stand hadn't really changed other than her looks. She was the same bossy, over bearing, know it all she had been as a little girl and because of that, had no real friends other than me. But like the fool I was, I just ignored all the signs and warnings from my friends.

That next summer, my father was offered a job to head up the Vocational Department for the Galena Park Independent School

District. The Superintendent told him that he had pulled some strings so that he could take the job if he would go to night school to complete his degree in education. So once again we moved back to Galena Park.

The next part of this story is going to be hard for some of you to believe, and as I look back remembering it, I'm sure that in today's world, on one hand my father may have been accused of bad parenting or perhaps even child neglect for what he allowed me to do. But on the other hand, what he did after that, should qualify him for the award of Father Of The Year.

As you can imagine, I was devastated to leave Gail and move back to Galena Park and was determined not to let that distance between us break up our love story. Although I was only 15 years old and did not have a driver's license until I turned 16, every weekend for the next two years I borrowed my fathers second car and drove the 77 miles north to Huntsville to spend the weekends with Gail, sleeping on the couch in her parent's den.

Throughout those two years, my father taught auto shop and headed up the vocational department every day and then three nights a week drove 100 miles round trip to college to earn his degree. Dad had the job he'd worked hard for and because of his new degree was in line to receive a nice raise and finally be able to stop worrying about paying his bills without working on the weekends to earn extra money.

Three weeks before my senior year began I asked my parents if I could talk to them.

"Sure, what's on your mind?" Dad said.

"I don't really know how to say this, so I'm just going to come out with it," I said. "I don't want to go through my senior year without Gail. You guys have to know by now how I feel about her. This is going to be a special year in our lives and I want to share it with her."

They were both speechless and didn't respond.

"I've already talked to Uncle Donald and he said I could live with him rent free as long as I pay for my food. Huntsville only requires 22 credits to graduate and I already have 18. All I have to take is four classes and that will allow me to sign up for Distributive Education. In D. E. I'll only have to go to school until noon and then I can work in the afternoons at Piggly Wiggly to earn the money to pay for my food."

Still a bit shocked, my father said, "When did you figure all that out?"

"Gail and I have been working on it for months" I said.

My dad looked at my mother and then back at me, "Spending your senior year with Gail means that much to you?"

"Yes sir. It's an important time in our lives and we want to be together all the time, not just on the weekends."

What my father did next was unbelievable. He drove that very night to the Galena Park Superintendent's house and resigned. Then he sold our house in Galena Park, bought a mobile home and had it delivered to Huntsville. One week before my senior year started we moved into our new place.

I said in the opening of this book that I've lived a life that most people only dream about, so I can't say that moving back to Huntsville for my senior year was a mistake. However, that move did have a prodigious effect on my future and was the cause of an epic family argument between my brother Ron, my parents and me.

My brother and I fought like cats and dogs most of our lives, so I had experience with his wrath, but I'd never seen him display this kind of anger towards my parents before.

"This is a terrible mistake!" He screamed at my father. "You're enabling him to completely ruin his life, his entire future and possibly yours too!"

What he was so upset about was one of the interscholastic high school rules that would prevent me from playing football or running track if we moved. The rule stated that to play varsity football, a student had to be a resident for a year. This rule prevented "recruitment" of the best players from other schools to form a power house team. If we actually moved to Huntsville, I would be disqualified and

Ron couldn't believe they were willing to let me throw my future away over a girl.

Ron was trying to explain to my parents that he was convinced I would be offered a football scholarship because I'd done so well my junior year playing on the varsity team at Galena Park. He also reminded them about the full ride track scholarship to Rice University I had already received in my sophomore year.

For almost two hours Ron ranted on and on, but foolishly, my mind was made up. As a result, I didn't compete in any sports my senior year, so obviously I had no offers for a football scholarship and the Rice University track offer simply went away. So apparently, love is not only blind, it's also stupid.

I will admit to fantasizing many times about how different my life would have turned out if I had listened to my brother that night. Would I have gone down the same path, but just a few years later? Would I have been any happier, or richer? Probably richer for sure, but I seriously doubt I'd been any happier. However, the happiness I'm referring to wasn't a result of this move... that came several years later.

My senior year flew by in a flash and truthfully wasn't as memorable as I had hoped. I did get to spend it with Gail and made sure my parents knew how much I appreciated all they had sacrificed to make it happen. I also tried my best to convince myself it had all been worth it, but deep down inside I knew the truth...

I wish I could tell you that I finally woke up and started making better decisions after that experience, but I wasn't quite through; I had one more colossal, brainless mistake to make... I asked Gail to marry me.

The comedian Richard Pryor in one of his routines described my feelings for Gail perfectly when he said, "I'm in love with a bitch I can't stand!"

I had been with Gail long enough to realize I didn't like the way she treated my friends, hated her arrogance and her selfishness, but at the same time, I was madly in love with her. So, bowing to the pressure from Gail and her parents to take the next obvious step, we set a date for a December wedding.

Of course, my parents appeared to be happy about it, but my brother Ron... well I'm sure by now you can imagine his reaction.

For a few months he wouldn't even talk to me, but eventually he started trying to convince me that it was the worst decision I had made so far in my life.

"And little brother, that's saying a lot, " he said, "because so far, you have made some real doozies!" But like I've already said, my love for Gail was blind and stupid, so the wedding plans continued.

The night of our rehearsal dinner, Ron insisted on driving me there, because he figured it was his last chance to talk me out of it.

"I promise I won't bring this up again,"he said as we pulled out, "but I have to try one last time. Benny, true love will always prevail. Nothing can stop it. So I want to make you this offer. I am dead serious about this so don't just blow me off."

"If you will just put this wedding off until you finish college, I will pay for all of your tuition, all of your books and your rent. And as a bonus..." He paused and turned to look at me. " I will buy you a brand new Corvette. All you'll have to do is work part time to pay for your gas. It's a one time only offer. If Gail really loves you, she'll wait and you guys will have a much brighter future with a college degree."

This wasn't the first time Ron had offered to help me pay for college, but it was the first time he'd offered to pay for all of it. But his final coup de gras was the Corvette.

I had been obsessed with Corvettes from the first time I saw one driving down the road. The walls of my bedroom were covered with pictures of them. On the shelves were Corvette model cars I had spent hours assembling piece by piece and I had every year from the first to the current 1968 version. Owning a Corvette had been my dream and my life long fantasy. So this wasn't just any offer, Ron was going for my jugular.

But... I was in love and nothing, not even a new Corvette could change my mind. So far in my life, that brilliant decision ranks as number 5 of my all time bonehead moves.

In an effort to keep this book G rated, sparing you all of the gory details, I'll just say that my marriage to Gail turned out to be a disaster, lasting three and a half miserable years.

I WAS ONCE AGAIN... STUPID STUPID STUPID!

# 6

## MARCEL MOTEL

No doubt I could write a book on why my marriage to Gail didn't work, but nothing good would come of that. I will admit that it wasn't all her fault, I was as much to blame as her. We were simply too young, had completely different personalities and each had different life goals we wanted to accomplish. The real tragedy was, we didn't realize this until after we had married and lived together for a few years. We had our first major fight about three days after our honeymoon and it went downhill from there. There were too many problems between us to list here, but the major obstacle and final straw we both knew we would never be able to survive was my decision to make my living as a musician. It wasn't something we said out loud to each other, but I think we both knew my music career was going to lead to our eventual demise.

With the blank check my brother had given me, I bought a guitar, a mixer, two speakers and a microphone. It was all the state-of-the-art equipment at that time and after a few weeks of practice, I had about 6 or 7 songs down pretty good, but needed a lot more. I wasn't ready for a gig yet, but once again my brother Ron had a different idea. He called and told me that he'd talked to one of his friends and had set up an audition for me the following day.

"I'm not ready yet." I insisted.

"Just play the songs you know," He said, "if you're worth a shit like Jackie Mills said, that should be enough."

Ron was right, I only had to play five of the six songs I knew to land my first professional gig. It was a private bar inside an apartment complex. I performed as a solo act from 5 o'clock till 7 o'clock Monday through Saturday for a whopping $87.50 a week. During my second week, a man approached me and asked me if I would be interested in playing for him after I got off from my gig there. Of course, I jumped at the chance. So after my 5 to 7 gig at the apartment bar, I packed up and moved a few miles down the road and (setting up in a corner next to the cigarette machine) I played from 8 to 10 at Bud's Fish and Chips. It was a combination pizza and fried fish restaurant and they paid me another $87.50. I was making $175.00 a week and excited it had come so quickly.

After I'd played at both gigs a few months, I was approached by Larry O'Keefe, a booking agent from one of the largest entertainment agencies in Houston. He offered me my first road gig. It was for 4 weeks at the Ramada Inn, in Lafayette, Louisiana and it paid $385.00 a week. That may not sound like much now, but that was big bucks in 1969.

Before I get into the Lafayette story, I want to rewind and tell you a famous story my brother laughed about for years.

Apparently Bud, of Bud's Fish and Chips was excited to have live entertainment at his restaurant, so he made arrangements to use the large shopping center marquee, where his restaurant was located to advertise my performances. It was the first time I'd seen my name up in lights. In huge glowing letters, big enough to see for miles it said: BEN MARNEY - MUSIC TO EAT BY.

One night Ron and several of his friends came to hear me play. When they walked in they were laughing.

"What's so funny?" I asked Ron.

"Have you seen the marquee tonight?" He said still laughing hard.

I walked to the door and looked at the large glowing sign, it said: MUSIC TO EAT BEN MARNEY BY.

Ron told that story and laughed about it for years. He always denied it, but I'd still bet my house and guitar that it was Ron who had climbed that ladder and did a little rearranging or at the very least paid someone to do it.

Years later Ron told me that on that first gig at the apartment bar, he had put in a fix and had offered to pay my salary even if his friend didn't like me, but when he came by the first week to pay the $87.50, his friend wouldn't take his money and told him that I was doing a good job and he was glad to have me. What an amazing brother he was...

The day before I headed out on my first real road gig to Lafayette, my father asked me to drop by his shop. Although I was 6 foot tall, my father in his cowboy boots stood about 6 foot four and towered over me. He grabbed me by my shirt, pushed me against the wall and looked down at me.

"You are about to begin a new chapter in your life out there on the road. I just want to make one thing perfectly clear to you," He said sternly, "If I ever hear about you taking any kind of dope, I will track you down and kick your ass all over that night club you're playing in. No son of mine is going to become a drug addict. Are we clear on that?"

"Crystal clear." I said. "Dad, you don't have to worry about that, I don't even drink."

"I know that and I'm proud you don't, but you're about to enter into a world you don't know exists. There will be a lot of temptations. Just remember, there are a lot of stupid people out there in the world, try not to be one of them."

To this day, I can vividly see my father's face saying those words. He was not a violent man, but there was no question in my mind that he wasn't joking. He would have kicked my ass for sure, and every time I was offered pot or cocaine, my father's words and angry face flashed in my head.

I had heard the term, "paying your dues," but had no idea what it meant until I loaded my car and took off to Lafayette. I didn't make it to Beaumont before I had to pay the first installment on those dues, when my right rear tire blew at 70 miles an hour. I almost lost it, but was able to pull over as far as I could on the I-10 Freeway. That's when I remembered that I hadn't got around to fixing my spare from my last flat. Three hours later, I finally got back on the road, but was barely going to make it to the gig in time to set up and play.

When I found the Ramada Inn, I flew into the parking lot and ran inside, but the girl behind the counter told me that they didn't have a bar in that hotel. Totally confused, I ran back to my car, found my contract and realized it didn't say the club was "inside" the Ramada Inn, it said it was beside it. I looked around and saw a small building on the corner of the property.

When I walked inside, the bartender scowled at me and said, "We've been wondering if you were ever gonna show up." He pointed at a grand piano surrounded by bar stools, "Set up over there behind the piano," he barked, "and you better hurry, you're supposed to start in 20 minutes."

This was not how I'd dreamed my first big gig would begin, but somehow I started my first song on time and the customers seemed to like it. By the third song they were all singing along and the bartender and waitress were smiling for the first time since I'd walked in the place.

Each set seem to get better and the crowd got louder, but when my last set ended I was worn out and ready to get some sleep.

After I finished my last song, said goodnight and started packing up my guitar, a very drunk woman yelled across the piano bar, "Where do you think you're going?"

"I'm only supposed to play until 1," I said.

""Where is your tip jar?" She asked.

To be honest I had no idea what that meant, I was really that green. "I don't have one." I said, still not sure what "one" was.

The waitress walked up to the piano and set a very large Brandy Snifter in the center. "Here you go," She said and walked back to the bar.

The drunk woman dug in her purse, pulled out a 10 and dropped it in the Snifter, "Will that get me one more song?"

I grinned and said, "For that, you get two."

"How about three," Another customer said dropping more money in the Snifter.

"Four!" Someone else said adding to the cash.

"OK, four more, but I'm fried guys. I'm done after that."

I'm sure some of you will think I'm embellishing this next part, but I swear It's the truth. Remember my flat tire on the way? The money I had to spend to get it fixed and the money for the gas it took to drive from Houston to Lafayette had taken every cent I had. When I counted the money from the Snifter, it totaled 33 dollars. *Manna from Heaven.*

I think I need to remind you again about how green and naïve to show business I was. Because I had not read the contract carefully, I had assumed that the Ramada Inn would be supplying a free hotel room. After all, I was going to be performing in their bar. But no, it wasn't their bar and they weren't connected to the actual bar at all, so I had nowhere to sleep.

I did have a few credit cards in my billfold, but have I mentioned my wife Gail? She was a shopaholic and kept those cards maxed out. I was exhausted and knew that my $33 wasn't enough for a room, so I decided I'd take the chance and use one of my credit cards and rent a room at the Ramada Inn.

Crossing my fingers behind my back, I handed the probably maxed out card to the desk clerk. He rolled the impression stamp over the papers, handed me back the card and gave me a room key. For those of you too young to remember, credit cards were not hooked up to the internet back then for instant approval. They had to be approved manually via a telephone line.

The second I laid my head on the pillow I was out, but was awakened by a loud knock on my door at 4:00am. It was the night manager. He had ran my card and proceeded to kick me out of the room.

I was so tired, I curled up in my back seat and slept in my car in the hotel parking lot until daylight. At 7:00am I walked into the lobby of the Ramada Inn, found the payphone and made a collect call to

Gail. I wasn't sure she was going to accept it for a moment, she actually paused to think about it before she said OK and accepted the charges.

"The credit cards are maxed out and they kicked me out of my room last night." I told her.

"Kicked you out of what room?" She asked. Her voice was cold as ice. "I thought a free room was part of the deal?"

"I did too, but I screwed up and didn't read the contract right. I'm not actually playing at the Ramada, it's a small club next door to it. That's not important now. I need you to either wire me some money or figure out how to pay down the balance on one of our cards, so I can rent a room till I get paid Saturday."

Cold silence was her response. "Did you hear me?" I asked.

"I don't have any money to wire you. The money in the bank is for the bills. You wanted this Ben, not me."

"I'm not the one who maxed out the cards on clothes I didn't need to buy," I yelled in the phone. "That was you. I'm in trouble and I need your help."

In a voice I'd never heard before, she said coldly, "How's your music career going so far?" And without another word, she hung up in my ear leaving me broke and stranded. I walked back to my car in a daze, not sure what I was going to do next.

Since the car was almost out of fuel, I spent 10 dollars on gas and drove to a truck stop a few miles down the road and spent $3 more on breakfast. I only had $20 left. This was February and it was cold, so I found the public library, hung out there until 5:00pm, then drove back to the bar. For happy hour, they had hors d'oeuvres, so that was my lunch and dinner.

Throughout my life when things looked the darkest, out of nowhere something has always seemed to fall from the sky to solve my problem. I know now that it was God's hands on my shoulders looking after me, but as I'm writing this memory down on paper, it makes me wonder how I could have been stupid enough to have taken off on that trip to Lafayette so unprepared in the first place.

Before I started my first set that night, I asked to borrow that over-sized Brandy Snifter again for my new discovery, a tip jar.

Apparently, the word had spread about me, because the bar quickly filled to capacity and stayed that way all night, but when I finished my last set, this time it was a twenty from a drunk for one more song, then another twenty and another and another. When I finally finished and counted the cash, it totaled $172. I was so tired from playing all night and from lack of sleep, I stumbled into the Ramada Inn and slapped down the 38 bucks cash for a room and slept until noon the next day.

Finally thinking with a rested brain, I realized I couldn't afford to pay 40 bucks a night at the Ramada, so I decided to take a drive around Lafayette to see if I could find a cheap place to stay for the month. I found a place and moved in that afternoon, it was called the Marcel Motel.

I've always planned on writing a song about the Marcel Motel, but never have, so I guess including it in this short story will have to do. I just hope I give it justice.

It was located on the old highway and I assumed it used to be a nice place to stay before the I-10 Freeway was built and took all the traffic away. It only had 15 rooms that lined the rectangular parking lot; 5 on each side and 5 in the middle.

To be honest what attracted me to the Marcel Motel was the price, but I didn't read it on the big marquee sign out front, because the Marcel Motel didn't have a marquee, in fact it didn't have a sign at all. I saw the price painted on a piece of cardboard stuck in the office window. It said King bed, AC & TV $55 a week. I'd just spent $48 for one night, so I figured if the TV and heater worked, and the roof didn't leak too bad when it rained, it would suit me just fine.

When I opened the door, the brown carpet looked like it had a random pattern of black dots, but on closer inspection I realized that the black dots were actually cigarette burns in the carpet. The AC/Heater worked, but the cover was missing exposing the fan, wires and tubes. The bed was not bad, but there was no way I could sleep under those sheets. The TV was actually a color set, but would only get two channels. The bathroom was pretty bad too. I had passed a shopping center a few miles away, so I drove there and bought some new sheets, towels and a pillow. Next I bought a scrub brush and some Comet Cleanser. Then I borrowed the vacuum from the manager and went to work.

I stayed there for the full 4 weeks and never one time saw a maid. I washed my own towels and sheets and vacuumed my floors, but for $55 a week it was worth a little extra work. With my beloved Comet Cleanser, scrub brush and daily vacuuming, my room was always the cleanest at the Marcel Motel. I have fond memories of sitting on the bed drying my long hair from the open face of the AC/heater fan each night before the gig. The Marcel Motel was the definition of a dump, but actually I loved the month I lived there. It was all part of the experience. The owner of the Marcel Motel and his wife were great friendly people and of course, I loved my gig at that small bar beside the Ramada Inn.

The regulars at that bar were completely nuts, drank way too much and had sort of adopted me as an honorary Coonass. One night a group of them invited me out for a late night breakfast. I followed them to an apartment complex on the west side of town. When I got inside the apartment, they handed me a pair of pliers and told me to have a seat at the table. For the life of me I couldn't figure out why they'd given me the pliers, so I walked into the kitchen and asked what they were for. One of them opened the refrigerator and pulled out the vegetable drawer... it was full of live crabs. It was 3am and they were having a crab boil for breakfast. Crazy Coonasses!

I use that term with great love and affection. Coonasses (that's what they called themselves) are the nicest, craziest and wildest party people on this earth.

Each night playing that gig I averaged over $100 in tips and when I drove out of Lafayette on my way home, with my weekly salary of $385 and all my tips, I had a little over $4,000 in my pocket. I couldn't wait to get home and throw it in Gail's face and tell her that yes, my music career was doing just fine.

I loved flashing all that cash, but of course, she wasn't impressed.

She just took the money from my hand, stuffed it into her purse and walked away. Over her shoulder she said, "Maybe now we can pay our bills on time."

AT THAT MOMENT, I started missing those happy days living at the Marcel Motel.

# 7

# THE RED RAIDER INN

I performed the next few months doing my solo act, 6 nights a week back at the apartment bar and Bud's Fish and Chips. During the day, I began rehearsals with my new band. My agent, Larry O'Keefe had helped me line up a drummer, Lynn Myer and a keyboard player, Beaux Williams and "The Ben Marney Trio" was born.

Gail had always been an amazing typist. She could type over 100 words a minute with very few mistakes, so finding a clerical job had always been easy for her. She had discovered that rather than working a full time job that came with all the office politics, she could make more money working temp jobs, so she signed up with an employment agency in Houston called "Kelly Girls" and stayed busy working temporarily at several businesses a week or two at a time. Because of her amazing typing and filing skills, she was always in demand and could pick and choose when she wanted to work. I hadn't made a bone head decision for a while, so I guess it was time...

In an effort to somehow get Gail to accept my new music career decision, I came up with a brilliant plan. My new trio had been booked for 4 weeks at a bar in Lubbock called the Gaslight and I convinced Gail to take some time off and come out on the road with me.

You need to understand that Gail's talent was as a great typist and anything clerical. When it came to music, she was tone deaf, she couldn't sing a lick and she was rhythmically challenged. However, she was very beautiful and looked amazing in hot pants! I wanted her to experience what it was like to be on stage, so on our first night at the Gaslight, I gave her a tambourine and told her to just have fun and dance to the music. So that's what she did and it seemed like she actually enjoyed doing it.

During our second set, a drunk started yelling, "LET THE GIRL SING!"

She couldn't sing, so I ignored him. A few songs later he yelled again, "LET-THE- GIRL- SING!"

This went on all night. After we'd finished our last set, the club owner asked me to come to his office. "Why didn't you let the girl sing? Is she sick or something?"

I did my best to explain that he'd hired us as a trio and that Gail was just sort of eye candy for the stage. Although he was happy with our music as a trio, he was concerned that if Gail never sang, knowing his regulars, the yelling might get out of hand and asked me to not put her on stage again.

The problem was, Gail had actually loved being on stage and when I told her she couldn't do it anymore, she went nuts, screaming and throwing things at me in our hotel room. She was out of control and when she got that way, I knew there was nothing I could do or say to console her. She began throwing her clothes into the suitcase and actually left that night and drove back to Houston. That was the last time she traveled with me and the last time in our marriage she heard me play.

The Ben Marney Trio soon developed a good reputation and as a result the gigs and the money got better and better. Ironically, I played in many of the same hotels I had watched all those bands during my years of traveling with Career Enterprise. One of the hottest rooms in Houston at that time was at a large Ramada Inn, located in South

West Houston. When Larry told me he'd booked us there for a four week gig I was ecstatic. Since it was close to my brother's house he was there often with a large group of his friends. It was an exciting time for me. The fact that my brother and his friends kept coming back so often and seemed to love my music was validation that I had finally made a good decision with my career and life.

One night when my brother was there with a large group, a girl walked up to the stage and said, "You need a girl in the band."

"You think so?" I said smiling at her. "We're doing pretty good without one so far."

"You sing pretty good," she said, "but you need a girl to give the people a break so they don't get sick of hearing you sing every damn song."

Her name was Carla Christian. She was a large woman, not fat-- just a bit chunky, tall and big boned. And not what you'd call pretty. Sort of plain.

Normally, I would have just ignored her and started playing my next song, but there was something about her.

"I don't suppose you know of a girl singer do you?" I asked knowing the answer.

"Yes I do. I'm talking about me and I'm great!" She said arrogantly.

I laughed, "Oh yeah? And you're humble too."

She frowned, "Just give me the mic and play something. I'll prove it."

"What song?" I asked her.

"I can sing anything in any key, just pick one." She said with a smirk.

Carla was something. I was pretty sure I'd finally met someone more cocky and arrogant than my wife Gail, so I couldn't wait to see if she could back up her bullshit.

One of the hottest songs out at that time was "Respect" by Aretha Franklin. Although I had some soul in me and did the song OK, I'd never really given it the justice it deserved. It was a tough song to sing, so I counted it off as a good test to see what she would do with it.

When she started singing, she brought down the house. She could give Aretha a run for her money and just killed it! The crowd went wild.

She gave me a big cocky grin, handed me back the microphone and said, "I'll be at the bar."

I had her sing a few more times during the night and told her that I'd talk to my agent and see if we could increase our price enough to afford to hire her.

Carla was working at a Burger King across the street from the Ramada Inn and after her shift, almost every night, she would come and sit in with us. Once Larry heard her sing, he raised our price and the Ben Marney Four was born. Terrible name I know, but it was all I could think of on short notice.

When she sang, she had an awkward movement. My brother described it best when he said, "Your new girl sings great, but she looks like she's trying to wipe cow shit off her shoes while she's singing. Anything you can do about that?" Unfortunately, I never could.

The first major gig we played as the Ben Marney Four was at the Red Raider Inn in Lubbock. Like I've said, the city of Lubbock, Texas has been the backdrop of many major events in my life. I had played The Red Raider Inn successfully two times earlier with my Trio. I have mentioned several times that I'm not a drinker and there are several reasons why. One of those reasons took place at the Red Raider Inn.

On our second gig there, they had what they called a "Rag Peddlers Convention." The hotel was enclosed with all the rooms facing a large open area where the swimming pool and Cafe were located. The "Rag Peddler's Convention" was actually a wholesale clothing market and the salesman would set up their samples in their rooms and the local retailers would come, browse the big circle of the displays in the rooms around the pool, and purchase clothes and shoes for their stores.

This clothing market lasted a full week. The prior week before the convention, the waitresses began hanging signs around the bar that said: THE F-TROOP - WELCOME BACK!

When I asked what the signs meant, the waitresses just laughed and told me that the F Troop was a drinking club and I'd find out more about it next week when the rag peddler showed up. Unfortunately, I found out a little too much about that club.

My trio was a huge hit with all the rag peddlers and they were in there every night raising a lot of hell. All week they kept trying to talk me into joining the F-Troop, but being a nondrinker, I just laughed and passed on their offers. Finally, on Saturday night, the last night of the convention I gave in and joined the F-Troop.

To become an official member, you had to be initiated. The initiation was a formal presentation of drinking ten swallows of what they called a "Shabonga." To make a Shabonga, they took a large water pitcher, filled it with a shot of every single liquor behind the bar plus one full beer and a Dill pickle floating on top. Then they lined you up with a member on each side.

The initiation went something like this, "Ready on the right?"

"Ready Sir!"

"Ready on the left?"

"Ready Sir!"

"Begin!"

Then they lifted the pitcher of the Shabonga and began pouring it down your throat, counting your swallows backwards from ten. "Ten, nine, eight, seven..."

It tasted horrible, but somehow I made it all the way without gagging. After me, my keyboard player Beaux, joined the group and finally my drummer Lynn became a member as well.

I had no experience with serious drinking at that time, so I was amazed that I felt absolutely nothing, not even a slight buzz. I just figured, because I'd never drank before I must have had a large resistance to the effects of alcohol.

One of our signature songs back then was "Evil Ways" by Santana. We had a great arrangement of that song with several instrumental breaks and it took a lot of energy for all three of us to get through it. Everyone started yelling for us to play it, so we jumped on stage and cranked it up.

The next thing I knew, I was sitting on a stool singing a James Taylor song, but wasn't sure how I'd gotten there. There was a loud low bass roar coming from my left, so I slowly turned my head to look at Beaux, but he wasn't there. Somewhere between Evil Ways and Fire and Rain, he'd slid off his organ seat and was passed out curled around his bass peddles.

I looked back at Lynn behind his drums and he just smiled and lifted up his second glass of Shabonga and said, "This shit is pretty good!" Did I mention that Lynn was the drinker in the group?

That was one of the five times in my life I've been drunk, but it was by far the worst. I have no memory of the following 24 hours. The General Manager, who was also an official member of the F-Troop gave us Monday night off to recuperate.

We were one of the Red Raider Inn's favorite bands and it was the best possible venue we could have landed to debut the Ben Marney Four.


I ASSUMED it would be another positive forward step in my music career, but in my wildest dreams could not have imagined how those next four weeks at The Red Raider Inn would completely change my life.

Ben Marney Four - Ben - Lynn - Beaux - Carla

# 8

# DANA DAMRON

In 1971, The Red Raider Inn was apparently "THE" place to stay in Lubbock, Texas. Performing there, I got to meet Roy Clark, Tom Jones, Roger Miller and Bob Hope. Amazingly, Roy Clark was the most unfriendly. He wouldn't give anyone his autograph and tried his best to be invisible.

Bob Hope was very friendly as you might expect. He was there several days and tried his best to talk to everyone.

One day his handler ran up to us at the cafe in a panic, "Have you seen Mr. Hope? We can't find him." They eventually found him in the laundry room, sitting on the washing machines telling jokes to the housekeeping staff. He was a great man.

When I met Tom Jones, he was butt naked. After the gig at about 3am, I decided to take a swim in the indoor heated pool. When I walked to the pool area, there was a very large man standing near the edge and I could see someone swimming. It was Tom Jones in the pool and the large man by the edge was his body guard. When I realized it was him, I immediately turned around and started to walk away. I've never been one to fawn over stars, understanding how little private time they get, but when I turned around Tom Jones yelled, "Come on in Mate, the water is warm!"

It wasn't until I was actually in the pool that I realized that Tom was skinny dipping. He had performed that night to a sold out concert and was in a great mood. When I told him that I was a musician and was playing in the bar of the hotel, he started talking about the music business and told me how he'd gotten started. We talked for almost an hour. He is on the top of my list of one of the nicest stars I've met in my life.

Roger Miller and his entire band walked into the bar one night while we were performing. Before the night was over, he was on stage singing with us and we partied with him and his band until daylight. He was drinking pretty heavy, but never appeared drunk and was full of hilarious stories. Singing with him and getting to know him that night is one of the highlights of my life.

Yes, the Red Raider Inn was a special place and I loved meeting all those stars, but the most important person I met there, happened accidentally during the debut booking of The Ben Marney Four.

Adding Carla to the band had no doubt improved our repertoire and range. Larry had booked us in a few small bars around Houston to work her in, give her some on stage experience and get us ready for some upcoming big and important gigs. I had hoped that her over the top, egocentric first meeting with me was just an act to get my attention, but unfortunately it was no act. With every compliment she got from a fan, her head got a little bigger and she became more and more difficult to deal with.

As I had expected, she was a big hit in Lubbock at The Red Raider Inn and because of that her ego had grown enormously.

On the third Saturday of our four week contract, she knocked on my door a few hours before show time.

"Ben, I think I'm going to skip the first two sets," she began, "You know they're all coming just to see me anyway, so I thought it would be more effective if I didn't do the first two sets and made a grand entrance for the third one. Maybe you could make some kind of announcement during the first two sets about when my show would start. What do you think?"

I don't know about you, but my brain has a special place it has stored a few memories I've lived through in my life in vivid, total recall detail. This is one of those memories.

There is no doubt that Carla was an amazing singer and performer. Even with her "wiping cow shit off her shoes" dance, she was electrifying to watch on stage. I knew that, my agent Larry knew that, and of course Carla knew that too, but she had made one slight miscalculation. It was something she hadn't realized yet, but something I'd learn early in my career from, of all people, my non musical, but brilliant brother.

"Little brother, there's something I want you to always remember when you're up there on that stage and people are yelling and screaming, telling you how wonderful you are," he told me one night after a gig. "You're a good singer no doubt, but never forget that you're not the greatest singer in the world. There's always someone out there better than you, who would love to have your job. Always remember, the worst thing you could ever do is to start believing your own bullshit."

That was Carla's miscalculation. She honestly believed that she was the greatest singer that ever lived, and completely and totally believed her own bullshit. What she didn't know, was that I had been expecting something like this, and had already contacted Larry O'Keefe about finding me another girl singer.

She was standing there with all her cockiness, waiting in the doorway for my answer. "Carla, I have a better idea," I said, "I think you should miss the first, second, third and fourth set tonight and spend that time packing your bags, because you're fired!"

The problem with believing your own bullshit, is how shocked you are when you realize that there are actually other people out there who don't believe it.

"What? You can't fire me. I'm the whole show!" She actually said those words.

I just smiled, "Carla, this is my third contract here. They keep bringing me back because they love my trio. I just added you here to let you get some more on stage experience. I didn't need you on the first two contracts and I damn sure don't need you on this one. Go pack your bags, I'll buy you a bus ticket to Houston in the morning."

I wish there was some way to print the picture I still have in vivid detail in my mind of her standing there in shocked disbelief. My father had a funny saying that fit this scene perfectly.

"Never let your alligator mouth say something your mosquito ass can't back up."

Like the scene from Gone With The Wind, I wanted to say, "Frankly my dear, I don't give a damn," but actually my words were, "Have a nice life." Then I slammed the door in her face, and it felt good.

That night, the bar was packed and Beaux, Lynn and I kept the joint rocking. As I had hoped, none of the bosses or customers asked anything about Carla all night. The only time anyone asked about her was when I was leaving.

"What happened to the girl?" A guy asked as I passed his table.

I smiled and as a joke I said, "I fired her. I'm looking for a new girl singer, do you know one?"

He pointed to a cute blonde sitting next to him. "This girl says she can sing."

We had played over our normal stopping time and I was running late. I had promised to call Gail after the gig and knew she was probably already pissed I was late.

I held out my hand, "Hi, I'm Ben, so you're a singer?"

She smiled at me and said, "I sing, but not professionally."

The guy with her said, "She must be pretty good, she's got a singing scholarship and studying music at Texas Tech."

"Want to audition?" I asked her. "I really 'am' looking for a new singer."

"Sure," she said.

"Great! Sorry, but I've got to go make a phone call. I'll hook you up with Beaux."

As I ran out the door, I yelled, "Beaux, chick singer," pointing at the blonde, "Audition her." I didn't even get her name.

Beaux dropped by my room later and told me that she'd done well in the audition.

"Not a real poppish voice," He said, "more formal, but she's got good range, pitch and timing."

He told me her name was Dana and that she was supposed to call me the next day. When she did, honestly I was a little surprised. I'd assumed her boldness to audition had more than likely come from the scotch she'd been drinking, but when she called she said she was interested in learning more about the job.

Since I hadn't heard her sing yet, I asked her to come to my hotel room and audition for me. Thinking about it now, I guess that did sound a bit suspicious and explained why she showed up with Trudy, her roommate.

I'd been in such a rush the night before, I hadn't really noticed how beautiful she was, but when she showed up at my room she looked incredible and it was the first time I saw her amazing smile.

I had her sing a few songs for me acappella. Beaux had given me an accurate account of her voice. She had obviously been formally trained and sounded a bit too operatic. I wasn't sure if she'd be able to overcome all that training to sing pop and rock, but I liked her, and offered her the job. It was supposed to be just for her summer break from college.

"I'll have to talk about this with my parents first." She said.

I shook my head understanding, "Where do your parents live?"

I'm not sure what I expected her to say, but when Dana said that her parents lived in Muleshoe, Texas, my immediate thought was to forget about this girl. In my mind, I saw Ma and Pa Kettle standing there, holding a pitch fork, posing in front of their barn. There was no way in hell her parents were going to let their innocent, farm raised daughter from Muleshoe, Texas go on the road with a group of long haired rock and roll musicians. No way, so I just scratched Dana off my list.

What happened next is why I am convinced God has always had his hands on my shoulders, leading me along the way in my life.

Dana's parents were not farmers, in fact they were very sophisticated and well educated, both graduating from the University Of Texas. Her mother was a classically trained pianist with a degree in music and child psychology. Her father was a Pharmacist, owned the local Rexall drugstore in Muleshoe and at that time was on the Texas State Board Of Pharmacy. They were not the Ma and Pa Kettle country bumpkins I had imagined.

Her parents had been at a pharmacy convention in San Antonio and had just arrived home on that Saturday, so Dana drove back to Muleshoe to have a Sunday morning breakfast with them to ask about joining my band.

But before she brought up the subject, her mother said, "Oh Dana, the convention was so much fun. They had a great band there and we danced all night. Your father and I have been talking about it and we think that's what you should do. You need to sing in a band."

Dana smiled and said, "Well, guess what..."

I couldn't believe it when she called to tell me that her parents wanted to meet me, and were actually considering letting her join the band.

They all came out to meet me on Friday night. Dana and her mother walked in first. It was easy to see where she got her looks, her mother was beautiful. They took a seat at a table, waving at me on stage. Then the door opened and her father walked in, but he didn't join them at the table, instead he started dancing and before he finally sat down, I think he'd danced with every girl in the place.

It became apparent to me, and everyone in the room, Sam Damron, Dana's father was (and still is) the life of the party!

After my set, I join them at the table, honestly a little nervous not knowing what to expect. Remember, I was still envisioning Ma and Pa Kettle at this time, but it didn't take me long to figure things out.

"Do you know what I do for a living?" Dana's father asked me the moment I sat down.

"No sir, I don't," I answered.

He grinned and said, "I sell dope!"

Dana's mother yelled, "Sam, stop that. Be nice." Then she smiled at me, "He's a pharmacist. Nice to meet you, I'm Elaine."

For the rest of the night, I sat with them on my breaks and answered about a million questions. Her mother wanted to know about my family and how I was raised, but Sam continued dropping hints, trying to find out if I was a sex maniac, alcoholic or drug addict. I'm pretty sure I convinced her mother I was an OK guy, but Sam couldn't believe I didn't even drink. For years, Sam would show up unannounced at our gigs, and make a point to talk to all of the waitresses, bartenders and club owners, checking up on me. I thought it was funny and didn't blame him, because I certainly looked the part with my long hair and beard, and it was after all, the 1970's smack in the middle of the sex, drugs and rock and roll era.

Because I was a married man, and promised to look after Dana like she was my little sister, amazingly they said yes and let Dana join the band for the summer break.

Before I go on, I need to go back to Carla. Remember her, the girl I fired? What I didn't know at this time was that she had hooked up with my drummer Lynn Meyer about a month earlier, so when I announced to the band that I had hired Dana, Lynn came to me and asked if it would be OK if Carla hung around and stayed with him in his hotel room instead of me buying her a bus ticket and sending her back to Houston.

I reluctantly agreed, but told him to make it clear to her that if I ever saw or heard her be rude to Dana, she would be on a bus that afternoon. A few hours later, Carla called and asked if she could talk to me. When she knocked on my door, the arrogant, overconfident, know it all Carla that I had always known was not there. In her place was a humble, very regretful person that I'd never met before. She begged and pleaded with me not to fire her and let her stay in the band.

Trying to be as nice as I could, I said, "I'm sorry Carla, I've already hired another girl. You know that, and I can't afford to have two girls in the band."

"If you let me stay, I'll work for expenses. I can stay with Lynn, just pay for my food until you can afford me. I will work with the new girl and show her the ropes. With two girls, just think about it, I bet we can get more money pretty quick."

"Carla," I said smiling, "Dana is a sweet, innocent country girl. I'm not sure I want her to learn how to be a pain in the ass chick singer like you."

"I promise I'll be nice to her and take her under my wing and protect her. Please Ben, I don't have any place else to go. Please, let me stay."

I told Carla I'd have to think about it, then made a few phone calls. The first one was to Dana to see if she would care if I let Carla stay. The second, was to my agent and Larry O'Keefe, who actually like the idea of having two girls in the band. Of course, he wasn't the one who would have to deal with them, but I reluctantly agreed to let Carla stay.

"Carla, if I do this," I said, "you've got to promise me that you'll cut out all this primadonna egomaniac crap. You don't have to tell everybody how great you are, just prove it to them when you're on the stage. I think everybody deserves a second chance, but I'm warning you, I don't give a third. The moment that giant ego of yours rears its ugly head again, you're out for good."

I know what you're probably thinking and trust me I was thinking it too. I was not delusional, I knew that Carla hadn't suddenly changed into a nice person, she had really screwed up this time and egomaniac or not, she knew it. I knew it wouldn't be too long before the real Carla showed back up, and I was right.

The plan was for Dana and her roommate Trudy to stay with me and my wife for a few days until they could find an apartment. We were booked for 8 weeks at the Holiday Inn located near the Houston Intercontinental Airport. I had discussed this plan with my wife Gail a few different times and she seemed OK with it, but when we arrived at my apartment around 8 o'clock pm, she wasn't there.

This was before cellphones, so I had no way to call her and honestly, had no idea why she wasn't there, or where she could be. When it got to be 10 pm, I helped the girls make up their bed in the hide-a-bed couch in the downstairs living room, then went upstairs and waited on Gail to come home.

She finally showed up at about 2 am. She was distraught and crying. When I asked her what was wrong and where she'd been, she blindsided me and dropped a bomb on my head. It was true confession time.

Apparently, she had been sleeping with her boss for the past year, that's where she had been. To quote her, "We decided that it was finally time to tell you the truth."

If that wasn't enough, she also let me know that our marriage was over... and as a bonus she told me that she and (what ever his name was) planned on getting married as soon as our divorce was final.

I had talked to her that morning, right before I started driving from Lubbock to Houston and she was all lovey-dovey, telling me how much she'd missed me and how excited she was that I was coming home. It was an Academy Award winning performance.

After a lot of screaming and yelling, I grabbed one finger full of the few hanging clothes I had in the closet, loaded up the girls in my car, drove to North Shore and woke up my parents.

It was four in the morning when I knocked on their door, but my loving parents didn't say a discouraging word. They just welcomed Dana and Trudy and got them settled into one of the guestrooms. My dad made a pot of coffee and after the girls were asleep, mom, dad and me settled in the living room to talk about what had happened.

After filling them in on all the gory details, my mom asked, "Are you sure it's really over? Are you going to file for divorce?"

I shook my head, "Yes... This has been coming for a long time. Gail hated my music and this is the final nail in the coffin. I still love her, but I could never trust her again, so yeah, it's over."

"Great!" My mother said enthusiastically. "I never liked that little smart ass bitch anyway."

We stayed with my parents for about three days until we located some apartments to move into. It was call the Oakwood Garden Apartments. Dana and Trudy moved into a nice two bedroom, and I took a small efficiency a couple of floors below them.

Other than my marriage blowing up and Gail driving me nuts with all her outrageous demands, the gig at the Holiday Inn Airport and everything else in my life was going pretty good. Carla kept her promise, went above and beyond and was actually a huge help to Dana. Before long, my band, now called the Ben Marney 5 was the talk of the town.

I knew the best thing for me was to get back out on the road and the hell away from Gail, but Larry had booked us solid for the whole summer in Houston. I was sort of stuck, doing my best to deal with the gig, and all of Gail's hell, but once again fate stepped into my life and changed everything.

I was surprised to see Larry O'Keefe at the gig on a Tuesday night, he normally only came out on weekends, but there he was, walking in carrying a large book in his hands.

When I sat down next to him he said, "Guess who is the worldwide Entertainment Director for the Marriott hotels?"

I shook my head, "I have no idea, who is it?"

He gave me a wide grin, "Me!" Then he opened up the book and said, "Where do you want to play?"

For our first gig, we selected a place starting in two weeks in Washington DC called The Port of Georgetown.

After we selected some great gigs all across the United States filling up the rest of our year, Larry picked up his book and headed out.

On his way out he stopped, turned around and said, "Oh, by the way. These are all showrooms, so you'll need to do two shows each night."

"Show? What kind of show?" I asked.

"Do the same thing you're doing now, but do it on the dance floor with the girls, and talk a lot more."

"Talk about what?" I yelled, but he was already out the door.

SUDDENLY WE WERE no longer a dance band playing to drunks in

Holiday Inns, now we were a show-band booked in some of the top show rooms all across America, and I had no friggin' idea what the hell a show was!"

Dana in 1971

# 9

# WILLARD AND ALICE

I t was 1971, I was 21 years old, and I had started my professional
music career only two years earlier, sitting on a stool playing
my guitar, performing as a solo act for $87.50 a week. Now
suddenly, I was booked for a solid year in some of the top show rooms
all across the US and my weekly share was over $1,000! All I had to do
to earn it… was to figure out what the hell a "show" was. And I only
had three weeks to do it.

Through the next two weeks, I didn't play the last two sets at the
Holiday Inn Airport, instead I spent that time checking out some of
the top showrooms around Houston. At that time, Bill Nash, Gary
Smith and Dean Scott were considered to be the best, so that's where I
went for my research. Each of them were unique performers, but Bill
and Gary had similar shows, playing guitar, singing the hot songs of
that time, telling jokes and messing with the crowd in between the
songs. Dean did the same thing, but with the addition of doing some
amazing and hilarious impersonations of Ray Charles and of all
things, Dolly Parton. He was a fantastic performer.

Over the two weeks, I had a chance to see 2 Bill Nash shows, 2
Gary Smith shows and 3 of Dean Scott's. I now knew what a show
was, but honestly wasn't sure that I had the talent to pull it off.

Although Bill, Gary and Dean's shows were all different, the one common denominator that ran through all three was their amazing on stage charisma. They all had that amazing, unique ability to hold everyone's attention and have them hang on every word they said, and all three of them were funny as hell.

I knew I could sing, play guitar and talk to the crowd, but funny... I was not funny.

I decided not to worry about the funny part and put together two shows that included what I thought were the best songs Dana, Carla and I did. I was praying that the strength of our music and power of our voices would be enough to pull off the shows.

It was a Friday night after we'd finished playing and we were in the middle of our second night of rehearsals of the new shows, when Carla, the "real" Carla with her giant ego, decided to show up again.

She was not happy with my song selections and only getting to sing 4 of the 12 songs in each show.

"I need to be singing at least half of the show," she boasted, "you and Dana can split the other half." Oh boy, here we go again, I thought.

The facts were, she was probably right. Dana was very inexperienced and when it came to doing a show, so was I; however when Carla was performing, it 'was' a show. She was an amazing singer who had great on stage charisma.

I knew that featuring Carla more would absolutely make the show work, but I also knew that if I did, she would make my life a living hell. With everything else that I was living through at that time, specifically my divorce with Gail, there was no way I could add to that load, so I told her no.

"These are the shows we're doing, take it or leave it!" I said.

Knowing Carla, I'm sure she thought that finally, she had me trapped. The Washington gig was only 10 days away, so she said, "OK then, I'll leave it. Either give me half the show or I'll quit, and I'll take Lynn with me."

I looked at Lynn, "After all we've been through, you'd leave me like this?" He dropped his head and shrugged.

By now, if you've read this book from the beginning, you should know that I am capable of making really stupid decisions, so can you guess what I did next?

"OK guys, here's the deal," I said pissed, "Carla, this was your last chance. Lynn, I know she's got you so pussy whipped you're not thinking right, so you have one more chance coming, but for now, neither one of you are going to Washington with me. You are both off that gig, but if you want to get paid for this week and the next, you'll finish out this gig, playing and singing at your best. Otherwise, there is the door." Then I stood up and walked out of the bar.

It was 3am, but I didn't care. From a payphone in the lobby I called and woke up Larry O'Keefe and told him what I'd just done.

Because Larry was now the entertainment buyer for the Marriott hotels, he had a lot of pull and a lot of connections. By noon the next day he'd found me a new drummer. His name was David Ka-tie-ah. Because the contract called for five musicians we also needed to replace Carla, and Larry had three other girl singers lined up, but I'd had my fill with egocentric chick singers, so I decided to go with a utility musician instead. His name was Dale Beuall and he played amazing guitar, sax and flute. We met for the first time on Sunday and had 8 days to learn two shows and three dance sets.

Larry was worried about how Lynn and Carla would act the last week of the Holiday Inn gig, so to give me extra rehearsal time and avoid any problems with Lynn and Carla, he booked another band to replace us.

So, much to Lynn and Carla's surprise, at the end of the gig the next night, I handed them their paycheck and savoring the words said, "I've already found new musicians to replace you, so... you're fired! Bye-bye guys, I hope you two have a nice life!"

If you're thinking that Carla, realizing she had made another big mistake, suddenly changed her mind and started begging me not to fire her, you'd be right.

Taking her and Lynn back would have instantly made my life easier, but I'd had enough of her. Right before my eyes I watched her transform back to the nice Carla, but I'd seen that rodeo before.

I understand that she and Lynn joined a new band about a month after I'd fired them, but that band leader was much smarter than me. He fired Carla after only two weeks of her BS. That was the end for them as well, because Lynn stayed with the band and finally came to his senses and kicked Carla out of his house. That was the last anyone heard from Carla. It was such a shame; all that talent, but she just couldn't control her enormous ego.

The rehearsal with the new band members went surprisingly well. Dale knew a lot of great instrumentals that worked out perfectly for the dinner set, and between Beaux, David, Dana and Dale they quickly came up with enough songs to fill up the rest of the dance sets. They were both great musicians and also learned the music for the shows at lightning speed. Because things had gone so well in rehearsals, we decided to leave a few days early and catch the show of the entertainer we were following at the Port of Georgetown.

When we pulled up to the Port of Georgetown to see the Saturday night show, the parking lot was full of large television broadcast trucks. It turned out that the entertainer that we were following was filming one of his television specials that would be airing in New York City and Washington as well. His name was Clint Holmes, and had a hit record called "Playground In My Mind" on the Billboard charts at the time.

When I watched his show, my heart sunk deep in my chest. This guy was Sammy Davis Jr., Elvis Presley and Frank Sinatra all in one package. He was a great singer, dancer and entertainer. He eventually ended up with his own theatre in Las Vegas.

Oh My God! This was who we were following in two nights with a band that had only been together for a week and two shows we'd never ever performed. There was no doubt in any of our minds that we were destined to bomb and lay a huge egg right in the middle of the stage on our first night.

After the show, we found a late night breakfast joint and sat around a table staring at each other in stunned silence.

Finally Beaux said, "You think they'll fire us the first night or let us at least finish out a week?"

I shrugged, "I'm not sure I'd want to suffer through an entire week. I hope they let us go home after the first night."

"We have a contract," Dale said, "Won't they have to pay us off or something?"

"I don't know." I said. "Guess we'll find that out pretty soon."

We all ordered breakfast but none of us had much of an appetite.

"I don't know about you guys, "I said after we'd eaten, "I've never been to D.C. before and it looks like I may never be here again, so tomorrow I'm going to at least check out this city while I'm here." And that's what we did.

That Sunday, we visited all of the amazing monuments, drove around the White House and took in as much as we could in one day. We finished the day walking through the Smithsonian museum. That was by far our favorite stop. If you haven't been there, you need to go. It's incredible.

Dreading the awful outcome, we begrudgingly made our way to the Port Of Georgetown Monday afternoon and set up our equipment. We were all praying that because it was a Monday night, maybe the showroom wouldn't have much of a crowd so we could perhaps last a few days before we got the axe.

To give the appearance of some kind of an actual show, I decided to just have Beaux, David and Dale play the first pre-show dinner set and make a big entrance with Dana and me at showtime.

When the band started playing there were only two tables of customers, but after their 45 minute set, I looked around from backstage and almost fainted. The room was packed with 400 smiling folks, all giddy with anticipation, waiting for our "BIG" show.

That $87.50 a week at Bud's Fish and Chips was looking pretty good to me at that moment. I wanted to run, but I didn't. When the band started playing our opening song, I took a deep breath and walked onto the dance floor and started singing.

Earlier that day, we had adjusted the show lights so they would shine evenly on Dana and me during the show, but when I looked to my right for Dana, she was standing too far back, and the lights were hitting her at about her knees.

"Move up," I whispered.

With a terrified look on her face she just shook her head and mumbled, "No way." She was wearing a long, form fitting, slinky gown and I could actually see her knees shaking underneath her dress.

"Move up." I said again, but she just shook her head and stood there like a statue until the song ended.

After the applause died down, Larry O'Keefe's words flashed through my head, "Just do what you do and talk to the audience more."

I wasn't sure what to talk about, so I started by introducing myself, the band members, and then Dana. When I told the audience where she was from, Muleshoe, Texas, they instantly roared with laughter. Because I was from Texas I'd never considered that the name "Muleshoe" might sound funny to some people, so honestly I wasn't exactly sure why they were laughing.

What happened next was, I swear, a gift from God. Taking advantage of my ignorance and red-neck-ness, God put these words in my mouth.

Not really meaning to, but sounding a little like Andy Griffith, I said, "I think I need to tell you all that this here is my first show and I ain't real sure what to do next. I'm hoping you all didn't come here tonight to see me do some dancing, like ole Clint Holmes was doing here last week. The only dance I know is the Cotton Eyed Joe and honestly, I can't do it worth a shit." The audience, the waitresses, the club manager and the bartenders all roared with laughter.

I was still completely clueless as to why they were laughing and must have had a goofy, confused look on my face, so I asked them. "Did I say something funny?" They laughed harder. I swear, I honestly had no idea what they were laughing at. Just to make sure, I looked down and checked my zipper to see if it was open and when I did, they actually started clapping.

I slid back to the stage and asked Beaux, "What the hell is so funny?"

"I don't know," he said, "but whatever it is, keep doing it."

I smiled back at the audience and continued innocently revealing my total lack of sophistication. "I tell you what, this here War-shington DC is a real nice place. Yesterday, Dana, the boys and me checked it out. We went to this place called the Smith Stoneian."

The second I said that, I heard a woman scream with laughter. I looked at her confused, "You ain't never been to the Smith Stoneian?" The room exploded with laughter.

Continuing with my red neck ignorance, I said, "Honey, you need to get on over there to that Smith Stoneian. They even got a fella there that turned into a giant bar of soap."

Eventually, I caught on, but not completely. I thought they were just laughing at my Texas accent, and they were, so I laid it on thick. It wasn't until after our second show, repeating everything I'd said in the first one, that I realized that, the Smith Stoneian was actually pronounced Smithsonian. What a moron I was back then.

With each performance after that, my Andy Griffith routine got more and more Southern and my misspronunciation of famous landmarks became legendary. We packed the place every night for the four weeks we were there.

On the last weekend, the manager came up to me, right before the show and told me that Mr. Marriott was in the audience. Mr. Marriott Senior, the friggin' founder of the Marriott corporation.

I purposely didn't tell the band or Dana he was there, so they wouldn't freak out like I was. Fortunately, the show came off without a hitch, ending with a standing ovation. After the show, the manager came back stage and said Mr. Marriott wanted to meet me.

He was there with his wife Alice and they were incredibly gracious and very complimentary of the show.

"It's nice to meet you, Ben. Call me J. Willard," He said holding out his hand to shake. "This is my wife Alice. Is that your wife, singing with you?"

I shook my head, "Not yet, but I'm working on it."

They both laughed. "I don't blame you son, she's very pretty. I really like the fact that your show is funny and clean at the same time. That's a hard combination to find these days. I think we can do a lot of business together in the future if you'll fix just one little thing."

I turned toward him, confused. "What do I need to fix?"

He smiled, "Well, my wife Alice, doesn't think your future wife Dana, has enough clothes on."

I racked my brain trying to remember what Dana had been wearing in the show. I've never been real observant of Dana's wardrobe, but I was pretty sure she was wearing another one of those long slinky dresses. I was a bit confused, because it wasn't revealing at all. Then it hit me. This was the early 70's and the no bra look was all the rage.

I smiled at him, "Can you recommend a store that might sell brassieres? I'll take her there first thing in the morning."

We performed at the Port Of Georgetown three more times over the next few years and for almost six years we crisscrossed the country performing our shows exclusively in Marriott Hotels. Mr. Marriott trusted us enough to open up several of his new hotels in Chicago, Denver and, as a reward for our hard work, he booked us for 16 weeks in Acapulco, Mexico.

Dana eventually learned to stand in the lights, but even now, after 40 some odd years and thousands of shows, right before the show starts, her knees still shake.

To this day, I'm always a touch more southern when I'm on stage. My Texas accent has been one of my biggest blessings and assets in my life.


A NOTE to all you non-southern, yankees out there. Don't let the accent fool you. Just because we may look a little goofy, talk a little slow and sound a little dumb... don't mean we are!

Ben Marney Show - 1972

# 10

# JOHN SIVIL

When I was about 12, my brother Ron, lost his best friend in a car crash. His name was,Gibb Jones. He ran into a bridge, trying to eat a hamburger while he was driving back to the University of Texas in Austin. The night before he was killed, he was at our house, hanging out with Ron in the living room most of the night, listening to music on our stereo.

Gibb was into the blues and had brought over his new Bobby Blue Bland LP. It wasn't my kind of music, or my parents, so after listening to a few of the songs, we left them alone and retired to our bedrooms. I've always regretted not staying and spending a little more time with him.

I heard about his accident at school the next day. The news had spread like a wildfire through the halls, but because my brother had already graduated and was attending the University of Houston, he hadn't heard the news, but I didn't know that.

The minute the bell rang, I jumped on my bike and flew home so I'd be there when he drove up to tell him how sorry I was.

When he walked in the house, he was singing, holding a package under his arm. I wasn't sure what I was expecting, but singing was not it. I started to say something to him about Gibb, but his singing threw me, so I just kept quiet and let him walk on by.

He walked into the living room and opened the package. It was a new Bobby Blue Bland LP; the same one Gibb had brought over the night before. Still singing, he ripped open the plastic, pulled out the album, placed it on the spindle and hit play. He settled on the couch, leaning back with his eyes closed listening to the music. I sat next to him not talking, listening to the music with him.

It was almost like he was in some kind of trance. I assumed it was just his way of grieving. After the third song ended, I finally said something. "Ron, I'm really sorry about Gibb."

He cracked open his right eye slightly, looked at me and wrinkled his forehead. "Sorry about what?"

"You don't know?"

He raised up and turned toward me, his eyes open wide. "Know what?"

"He was killed in a car wreck this morning. I thought you knew."

Locking his dark black eyes onto mine, he froze, still as a stone. His eyes filled with tears and his body began to tremble. Barely able to get out the words, he whimpered, "Gibb is dead?"

"Bubba, I'm so sorry... yes."

Before my eyes, I watched in horror,as my big. strong brother literally melted off the couch, curled into a fetal position on the floor and cried a cry so deep and full of pain it broke my heart. It was my first time to experience true, unbridled, raw human emotion.

I didn't know what to do, so I slid down beside him and patted his shoulder as he wept.

A few minutes later my mother walked into the room. She'd just heard the news as well, tears were rolling down her face. She laid down on the floor next to Ron and pulled him into her arms. They cried together for a very long time.

The next night, Dad drove us to the funeral home and we viewed his body.

I didn't really want to, but for some reason Ron needed me. "Will you go up there with me little brother? I'm not sure I can do this alone."

He didn't resemble the Gibb I'd seen only a few nights earlier, but Ron didn't seem to notice or care. I stood silently by his side as he gazed down, smiling at his friend. He stood there silently for a while then, started talking to him. "Gibb, I guess it's ok to tell you now." He whispered. "I never really did like the blues much, but I bought that stupid album anyway." He was laughing and crying the words at the same time.

We stood there together looking down at Gibb for ten or fifteen minutes while Ron talked. Then he reached down and touched Gibbs hand. "I promise I'll look after your mom and dad." He said. "And don't worry... I'll never forget you."

When Dad said it was time to go home, Ron wouldn't get in the car. Ron and several of his friends stayed all night at that funeral home. He told us later that they'd pulled chairs up close to his casket and told each other Gibb stories all night.

After that, Ron changed and always seemed different somehow. He withdrew into himself and didn't talk as much. And almost every day until he moved out into his first apartment, Ron played that Bobby Blue Bland album.

That was my first experience with death, grieving and how people react. I was too young to understand and honestly was a little mad at my brother for not snapping back to normal. He stopped messing with me, even when I acted stupid. Playing with him, he didn't react. Nothing I did seemed to matter to him.

I talked to my father about how sad Ron seemed to be and asked him when he thought he'd get back to his old self.

"Ben, I'm not sure he ever will." Dad said. "He took Gibb's death hard. Son, in life you don't have many true friends. If you can use all of your fingers on one hand counting them, then you are a lucky man. Most of us only have one or two in our whole life. When you lose one, a part of you dies with them and that changes you forever."

I still didn't get it. I remember thinking, one or two? I've got more friends that I can count. I was too young to grasp the concept of a "true" friend versus just a friend. Fortunately, I didn't have to deal with death and funerals for the rest of my childhood.

I mentioned before I was moved up a grade. The day the principal took me out of the 5th grade and walked me down the hall to my new 6th grade class, the teacher introduced me and made a big of deal explaining why I was there.

Embarrassed from all the attention and stares, I slowly walked to the back of the room and took a seat next to John Sivil.

When I sat down, he started grinning from ear to ear and immediately introduced himself. "Hey Benny, I'm John, nice to meet ya!" That was the day I met one of those "true" friends my dad had talked about. It was a friendship that bonded us together forever.

John was a good athlete like me and we played side by side on the same baseball, basketball, football and track team all the way through high school. If you couldn't find us together on some sports field, then we were either at John's house, my house or in the woods on one of our pretend African safaris. We were inseparable. My parents considered him part of our family, just like his parents considered me as part of theirs.

In my effort to keep this book under a thousand pages, I've racked my brains trying to pick only a few John stories that do him justice and help explain what a special person he was.

I guess the best words to describe him would be handsome, positive, gentle and kind. He was a real lady killer, with his dark complexion and brown eyes, but his good looks were not what made everyone love him. He was just simply one of the nicest guys you'd ever meet. Honestly, I'm pretty sure my first real girlfriend liked John better than me, not romantically, but as her best "boy" friend. Her name was Linda Tice, but I was the only one who ever called her Linda. John always just called her Tice.

I don't think I ever saw John in a bad mood or angry. I've seen him sad enough to cry, I've seen him confused and hurt, but I can't remember ever seeing him really mad. John was one of those rare people that seem to always be in a good mood, always smiling and only saw the positive side no matter how dark the situation may be.

I was just the opposite, a moody kid and easy to anger, always getting mad over the silliest things. No matter how mad I got, even if it was at him, he had a way of saying just the right thing to make me laugh and calm down. We were so different that I've often wondered how we remained such good friends all those years.

When I had to move away my freshman year, John met Kelly Smith and they became fast friends. When I returned the following year, the three of us became known as the three musketeers, doing everything together.

Probably the dumbest thing we ever did was let John's father, Noris overhear us complaining about our football coach. It was 1964 and the Beatles had just hit America and soon everyone started wearing their hair a little longer. The girls loved it, but our football coaches didn't like it at all. The three of us had to do extra laps that day because the coaches thought our hair was too long.

We were trying to come up with some way to get back at the coaches when Noris suggested that we get back at them by shaving our heads. "That'll show em!'" he said.

I swear we weren't stoned or drinking that day, but before I knew it, Noris had his clippers, razor and shaving mug all lathered up and we followed him out to the garage. None of us had a date for three months after that.

The worst part was how the coaches reacted. I'm not sure why now, but we honestly thought they'd feel bad, but when they saw our shining bald clean shaven heads, they gathered the team around us and said, "Boys, now THAT'S what we call a hair cut!" They loved it.

Galena Park, where we lived, was a small suburb of Houston. If you're not familiar with Houston, let me tell you, it's a hot and humid place. In those 100 degree summers, one of the dumb things we loved to do was find a large patch of clover and lay in it. We did it all the time. The clover was always cool and felt good against our skin. John, Kelly and I would lay there for hours, watching the clouds, talking about our lives and what we wanted to be when we grew up.

Kelly was never sure. He flip flopped between an engineer, a doctor, or working construction. We never knew what he might come up with. John always wanted to be a football coach. Not pro, or even college--he dreamed of being a high school football coach. That made sense to me, considering how good of an overall athlete he was, and I always encouraged him to do it one day. His only concern was his fear that he wasn't smart enough. John wasn't what you would consider slow, but he did struggle in school, making C's and D's on most of his report cards.

In those days, if you were on the football team and didn't make A's, B's or C's, you got licks from the coaches; one for a D and two for an F. John's ass was usually bright red on report card days. I'm confident that he would have never made it through algebra or biology if his desk had not been next to mine. Over the years, we developed a pretty sneaky system for him to copy my answers.

My dreams in those days, laying in that clover, were always, according to John, never big enough. No matter what I said I might grow up to be, he would say, "Naa, that's not you. You're gonna do a lot more than that."

He seemed to know somehow, even when we were just kids, that I would take a different path to walk down for my life.

We did spend some time apart: me practicing hours and hours with my guitar, Kelly practicing baseball, John either shooting hoops in his driveway or chipping golf balls into a wash bucket.

John's true talent was golf. There's no doubt in my mind he could have qualified for the PGA tour if he wanted to. He was that good. While I was changing my guitar strings, John was retrieving the hundred or so golf balls he had chipped into the 24 inch wide wash bucket from 100 yards away. He never missed the bucket by more than a foot.

In high school, my music was just something I did for fun and to get all the girls' attention. The thought of being a professional singer and musician had seriously never crossed my mind. The facts were, if you grew up in Galena Park, if you were honest with yourself, you dreamed about getting a good shift at Armco Steel or one of the other factories lining the Houston ship channel. Touring the world, singing and performing shows was unfathomable.

One night, John was in his usual place when he was in my bedroom; lying on his back on the other twin bed throwing and catching a ball in the air as he listened to me practice a new song. It was 'The House Of The Rising Sun' by the Animals.

When I finished, John rolled over on his stomach and said, "I like the way you sing that better than that Animal guy!"

I laughed. "Yeah, right."

He sat up and looked at me. "I'm serious Benny! You sing and play great. I bet you could do that for a living."

I laughed again. "I'm serious. I'm not kidding. Then, when you become a big star, I could be your manager. Just think about all the girls we would meet then." Then he laughed and snorted.

When John laughed hard, he snorted. When he snorted, that made me laugh more. When I laughed more, that made him snort again. This side-splitting chain reaction happened almost every day and could go on for hours.

When we finally stopped, he said, wiping his laughing tears away, "Will you at least think about it?"

John worked and studied hard and somehow graduated from the University of Houston. His dreams of being a high school football coach were within his grasp.

Not long after, he married Sandra, his high school sweetheart. But instead of pursuing coaching, surprising all of us, he decided to go into the trucking business with his new father-in-law. Soon Sandra got pregnant with their first child and they began what I thought was going to be a charmed life.

We were performing at the Marriott in St. Louis when Kelly called. He was crying so hard I couldn't understand him. "Calm down Kelly, I can't make out a word you're saying. What's wrong? Say that again."

I heard him clearly the second time and immediately broke down as well. "John has cancer."

We were in the middle of a four-week contract, but after a call to Larry O'Keefe, my agent, to cut the gig short and cancel the next one, we packed up and drove as fast as we could back to Galena Park

John had developed soreness in one of his testicles. When the doctors went in to check it out, they discovered the cancer. Although they removed it, they unfortunately felt that it was more than likely not the primary source. This was way before MRI's had been invented, so they immediately scheduled John for a full body, exploratory surgery.

I was sitting in a chair, next to his bed when he finally came out of the anesthesia and woke up.

"How bad is it?" He said in a garbled weak voice.

Although they had laid him open, very similar to an autopsy searching every inch of his internal organs, they found no more signs of cancer.

Trying to cheer him up, I joked, "Well, other than being one nut shy, I think you're going to be alright. They didn't find anything."

The one thing I haven't mentioned about John was his faith. He was, and had always been, a devout Christian. Back in the 6th grade when we first met, the first place he ever invited me to go to was to church.

Although my parents were Christians, they didn't attend church regularly. Dad often had to work on Sundays, so until I met John I had only gone to church occasionally, like Christmas Eve and Easter. Once we met, every Sunday morning after that, we sat together in the second row of the First Baptist Church, listening to Brother Ed and singing hymns.

We were baptized on the same day, joined the Royal Ambassadors, our church youth group, and always attended vacation bible school and church camp together every year.

It's clear to me now, the reason behind John's consistent positive and happy outlook on life was because of his unquestionable faith in Jesus Christ. So, it was not a surprise when I told him the doctors hadn't found any more cancer, he asked me to help him out of the bed, so we could both get down on our knees and pray. There was nothing I could say to talk him out of it, and the pain he went through to climb out of that bed and get down on his knees was immense, but somehow we did it.

For almost a year, all the doctors told us that John was cancer free, but 14 months after the discovery of his testicular cancer, they discovered seven more inoperable malignant tumors scattered throughout his body. His prognosis was not good. They told him he had about six months more to live.

I was back on the road, touring the Marriott chain when John called me and told me the news. We cried on the phone together for a while and then he made me promise him I wouldn't cancel any of my gigs because of the news. I kept that promise.

The last time I saw John, he was about 80lbs and bald from all the chemotherapy. Keeping my promise, we were back in Houston visiting my parents on a scheduled break.

The second I arrived, I called him to let him know I was coming to see him, but he said he wanted to come see *me*, and spend some time with my parents. When he arrived, he could hardly walk, but somehow made it out of the car, up the sidewalk and inside the house.

For almost two hours we all laughed and told stories about all the crazy things we'd done together. He even spilled the beans about a few things I'd never told my parents.

Just before he got back into his car to leave, he turned and held out his frail, withered arms and we hugged for a long, long time.

Finally he let go of his bear hug and whispered, "We did everything two kids could ever do, didn't we? You were a great, wonderful friend and I love you. Just promise me that when you think about me, you'll remember all the fun times we had and remember me the way I was. Not like this."

The next weekend, John fell into a coma and died on a Wednesday morning. He was only 23 years old. Of course, I was back on the road again and have always regretted not being there with him when he passed.

In fact, I didn't even know he had died when I finally had a break and dropped by his house to see him. Since no one had called me, I assumed he was still fighting.

I rang his parents doorbell and his mother answered. "I'd like to see John if you think he's strong enough for a visit."

Her eyes instantly filled with tears. "I'm so sorry Benny, but John died three weeks ago."

I froze and shook my head in total disbelief. I was filled with instant rage and screamed, "HE DIED THREE WEEKS AGO! WHY DIDN'T YOU CALL ME?"

Hearing my screaming, John's sister ran up to the door, grabbed me by my shoulders and shook me hard! "STOP THIS! STOP YELLING!" She said firmly.

I stopped and stood there bawling, hyperventilating, gasping for air trying to catch my breath.

Just above a whisper, his mother said. "His last words were, 'Don't call Benny.'" Her lips curled slightly into almost a smile. "At the end, he talked about you a lot. Benny, he was your biggest fan and he knew what you would do. He didn't want you to mess up your music career and... Honestly he didn't want you to see him in his casket. He wanted you to remember him the way he was."

I'm not sure what the odds are, for both me and my brother to lose our childhood friends right out of high school, but I assume they are astronomical. It *was* ironic.

That was over 40 years ago and I still break down and cry when I think about John. Some of the time, when I see him in my mind, it's the image of the healthy, handsome, happy John.

However...

John if you're up there looking down at me as I write this, I'm sorry, because I must admit the one image I think of most often when I think of you, is the night you showed up at my parents house, emaciated and bald. It's a memory I will always cherish and hope I never forget.

BECAUSE THAT NIGHT, I made you laugh hard and do that stupid snorting thing, one last time.

John Franklin Sivil 1949-1973

# 11

# PLAYBOY RECORDS

Although in my lifetime, my father never actually traded for a horse, he always called himself a horse trader. What he was trading for, or trading off, was not important. What 'was' important, and the part he truly loved, was the actual negotiation. He loved wheeling and dealing.

I've mentioned this earlier in other stories, but Dad wouldn't trade with just anybody, he only dealt with what he called his trading buddies. This was a very select group of 15 or 20 of his friends who understood the rules. And those rules were: number one, no matter what it took, or how big of a whopper of a story you had to make up to close the deal, always turn a profit. Rule number two, if you were stupid enough to believe that whopper of a story and got screwed, there were no hard feelings. You just had to take the merciless ribbing from the other members and try your best to get even the next time.

How you gained entry to this special group of trading buddies, to this day, remains a mystery to me. It was a very diverse group including a few of our neighbors, some of his teacher friends, three or four of his fellow grease monkey auto mechanics, his banker and even his doctor.

I honestly think the most important qualification to join this group was to have the ability to keep a straight face while looking you in the eye spewing a line of BS a mile long. When it came to spewing BS my father was apparently the Bull Shit Yoda. I attribute my creative story telling abilities to him.

Not only could my father spin quite a yarn, he had a unique ability to usually see right through his friends BS. Because of that, he was considered the master and always the main target to try and get the best of from his trading buddies. One of my favorite stories is when the president of our bank showed up at our house one Saturday morning.

The truth was, the bank had repossessed a car they had financed for a hot rodding kid. When they picked it up and cranked it, it was knocking like crazy. The banker was a pseudo mechanic (always calling my dad for auto repair advice) and instantly assumed that the kid had blown the engine and the repossessed car had thrown a rod. Knowing my father could fix it cheaply and hoping he could sell it to him at an inflated price to get some of the bank's money back, he had a wrecker drag it to our house and began telling Dad this long story.

"Truman, I financed this car for a poor little old lady who was just barely getting by on her social security each month. She's only had it a few months and wouldn't you know it, the damn thing threw a rod and left her stranded. So, I financed her another car and took this one back, but the banks really upside down on this. I need to get about $900 for it. I realize that it's not worth that to most folks the way it is, but I thought that maybe, if you could replace the rod yourself, you could sell it and still be able to turn a profit. What do you think?"

Dad lifted the hood and revved the engine a few times. When he did it, the loud knocking was deafening.

Hearing all the racket, our across the street and next door neighbors (two more members of the trading buddies group) walked over and stood by the car to see what was going down.

Dad walked around the car a few times, then opened the door and checked the interior and revved the engine with the accelerator pedal a few more times before he spoke.

"Well, it sure sounds like it's thrown a rod doesn't it?" Everybody enthusiastically agreed. "Jack are you sure you want to sell her for 900, it may not be a rod and worth a lot more."

Shaking his head, "I'm pretty sure it's a rod and the Ford dealership told me it would cost at least fifteen hundred to repair it, but that's mostly labor. I figure all it will cost you is parts. When you get it fixed, it should be worth at least two thousand. So, yeah 900 is good for me and the bank"

"One more question." Dad said, with a serious look on his face. "If I get her fixed, will the bank finance her again when I sell it to someone. I don't think I could carry a note this big."

"Yeah," Jack said, smiling. "I'll finance up to $2,000.

Dad smiled. "I'll go 800. You got the paper work with you?"

Fifteen minutes later, the banker had the $800 in his pocket and the car was in my dad's name.

To celebrate the deal, Dad pulled out some lawn chairs, served up some beers and they all settled, sipping their beer in the driveway by the busted car.

"Billy Joe, are you still looking for a second car? This would be a good one for you." Dad asked smiling.

Yeah, I'll buy it for two grand if you get the rod fixed, but I'm not sure I can wait that long."

"Jack, would you be willing to finance Billy Joe when I get it fixed?" Jack grinned, "Absolutely."

"Great. I'll be right back." Dad walked into the garage and came out with a large socket wrench. He bent over the engine, reached down and began turning the wrench. After ten minutes or so of tightening several bolts, he slid behind the wheel and cranked the engine. The horrible, deafening knocking sound was gone.

The banker jumped to his feet and yelled, "Truman, what the hell did you just do?"

Grinning, dad pitched the keys to Billy Joe, "There you go, all fixed good as new." He picked up his beer and sat down in the lawn chair, smiling at Jack, the banker. "Little old lady my ass! Somebody's been hot rodding that car." He said laughing. "The motor mounts had worked loose, I just had to tighten em' up a bit."

That day, Dad made twelve hundred dollars in about fifteen minutes and I'm pretty sure Jack the banker never lived that one down.

There is no doubt that I have inherited many things from my father: His thick hair, (thank goodness I've still got most of it); his looks (we could be twins); his obsession of being on time (he believed it was rude and selfish to be late) and way too many other things to list here, but the one thing I didn't inherit that I wish I had, was his trading skills. Unfortunately, when I buy something I own it for life. I can't seem to sell anything and normally just donate it or give it away when I'm done with it. However, I did pick up his ability to weave a pretty good bullshit story when needed.

MY AGENT, Larry O'Keefe had moved on from being the buyer for the Marriott hotels to securing a position working with Dick Clark. Yes, *THE* Dick Clark. Mr. Clark owned an entertainment management company called Entco. So as soon as Larry got established there, he called and asked me to come to Los Angeles to meet Dick. He was one of the nicest guys I've ever met and before long I was signed up and could boast that my manager was Dick Clark. Soon after that they arranged for me to sign a production contract with Lawrence Welk productions. Again, yes, *THE* Lawrence Welk.

The deal was for me to sign an exclusive six-month productions contract with the Lawrence Welk people  and in return, they would secure my first recording contract with a major label.

I signed that contract standing in between Dick Clark and Lawrence Welk, behind Mr. Welk's massive desk in his office. His office, I swear, was designed to resemble a champagne bubble, with a round ceiling and glass walls.

To get me that record deal, they needed a demo to shop, so the next week they booked recording time in the famous Hal Roach Studio in Hollywood. I was absolutely beside myself with excitement to record my voice for the first time in such a famous studio.

To this day, I'm not sure if the producer for my very first recording session was just messing with me because of my complete inexperience, or if he was actually serious with his directions. He was speaking English, but it might as well had been a  foreign language, because I didn't understand a damn thing he said.

After my first take, he hit the talkback button and said, "Ben, that was good, but just a bit too yellow. Could you add a touch of blue?"

That is an exact quote. "Excuse me?" I said back. "Yellow? Blue? I don't understand."

I heard his voice in my headphones, "Don't worry, you'll get it. Just add a touch of blue to this one." The music started, so still confused I sang another take.

When I finished I heard, "No. that was way too red.  Back it off slightly. I'm hearing green on this song. Let's try it again." The music started again.

This went on for several more takes, with more inexplicable, idiotic color references from the producer.

Finally I'd had enough. "Do you want it louder, softer, more gravel, less gravel, more punch on certain lines or less punch, more head tone, less nazily? Am I flat, am I sharp? Please, tell me anything but a color." He didn't respond, he just glared back at me through the window. "I realize I'm just a red neck from Texas and I'm here in the land of fruits and nuts, but honestly dude, I haven't got a friggin' clue what the hell you're talking about with all these colors! Is it possible for you to talk to me like a normal human or is that beyond your amazing hipness and super coolness to speak that way?"

Apparently, I had insulted his genius creativeness with my questions. He stood up from behind the mixing console, shot me the bird through the window and walked out. Needless to say, that was the end of the session.

In Houston a few weeks later, I found a studio with an engineer and producer that actually spoke English and recorded a two song demo and sent it off to the Welk group.

Unfortunately, six months later when that contract came up for renewal, I had not received any offers from any labels and was frustrated and impatient.

I flew back to Los Angeles to discuss whether or not to re-sign my exclusive Lawrence Welk production contract with Dick Clark and Larry O'Keefe. They were both all for it, but I didn't want to. We argued back and forth for a few hours till Dick had to leave for another appointment.

"Just sleep on it tonight, "Dick told me, "and we'll decide what to do in the morning.'

The reason I didn't want to re-sign with The Lawrence Welk group was because, as far as I could tell, they hadn't done a damn thing in six months.

I hope you don't hold this against me, but in those days I was an avid reader of Playboy Magazine and had bought the latest issue in the airport on my way there. Of course, I only bought it to read the articles. (I wrote that with a straight face. I told you I was pretty good at BS.)

That night in my hotel room, I opened up the Playboy and started reading the articles. Ok ok, it was after I'd checked out the fold out.

In one of the articles, I read that Hugh Hefner had decided to open a record label. His first signed artist was Barbie Benton, who had been on the Playboy cover several times and just happened to be Hef's girlfriend at the time.

I promise what I'm about to tell you is absolutely true. It's such a bizarre story I couldn't have made it up.

The next morning I took a cab to Dick Clark's office building and plopped down in a chair across from Larry in his office. Dick was running late, so Larry took that time to start hammering me to re-sign the Welk contract before he got there.

I have no explanation for what I did next, but on a whim, I picked up Larry's phone, dialed information and got Playboy Records' phone number and without hesitation, I dialed it.

"Hey there." I said to the cheerful receptionist who answered. "This is Ben Marney calling from Dick Clark's office. We just heard about Hef's new label. How long have you guys been open?"

"Almost a year now." She answered, I could hear her smiling through the phone.

"Who's doing your A and R?" She told me his name was Don Shane. "Boy that sounds familiar, where's he from?"

"I'm not sure. Hold on a second." When she came back she said. "He's from Tulsa, Oklahoma.

After I hung up, Larry looked at me, squinting his eyes, "What the hell are you doing?"

"I'm not exactly sure." I said, dialing the number again.

When the same voice answered, laying on my Texas accent I said. "Let me talk to Don. Tell him it's a voice from his shady past."

Almost immediately he answered. "Hello, this is Don Shane."

"Don!" I yelled into the phone, laying on the accent. "What the hell is a Tulsa, Oklahoma red neck like you doing out here in the land of fruits and nuts?"

He started laughing. "Just trying to make a living."

"Man, I haven't talked to you in a coons age." I said. "I think the last time I saw you was in Oklahoma City at that studio. What was the name of that place?"

"It had to be Cattle Row." He said. "I'm sorry, but I don't recognize the voice, who is this?"

"Oh boy, that figures, you come out here to Hollywood and get the big head." I laughed in the phone. "This is Ben Marney from Houston. How the hell are you!"

He had no idea who I was, but like I was hoping, being raised southern and not wanting to be rude, he wasn't about to let me know it.

"Ben!" He yelled. "Damn it's good to hear from you again. And I can ask you the same thing. What's a Texas redneck doing out here in Hollywood?"

"Well, I guess I'm still singing pretty good, because about six months ago they signed me up over here at Dick Clark's management joint and I'm in town kicking a little ass, trying to get them off theirs! Dick told me he'd have me a record contract by now, but you know how that shit goes."

"Where have they been looking?" Don Asked. "I've been here six months and they haven't called me." When he said that, I wanted to start dancing a jig, but somehow remained calm.

"That's exactly what I figured. That's why I'm here. I'm taking the bull by the horns and doing it myself. Look Don, Dick Clark just walked in and we've got a few things to go over. I know your real busy, but could I call you back later or could you call me back here in an hour or so?" I gave him Dick Clarks office number and hung up.

Larry was looking up at me with his mouth wide open. "Was that really someone from Playboy Records?"

I smiled. "Yep. It was my old buddy Don Shane, head of Artist Development."

"And you hung up before making an appointment? Are you crazy? How do you know him?"

"I've never met him in my life, but he doesn't know that. And don't worry, he'll call me back."

I was in the middle of getting lectured about the reality of how show business really works by Larry, two other agents and Dick Clark, when the secretary interrupted us. There's a Don Shane from Playboy Records on the phone for Ben."

What I would give to have a picture of their stunned faces. "Told you." I said grinning. "This may not be how things are done out here in Hollyweird, but apparently it's the way things are done in Tulsa."

The secretary put the call through and to my surprise, Dick hit the speaker button and said, "This is Dick Clark."

Don stammered on the other end. "Ahh, hello Mr. Clark, this is Don Shane from Playboy Records. I was trying to call Ben." I'm pretty sure he didn't remember my last name.

"Ben Marney?" Dick asked, winking at me.

Stammering again, Don nervously said. "Ahhh, yes sir, is he there?"

"Hey Don." I yelled into the speaker. "Yeah, I'm here."

"Is this a bad time, are you still in your meeting?"

"No we're done, hang on a second and let me find an office around here so we can talk in private."

"Hey Don," Dick said. "The next time you see Hef, tell him Dick Clark says hello."

Three weeks later, a picture of me standing in between Hugh Hefner, Tom Takayoshi and Dick Clark appeared in Billboard Magazine announcing my addition to the Playboy Label. I was the fourth person to sign on that label. Other than me, there was Barbie Benton, Lou Rawls and Mickey Gilley. A few months later, they signed an unknown group from Europe call ABBA. I wonder what ever happened to them?

I know what you're thinking and trust me, it's the same question I've asked myself about 1 million times. What the hell happened? The answer is... I honestly don't know for sure.

I will admit the two songs I recorded in Houston and used to bullshit my way through the Playboy Records doors were not my best work. My songwriting has come a long way since then and to be brutally honest, both of those songs sucked. However, Tom Takayoshi, the head of the label really liked them and began the wheels turning to release them as my first single, but I shot myself in the foot before that happened. Not literally, but what I actually did had the same effect.

If you were born and raised in the South, you will understand, but for those of you who were not, I'll try to do my best to explain.

When you're raised by southern parents, especially Texas parents, you are brainwashed from infancy to always be friendly and helpful when you can. If you don't believe me, the next time you're in Texas pull over to the side of the road, lift up your hood and see how long it takes before you have two or three people stop and offer to give you a helping hand. I wouldn't do this on an interstate freeway, but on any other road, especially in a small town, give it a try... we just can't help ourselves.

A few months after I had signed my deal with Playboy, I was back in Los Angeles for a few days when Larry O'Keefe asked me to go with him to listen to a new group they were thinking about signing. We met them in a recording studio not far from Dick Clark's offices. Larry and I listened to them play a few songs and they were absolutely great. After they finished, we all sat around the studio and talked a while. Their names were Joe Frank Carollo, Alan Dennison and Dan Hamilton. They were your typical broke musicians looking for work and hoped that by signing with Dick Clark's management company they might be able to land some good gigs. Joe Frank told us that the original group (with a different drummer named Tommy Reynolds) had a minor hit record in 1971 called "Don't Pull Your Love Out On Me Baby", but were now considered "one hit wonders" and couldn't get in the front door to even talk to any record labels.

I instantly remembered that song and had actually been performing it for years. "That was you guys? I love that song." I said. Then I opened my big mouth and said something that had a major negative effect on my life.

Joe Frank was from Leland, Mississippi, another southern boy, so I just couldn't stop myself. I wrote Don Shane's number on a piece of paper, handed it to him and said, "Call my friend Don at Playboy Records, he's one of us, from Tulsa. Tell him I said I told you to call, I guarantee you he'll talk to you. I just signed with them and I know they're looking for new acts."

This was October, 1974. My first single called "Oh Mama" was scheduled to be released in March or April of 1975. We were performing at the Playboy Club in Chicago when Don Shane called me to tell me that they had decided to postpone my release because they wanted to put all of the company's effort behind a new single they were all convinced was going to be a smash hit. That single was called "Baby Baby Falling in Love," by Hamilton, Joe Frank and Reynolds. It zoomed to the top of the charts and it was the biggest selling single Playboy Records ever had.

Playboy did eventually release my single, but I believe they only did it because they were legally contracted to. They put zero effort behind the promotion and "Oh Mama" became my first big flop. When Hef broke up with Barbie Benton a few years later, he lost interest in the label and it was eventually taken over by Electra who stupidly shelved everyone on the label. We all had to fight to get out of our contracts including Lou Rawls, Mickey Gilley and that other unknown group called ABBA.

That was my first hard lesson learned about show business. It was a humbling and heartbreaking experience, but I will admit that working all those Playboy clubs and getting to know a few of the Bunnies helped soothe the pain.

I suppose some of you might think that this was just another one of my stupid decisions giving Joe Frank Don Shane's phone number that day, but honestly I don't think it was. I think it was meant to be.

Show business is cutthroat, ruthless and can be very cruel at times. Trust me when I tell you, I've experienced all of that in my music career, but I've tried my best not to let those show business scars change who I am.

When those bad things have happened to me, I try to remember what my dad always said. "Life is short and a hell of lot harder to live when you're dragging old negative baggage behind you. You'll soon realize the more you're around people, the better you like dogs. Just don't let those assholes get you down." So far I don't think they have.

I CAN STILL SPEW a good line of BS when needed, I have no idea how to sing more blue or green, but I'm still Southern, relatively friendly and always willing to give a helping hand when I can.

Oh Mama - Playboy Records - 1975

# HOME COOKIN'

When I first signed with Dick Clark's management company and before I signed with Playboy Records, Larry O'Keefe told me I needed to record some new demos of my band. So I began saving my money and eventually bought a TASCAM reel to reel 4 track tape recorder and a small mixing board.

In the 1970s, multi-track recording equipment was very expensive, but because I believed having our own recording capabilities we could produce some really high-quality demos that would eventually lead to better paying gigs, I was willing to invest the two grand. If we were successful, then everyone in the entire band would benefit by making more money. To me, it was a no-brainer; however when I revealed my new multi-track tape recorder to my band and explained my plan, I was shocked by three of my musicians' responses.

I think I need to explain that in those days, because it was my show, my band and my gigs, and my financial responsibility to keep everyone paid each week, I made the lion's share of the money. It was not an equal partnership. My musicians were considered sidemen and earned sidemen money. Although these three musicians didn't have the talent or desire to front the show, because of the discrepancy in the money, apparently there was some resentment. They all had quickly forgotten that when I met them, they were broke, only working a few nights a week in beer joints and dives. With me, they had been working solid for years, earning top of the scale sidemen wages, living in five star Marriott hotels. The new cars they were driving and the new equipment they were playing didn't seem to matter.

We were in the fourth and last week of our gig at the Denver Marriott when I explained that we were going to start recording our sets in hopes of creating better demos. All but two of my musicians responded by saying, "What? You want to record us using our musical talents, so you can make more money? Are you going to pay us extra?"

I shook my head in disbelief, "No, but don't you get it? With better demos we'll all make more money."

"Yeah, we understand that, but when musicians go to a recording studio, they get paid for the studio time." I'm not sure which one of them said it, but they were all in agreement.

I couldn't believe what I was hearing. "Recording in a real studio is a hell of a lot different than what I'm talking about." I tried to explain. "I just want to record a few of our live sets, so we can get a better demo. I'm not asking you to do anything extra."

Bound in solidarity, all but Pat Vivier and Dave Abrams refused to allow me to record them if I didn't pay them extra.

For the past two years, I had been sending money to my brother Ron to invest, so fortunately I had a little cash saved up. The following Saturday after we finished the last night of the contract, I fired the entire band except for Pat and Dave. Then we drove to Los Angeles and with Larry O'Keefe's help, Pat, Dave, Dana and I put together a new one.

Up to this point, the music we were performing was top 40 pop and rock: Neil Diamond, Barbra Streisand, Tony Orlando and Dawn, etc.

Since we were starting from scratch with a brand-new band, I wanted to try something different. Dick Clark, Larry O'Keefe and everybody else at the management company didn't like the idea much, but I didn't care, I wanted to try something unique.

New bands like the Eagles, the Allman Brothers, Lynyrd Skynyrd and the Grateful Dead were flying high in those days and I absolutely loved their music. I wasn't exactly sure what it was that appealed to me so much, I just knew it was different. Also about that time, Hank Williams Jr., Waylon and Willie, the Charlie Daniels Band and Jimmy Buffett were getting more and more popular. I didn't know it at the time, but it was the beginning of what is now called Southern Rock and Outlaw Country and it fit me like a glove.

That was the kind of music I wanted my new show band to do, but to quote Larry O'Keefe and Dick Clark, "YOU CAN'T PLAY COUNTRY MUSIC AT THE HYATT REGENCY!"

Back then, in the mid 70's, all of the successful touring show bands were doing exactly the same thing: top 40 pop and rock. In fact, there were production companies all across the country making a fortune churning out these cloned show bands. They all wore matching shiny rhinestone studded, bell bottomed jumpsuits, did the same choreography and performed the exact same songs.

I knew it was a risk, but decided that it was about time for a little Charlie Daniels at the Hyatt or Marriott or wherever, and formed my new "country rock" show band, called Ben Marney and Home Cookin'.

Dave Abrams told us that he had worked with a guy named John Hamman who could play great lead guitar and also played piano. He and John had worked with Dan Rogers (Kenny Rogers nephew) in a band called Rogers County Line and in another band called Salt Creek.

Somehow we got permission to have rehearsals at the First Baptist Church in Reseda and had John come over to audition. That took about ten seconds before I said, "Your hired!" He was great and we all instantly liked him.

Next was a drummer. Pat had worked with a guy for years named, Gordon Martin and on his strong recommendation we hired him sight unseen and made arrangements for him to come to California.

Of all the show drummers I've worked with through my career, Gordon was the best. He never took his eyes off me during the show and was always smiling and into the music. If I wanted to speed up, slow down or build to a huge crashing ending, he was always right there. He was the sweetest guy you'd ever meet, but wasn't the brightest star in the sky--about as sharp as a marble.

I found out later that this was the result of something Pat didn't tell us about Gordon. He was an epileptic and occasionally, at the most in-opportune times, had full grand mal seizures.

I discovered this one afternoon during rehearsals when in the middle of a song I heard a crash. I turned around to see Gordon face down on his drums and his entire body was jerking violently.

Pat calmly took off his guitar, pulled Gordon off his drums, laid him on his side and stuck his billfold in his mouth.

He looked up at us and calmly said, "He does this sometimes. The billfold will keep him from swallowing his tongue. He'll be OK in an hour or so."

Amazingly, for the eight years he worked for me, he never had a seizure during the show--only during a few rehearsals and a few times right before. If he took his medications properly the seizures were controlled, but he always had a problem doing that. When they did happen, he would be out, sound asleep for several hours, then he'd wake up and everything would be Ok. Unfortunately, with each one of those seizures, he lost a few more brain cells.

With Pat on rhythm guitar, John on lead and piano, Dave on bass and Gordon on drums, we had a solid rhythm section, but were lacking the two instruments that would make us unique: a steel guitar and a fiddle.

At the first Baptist Church in Reseda, we auditioned several musicians that claimed to be able to play the steel, but their definition of actual playing was a lot different than ours. They all sucked.

I'm not sure exactly why, but in our desperate search for a steel player, John actually called Sneaky Pete Kleinow, from the Flying Burrito brothers, but we were a little out of his class or below it, depending on how you looked at it.

There is a major discrepancy in our memories on how we actually found Larry Campbell, but I won't get into that. The only thing that really matters is that we found him. What we all do agree on is that when he showed up we were all looking at each other wondering what in the hell we had gotten into with him. Larry was and still is tall dark and handsome; a real lady killer. He had long black hair, a big Fu Manchu mustache, an earring and talked with a very thick New York accent.

None of that was the problem. The problem was when he pulled out his piece of shit, broken down steel guitar. It took him at least thirty minutes to get it set up, and the moment he started to play and pushed on the knee lever, it fell apart in pieces on the floor. After another thirty minutes of watching Larry laying on the floor wiring his steel back together, John, Pat, Dana, Dave and Gordon were shooting me glances silently communicating, "Get this guy out of here, this is never gonna work!"

Eventually, Larry got it patched up, sat down behind it and Gordon counted off the first song. When he started playing, everybody started smiling. He was hired before we finished the first song.

John asked him if he by chance knew of a good fiddle player. "Yeah, I do." He said in his thick New York accent. Then he stood up and walked to his car and returned with his fiddle case.

Although Larry claims that the steel guitar is his first instrument, the fact is, he can play anything with strings on it: fiddle, mandolin, guitar and although I've never heard him play it, I'd bet you my house that he can play a mean banjo.

Without a doubt, Larry Campbell is one of the most talented overall musicians I have ever had the pleasure of working with. He worked with us for almost 6 years and eventually bought a new steel guitar that didn't fall apart. Since then, he has soared two amazing heights in the music industry. He's worked with Cyndi Lauper, Jackson Browne, Levon Helm and toured for several years with Bob Dylan. And, he has earned three Grammy awards along his way. I think all of us are honored to be able to say we played with him and very proud of all he has accomplished!

With the addition of Larry, Ben Marney and Home Cookin' was finally complete and we headed out on the road.

Not exactly sure what the hell to do with us, Larry O'Keefe started booking us gigs scattered around the country. We did pretty good in most of the jobs, but there were a few that absolutely didn't get it, the Marriott hotels being one of them. Almost weekly I would get a call from Larry O'Keefe begging me to cut the country music out and go back to the proven pop and rock repertoire, but I stood firm and wouldn't do it. Because our shows were so unique, it was difficult to find venues that would book us, but somehow he kept us busy.

I was even getting flack from Playboy Records, because my first single scheduled to be released was not even close to a country song. Mickey Gilley was their country artist and they were not interested in having two. However, Don Shane did come up with a great idea of having us open a concert for Mickey Gilley at a venue in Marina Del Rey.

That night, all my anxieties and questions in my head were answered. We had lost so many traditional "show room" bookings that I was beginning to question my sanity. Larry and Dick had been right, apparently the Hyatt Regencys and the Marriotts weren't ready for country music. As a compromise, I had added back in my show some Neil Diamond and Barbra Streisand, but kept the Willie and Waylon, Kenny Rogers and Charlie Daniels.

Opening for Mickey Gilley in Marina Del Rey was actually the first real country crowd we had ever performed for. I can't remember the exact songs we performed that night, but I do remember turning Larry loose on his fiddle playing the Orange Blossom Special and the room absolutely exploded. I think the technical show business term for our performance that night would be... we kicked ass! We had people literally standing in their chairs and screaming at the top of their lungs by the time we finished.

During Mickey Gilley's first performance, his stage manager called me aside and said, "We need you to pull it back a little on the next show. Mickey is more of a laid-back country artist. After all, you are just the opening act, he 'is' the star of the show and you guys sort of upstaged him. Just pull it back on the next one."

"Sure." I said. "No problem." After I told Home Cookin' what he had said, we all agreed to do our absolute best to completely blow his ass off the stage in our next show... and that's exactly what we did. As you could imagine, Mickey Gilley was not a happy camper that night, but I knew then that we were on to something, just not exactly sure what that was. For the next few years we traveled from one end of the country to the other doing a little better with each gig.

Home Cookin' was my very first real band and soon we all became good friends. It was sort of like having a big family, with a lot of brothers that were completely nuts.

Those years traveling with Home Cookin' in my 20's, were some of the best times of my life. We were all young, foolish, living large and having a blast doing it.

Lots of crazy things happen in those days. I still laugh when I think about the time the band came to me and asked if they could go buy some BB guns. We were playing a small club in Shreveport, called Sansone's Restaurant. It was a popular place, but the band accommodations weren't the best. They wanted the guns, so they could shoot the cockroaches in the band trailer.

In those days, because we were at most of the gigs for weeks at a time, everybody wanted to have their own vehicle, so we traveled as a caravan. We had a few cars and a couple of vans and one trailer full of our band equipment. My father had built me a custom trailer a few years back with The Ben Marney Show painted on the side. We were heading late one night from California to Olympia, Washington when I looked out my window to see a tire rolling past me and down an embankment. The tire was supposed to be on our two wheel trailer, but the axle had broken and the wheel had flown off. I think it was about 3:30 in the morning when this happened. We were in the middle of nowhere and totally screwed. I left the guys on the side of the road, drove to the next city several miles away and rented a U-Haul trailer. When I got back, the whole band was standing in front of the broken down trailer, posing for a picture, holding the busted axle in their hands like it was a Grammy award.

When I was renting the U-Haul trailer, I'd called my father and told him what had happened. He told me that luckily, he had a friend who lived not too far away and would get him to pick up the trailer and get it repaired. Unfortunately that never happened, because when he got there the trailer was gone.

I guess we should've taken the broken axle as some kind of an omen, but we were too young to think things like that. When we finally made it to the gig in Olympia, Washington, Gordon was unloading some luggage off the top of the van, fell off and broke both his wrists. We called the musician's union and they sent out a replacement drummer, but he was awful. When Gordon heard him play, even though both of his hands were in casts, he couldn't stand it, so he taped drum sticks to his casts with duct tape and somehow finished the night.

I have a great memory of us driving very early in the morning in our caravan across Oregon. It was a full moon and so bright that night, it almost seemed like we were driving in daylight.

I was usually the caboose of the caravan and remember coming around a wide corner to see everybody pulled over to the side of the road. I figured somebody had broken down so I pulled over behind them.

"What's wrong" I yelled.

"Turn around." They all said. When I did, I saw one of the most beautiful sights I've ever seen. The bright moonlight was shining on the snow capped mountains behind me. Running down the mountain were three sparkling, glistening waterfalls flowing down into a big stream. We were all mesmerized by the sight and stood there a long time listening to the sounds of the waterfalls splashing into the river. It was truly a breathtaking, magnificent experience I will never forget.

We all had CB radios in our cars in those days and on one of our all night trips, John was teaching us over the CB how to develop film. He had taken a class in college and was explaining the process. We were all talking back and forth on our radios asking him questions.

This had been going on for hours, when we heard a question about the film developing process from a voice we didn't recognize.

It was a trucker driving an 18-wheeler who had been following us and listening to us for miles. We thought it was funny as hell. That driver stayed with us for several more hours joining in on the discussion. When he had to pull into a truck stop for fuel, we pulled in as well and actually had breakfast with him.

We did a lot of crazy things over the CB in those days. I was still feeling a little damage from my divorce from Gail four years earlier and one night I picked up the CB microphone and sang, "The day you left, it was hard to stand alone."

After a few minutes, Larry sang, "I couldn't believe, that you'd really gone"

A few minutes later Pat added, "I didn't know if I could make it. "

Then John added, "And day by day, all I did was fake it."

I thought for a while then sang, "I didn't believe that you'd stay away, but I'm awful damn glad that things worked out that way. It's been four years and I'm still singing my songs... and darling life's a whole lot easier now that you're gone."

We laughed for hours coming up with more verses. The best and funniest ones were too explicit to write down and are probably still hanging in the ozone somewhere in the middle of Montana or Idaho or wherever we were driving through. But that song, "Life's a Whole Lot Easier" became the title and the first cut on one of our albums. If you want to hear it, it's available on iTunes. Just search for Ben Marney and Home Cookin'.

We traveled like this for years and there are about a million other Home Cookin' stories I could tell you, like the time in Natchez, Mississippi when we were all walking back to our hotel rooms after the gig. Larry was in the middle of telling us some story and not paying attention to where he was walking. Little by little we kept crowding him, moving him over, until we walked him into the swimming pool. When he realized he was going in, he yelled and pitched his fiddle case to Pat. My side hurt for days laughing about that.

I guess I should mention the story about when we were

performing in Austin, Texas at a Hilton hotel. John Hamman was quite a cook, and while we were there he decided to make Larry's girl-friend, Nancy, a birthday dinner. He broke into the hotel's kitchen, borrowed some pots and pans, plates and silverware and cooked a full course spaghetti dinner right there in his hotel room. Of course cooking wasn't allowed in the rooms and you could smell it all the way down the hallway, but somehow he got away with it.

We actually did get booked in a few Hyatt Regencys. We were playing at the Memphis Hyatt when my phone rang at 8 o'clock in the morning. It was the general manager and he wanted to talk to me about one of my band members. This particular Hyatt had a very successful breakfast service and was usually packed every morning with upscale businessmen and women all dressed up in suits and dresses ready to go to work for the day.

On this morning apparently John had woke up hungry and decided to go down for the breakfast buffet. Unshaven and without paying any attention to his very long and bushy hair, he threw on some clothes and jumped in the line standing in between all the suits. There was nothing really wrong with that, the problem was what he was wearing.

"He had on flip flops, a pair of ragged, too short, cut off jeans, " The general manager told me. "And, an old tee shirt."

Trying to be understanding, but still not seeing the real problem I said. "Are we not supposed to wear shorts in the restaurant?"

He smiled, "I would prefer you didn't, but that's not the problem."

Still confused I said, "OK, I'll tell the guys not to wear shorts, so what's the real problem?"

I was glad he was still smiling when he told me, "The problem is what was written on his T-shirt."

John had quite a collection, so there was no telling. "Oh God, what was it?" I asked, not really wanting to know.

He shook his head. "It said and I quote, I'm  A Fucking Genius"

Like I said, there's about a million stories I could tell you about the days on the road with Home Cookin', but rather than tell you the gory details about the night I grabbed Mr. Beasley, the food and beverage manager by the throat and threatened to kick his ass in the lobby of that very same Memphis Hyatt Regency, I think I'll just skip ahead to something more positive that changed all of our lives.

The bar manager at the very first Holiday Inn Dana ever worked with me, was Tom Bosik. Years later, he became the Food and Beverage manager at the brand new Holiday Inn Downtown in Jackson, Mississippi. While that hotel was still under construction, Tom called and asked me if I was available for the grand opening. Unfortunately, we were already booked for that date, but were open for the following month, so we were booked as the second band to ever play there.

Tom was a giant of a man, about 6 foot 6, close to 300 pounds. He always acted gruff, but really was just a big Polish teddy bear. When he didn't like something, he would fold his arms in front of his enormous chest and scowl down at you.

I hadn't told Tom about my new repertoire and when Larry began setting up his steel guitar, he pulled me aside and asked, "What the hell is that?"

I smiled up at him and said, "Tom, that's a steel guitar and it makes the prettiest country music you've ever heard."

Arms crossed, staring down at me with his famous scowl he yelled. "Country music! I don't want any fucking country music played in here!"

"Give me one night, that's all I ask. If you don't like it, we'll learn some polkas to play for your dumb Polish ass."

I've tried for years to come up with a reasonable explanation of what happened to us in Jackson, Mississippi. If you were not there at the time, I'm sure you're going to think I am stretching the truth, but if you were there, you know I'm not.

There was an instant inexplicable connection with Dana and me, Home Cookin' and with the entire city of Jackson. They absolutely fell in love with us and it started on that very first night.

The place was completely packed from the minute the doors opened until Tom had to forcibly throw them out. After the night was over, I walked up to Tom, who had been checking out the numbers for the night and said, "Well, what do you think?"

He smiled at me with his big goofy grin and yelled, "I fucking love that country shit!"

The next day, the crowd started building at 5:00 pm and it was standing room only by show time. It was that way every single night we were there for the entire four week contract. The same thing happened on our second contract a few months later and again on the third gig a few months after that. Tom told me that when we showed up the bar sales increased from an average of $30,000 a month, to over $90,000. Three times their normal sales.

Honestly, owning my own bar had never really crossed my mind at that time. I was 26 years old traveling up and down the country having a blast, so thinking about opening my own business was not in my head. One night in between my shows a man came up to me in the lobby. I recognized him as one of the regulars. He smiled and said, "Ben, have you ever thought about opening up your own club here?"

At that time in Jackson, Mississippi there was a 51% food to liquor ratio in their liquor laws. That meant, if you had a liquor license, 51% of your revenue had to come from food sales. As a result of that law, there were no night clubs in the city, only a restaurant or hotel could generate that much food revenue.

I smiled back at the man and said, "Not really, I've never even considered it. Isn't there some kind of ridiculous liquor law here?"

As it turned out the guy I was talking to was a state legislator and one of our big fans. He pulled me close and whispered, "That law is going to change next year. We're dropping it to 26% and you need to seriously think about building your own club here. I think you'd make a fortune."

It was about that time that I had my incident with Mr. Beasley, the food and beverage manager at the Memphis Hyatt Regency where I completely lost control of my temper. We had been on the road for almost two years solid and after that incident I realized that I needed a break. Dana flew home to Muleshoe and I drove to Houston to spent some time with my parents and brother.

I was burned out with all the traveling playing one gig after another and I guess it showed.

My brother knew I didn't drink much, but when I came over to his house, he handed me a snifter full of Remi Martin and we settled on the couch in front of his fireplace.

"You look troubled little brother, what's wrong?"

Actually I wasn't really sure what to tell him. All I knew is that my career was sort of at a standstill and didn't know what to do to change it.

"OK, let me ask you a question." He said, slurring his words from drinking a bit too much Remi. "If money was no object, what would you want to do with your life?"

You need to understand how much my brother intimidated me. By this time, Ron was a successful real estate developer, very rich, a multimillionaire, living in a beautiful mansion and driving a Mercedes. I was driving an old Ford van, barely scratching out a living singing, traveling the country like a gypsy with no real assets other than my talent and guitar. Every time I got around him, I changed back to that dumb little kid brother he knew when we were growing up. I would normally stare at the ground, shuffle my feet and mumble something stupid when I was around him. Intimidation is not a strong enough word, I felt completely inept.

However, the Remi Martin had given me courage, so I looked at him and said. "Well big brother, if money is no object, I would go to Jackson, Mississippi and build a nightclub."

He turned toward me and squinted his eyes. "Why in the hell would you want to go to Jackson, Mississippi?"

I think we actually finished off that bottle of Remi that night and although we were both drunk as hell, apparently Ron had listen carefully to every word I had said.

Before we both staggered off to bed, Ron went to the fireplace, grabbed one of those long matches and handed it to me, "Little brother, I'm behind you on this one and I'll get you what ever you need to do it. Like General Sherman said to his wife, a new burning has been inflicted on this afflicted town. Let's go burn down Jackson again."

Since I rarely drank, my liver processed the alcohol quickly, so when I woke the next morning I felt great. Ron on the other hand, was moving slow. To be honest, I wasn't sure if what Ron had told me the night before was just drunk talk or if he was serious, so I didn't bring it up.

After his third cup of coffee, he finally looked up from his Wall Street Journal. "Let this be a lesson to you little brother, never get drunk and talk business. So, how much is this night club gonna cost me?"

I left that day with his guarantee of a minimum of $500,000, but I didn't share in the profits until he got his money back. But before he wrote the check, he wanted me to do a test. To make sure we were the actual draw and not some weird mysterious combination of us and the Holiday Inn Downtown, he told me to book the band somewhere else in Jackson. Specifically, somewhere that was not doing well. If we packed that place, we'd know for sure.

About two months later, with one small ad in the newspaper, we started a four week contract at the Holiday Inn North. Over night, it went from basically empty, to completely packed with a long line to get in, and the crowds grew bigger and bigger each night we were there. There was no question about it, Dana, Home Cookin' and I, were the draw.

ON AUGUST 26TH, 1977, in the middle of a strip shopping center on North State street, the city of Jackson was introduced to a brand new night club called "Marney's."

Home Cookin'-1977 (Wayne -Ben-Pat-John-Gordon-Dana-Larry)

# 13

# MARNEY'S

Webster's definition of phenomenon is: something that can be observed and studied, that is unusual, difficult to understand or fully explain.

I added that definition to this story, so you know that when I use the word phenomenon to describe Marney's, I'm using that word correctly. Phenomenon is the only word to describe it.

When I told people where I was building Marney's, everybody thought I had lost my mind.

"You are opening a nightclub in the middle of an old shopping center, in between Baskin-Robbins and a SCUBA shop? Are you crazy?" That was the usual reaction.

I can't take credit for the location, I didn't choose it, my brother Ron did. I will admit I was a little skeptical about it too, but although Ron knew nothing about night clubs and even less about the music business, he knew real estate and understood people and traffic flow. He also knew that the rent in an older strip center would be a lot cheaper than in a newer, more trendy one. He was convinced our fans would follow us anywhere, and he was right.

The space was 75 feet wide and 125 feet long, with a small 400 square foot basement area. We started construction in May with plans of a Grand Opening in late August. For most of those months we were back on the road playing gigs so everyone could pay their bills, but not being there every day was killing me. Finally August came and we took that month off to get ready for the opening. When I walked in after being away for months, the place looked like nothing had been done. It was still a big empty space and I went nuts. When I called Ron and told him about the lack of progress, he flew to Jackson the next day and called for a meeting with the contractor he'd hired.

I never liked the contractor much. He was a very large, overweight guy with a cocky arrogance that rubbed me the wrong way the first day I'd met him. Ron had hired him on a glowing recommendation from a Jackson banker. When he walked in, it was obvious to both of us that our emergency, impromptu meeting was not appreciated.

He actually said something like, "I don't know what this is all about, but I'm a very busy man and this has screwed up my entire day."

It was the first time I'd ever seen Ron in action. "I apologize for the inconvenience," Ron said calmly, "and I hope we haven't totally screwed up your busy schedule, but don't worry, this shouldn't take too long."

In a huff, the guy plopped down in the chair and folded his arms in front of him. "It's too late for that, So, what's this all about?"

Ron smiled. "I just took a walk through the site and honestly, I don't see much progress since I was here last month. Can you explain that?"

Ron and I listened quietly to the contractor explaining why he was behind schedule, giving us one excuse after another. After the pompous ass had finished, Ron opened up his briefcase and took out a folded set of architectural plans. "Do you see that signature?"

The guy looked at the plans and said. "Yes."

"Is that your signature?"

This time he looked at the plans and dropped his head. "Yes, that's mine."

Ron pulled the construction contract from his briefcase, laid it on the table and flipped the pages. "Is this your signature as well?"

Realizing where this was going, he whispered, "Yes."

It says here, right next to your signature that for every day you go over the agreeed finish date, I can fine you $20,000. Remember that clause?"

Incensed, the guy jumped to his feet and shouted, "Yeah, but these delays were out of my control. You can't fine me for that!"

Ron stood up, folded the plans and the contract and put them back in his case. Then he smiled at the guy. "Yes I can, and believe me I will." Losing the smile, he glared at the guy with a fierce look in his eye. In a low, almost sinister growl he said. "I realize you are used to dealing with your good ole boy buddies and you may be able to get away with this kind of shit with them, but trust me when I say this, I am not someone to fuck with. I built out over 500,000 square feet of interior space last year. This is only 10,000. I know how long this should take and you've had more than enough time. We have a legal, reasonable signed agreement between us, and I have a team of blood thirsty, vicious lawyers. The grand opening is August 26. You've had 90 days to do this. Now, you've only got 24. If you miss that deadline, trust me, you will live to regret it."

Mr. Arrogant suddenly turned white and slid back into his chair, mumbling to himself as we walked out.

Before that meeting there were three workers in the space, within an hour it was crawling with them. When the week was done, the walls were up, the kitchen was being assembled and the  stage was built.

Construction went on in that building 24 hours a day for the next 24, but on the day of the Grand Opening, it still looked to me like it was a long way from finished.

Ron forced Dana and me to go home and rest, so we would be ready to perform that night for the opening. On our way out we both stopped, looked back one last time and took it all in. It was in shambles, nothing was in place.

When we arrived back later that night, the huge parking lot in front of the strip center was completely full. We parked in the back, walked up the stairs and opened the door. We almost didn't want to look, but when we did we were amazed. It was absolutely beautiful. Everything was in place: all the carpet was down, all the chairs and tables were in place. There were plants, decorations and glittering lights everywhere. The bartenders and waitresses were moving at full speed, because every single seat was full. It was completely packed.

For the next three years, by 6 o'clock every night, six nights a week, there was a line stretching to Marney's front door from Baskin-Robbins on the north end of the strip, and from Pasquale's restaurant on the south end.

Marney's had a total of 500 seats, although the fire code said we could only have 380 inside the space. Usually by 6 o'clock we were at capacity and could only let people in from the line when someone would leave.

As insane as it sounds people actually stood in those lines for hours just to get in every single night. It was against the law but I didn't care, so I sent my waitresses out and served the folks in the line. My regulars told me that because they could drink in line it was all part of the Marney's experience that they loved.

Since most of the businesses in the shopping center closed by five or six, we had full use of the parking lot and we needed every square inch. Suddenly that stupid idea of building a nightclub in the middle of a strip center didn't seem so stupid after all. Once again, Ron was right.

If you ask anybody who was there in those days, they will tell you that Marney's was THE place to go in the entire state of Mississippi. In fact I was the number one liquor purchaser from the state of Mississippi for almost 5 years.

There is no question that Marney's was a huge success, but that's not why I consider it to be a phenomenon. I've thought about it for years and truly believe it was a phenomenon, because it was much more than just a successful bar and restaurant. Marney's quickly became an integral part of literally thousands of people's lives. They didn't just come to Marney's to hear Home Cookin', watch our shows or to get drunk, they came, because all their friends were there... it was a big and very important part of their daily social life.

I believe that one of the major ingredients that caused Marney's to be a phenomenon happened by accident.

I met one of my dearest friends in Jackson on our very first contract at the Holiday Inn downtown. I was in the middle of my show when I noticed a uniformed police officer leaning against the bar, moving awkwardly to the music, while holding his police radio up next to his ear. I wondered if there was perhaps some trouble, but everybody in the room seemed to know him.

After my show he came up to me and I swear this is what he said, "Hi there Ben, I loved your show! My name is Herman and I'm gonna tell you now that we are going to become great friends. But I want to get something straight right from the beginning. I will kill for you, I will die for you, but I ain't moving no fucking furniture!"

Herman was right, we became great friends and yes, he is completely nuts. He had to be the craziest cop I've ever known. When Marney's was under construction, Herman got transferred to heli-copter duty and almost every day he made the pilot land in the parking lot, so he could get a Baskin-Robbins ice cream cone and check out the progress. About two weeks after we had opened, Herman came to me and said I needed to come with him, because the chief of police wanted to talk to me.

Apparently, my brother Ron's forcefulness with our contractor had scared the living shit out of him and he had dropped a few hints around town that perhaps we were mobbed up. The Chief wanted to talk to me to find out.

After I had assured him that the name Marney was Irish and that we weren't connected to the mob, he relaxed. "Can I make a sugges-tion to you that I think will make you a lot of money?"

I smiled and said, "Absolutely."

"Give all the peace officers a special rate, some kind of discount. If you do it, I'll spread the word and trust me, when people realize there are off-duty cops in your place, you won't have any trouble there."

When I told Ron what the chief of police had suggested, he said, "Do what ever you think. Whatever it costs us will be well worth the money for the security."

From then on, if you had a badge, city cop, county sheriff, highway patrol, any official peace officer that came to Marney's, you got a discount on your booze and if you were there with your wife or a date, your food was free.

It didn't take long for that news to spread and every night we usually had at least four or five off-duty cops in our audience. It was money well spent. For the five years we were open, we only had one or two minor scuffles.

I wanted them there because, not trying to sound sexist, but in those days if your bar was full of women, it didn't take long until it was full of men willing to buy them drinks. At that time, Jackson had a female to male ratio of eight to one and because single females quickly figured out that Marney's was a safe place for them, they came in droves. Marney's was always packed with the most beautiful women in town.

Marney's soon became famous and actually became a tourist attraction. Every week people drove for miles to get there, to see our shows, buy our albums and our t-shirts. We sold a ton of those albums and t-shirts.

Marney's fame is more proof of the phenomena. This fame wasn't the result of an expensive marketing campaign with radio, newspaper and TV ads. The truth is, we didn't advertise, we didn't have to. The word about Marney's spread like wildfire throughout Jackson and the entire state of Mississippi. We did take out a full page add in one of the small newspapers to announce our opening and ran it a few months, but eventually took it out. Marney's fame was all spread by word of mouth.

We also grew our fame when Home Cookin', Dana and I began filming TV specials that aired state wide on the ABC affiliate television station. Dana and I were also the on-air TV hosts for the statewide broadcasts of the United Cerebral Palsy telethon each year as well.

IT WAS an amazing time in my life. For the next three years, Marney's was packed every night, we were all over the television, our songs were getting some good air play on the radio, our albums were in the record stores and we even did a concert with the Jackson Symphony Orchestra to a crowd of over 30,000.

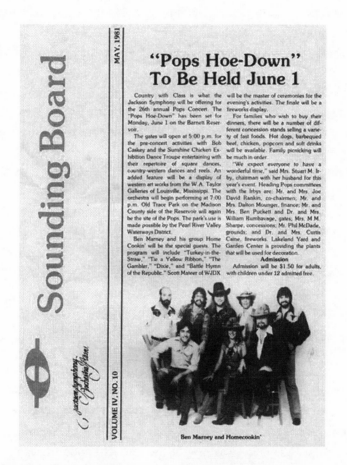

**"Pops Hoe-Down" To Be Held June 1**

Country with Class is what the Jackson Symphony will be offering for the 26th annual Pops Concert. The "Pops Hoe-Down" has been set for Monday, June 1 on the Barnett Reservoir.

The gates will open at 5:00 p.m. for the pre-concert activities with Bob Caskey and the Sunshine Chicken Exhibition Dance Troupe entertaining with their repertoire of square dances, country-western dances and reels. An added feature will be a display of western art works from the W. A. Taylor Galleries of Louisville, Mississippi. The orchestra will begin performing at 7:00 p.m. Old Trace Park on the Madison County side of the Reservoir will again be the site of the Pops. The park's use is made possible by the Pearl River Valley Waterways District.

Ben Marney and his group Home Cookin' will be the special guests. The program will include "Turkey-in-the-Straw," "Tie a Yellow Ribbon," "The Gambler," "Dixie," and "Battle Hymn of the Republic." Scott Mateer of WJDX

will be the master of ceremonies for the evening's activities. The finale will be a fireworks display.

For families who wish to buy their dinners, there will be a number of different concession stands selling a variety of fast foods. Hot dogs, barbequed beef, chicken, popcorn and soft drinks will be available. Family picnicking will be much in order.

"We expect everyone to have a wonderful time," said Mrs. Stuart M. Irby, chairman with her husband for this year's event. Heading Pops committees with the Irbys are: Mr. and Mrs. Joe David Rankin, co-chairmen; Mr. and Mrs. Dalton Mounger, finance; Mr. and Mrs. Ben Puckett and Dr. and Mrs. William Rumbavage, gates; Mrs. M.M. Sharpe, concessions; Mr. Phil McDade, grounds; and Dr. and Mrs. Curtis Caine, fireworks. Lakeland Yard and Garden Center is providing the plants that will be used for decoration.

**Admission**

Admission will be $1.50 for adults, with children under 12 admitted free.

Ben Marney and Homecookin'

We started getting calls from major stars wanting to play there for very little money. It was a convenient stop for them on their tours and helped cover their road expenses. We always opened for them and had the chance to work with Larry Gatlin and the Gatlin Brothers, Hank Williams Jr., Johnny Paycheck, Moe Bandy, John Anderson, Bobby Bare, and David Allen Coe.

Through the years, Ron and I fought like cats and dogs about the direction and operation of Marney's. Two or three times a year he would fly in unannounced and take a tour around Jackson checking out the competition. Every time he made one of these surprise visits, he would force me to raise the prices.

"The hottest joint in town, should be the highest priced." That was his never ending mantra.

Because he was rich, lived in a big expensive metropolitan city and hung out in the priciest bars there, I could never convince him that we couldn't turn Jackson into New York City.

It was a constant battle and his usual response was, "There you go again little brother, thinking with your heart and not your head."

Then he would fly back to Houston and leave me trying to justify to all my regular customers why I raised the price of the whiskey and beer.

Because of this constant battle with my brother, Marney's went through several evolutions. In the first few years, we didn't play there every week. Ron was afraid we might get over exposed and kill the magic. So we only played there four months a year. When disco hit and started giving us a little competition, we decided that we needed to stay there full time, add a few horns and give the discos a run for their money. Stupidly, we actually renamed the band Discovery and started playing the disco music live during our dance sets. In my shows I took out some of the country and added in some of the hot songs of the day. I didn't really want to do it, but our numbers had fallen and Ron insisted that I change with the times to save the business.

Although Discovery was one of the hottest bands I ever had, our true blue Marney's fans were not impressed and the numbers kept falling. We were still doing pretty good but not jam-packed every night like we were in the beginning.

About that time the movie Urban Cowboy was released and the world went cowboy crazy.

We were still fighting the disco craze, when Ron called me and told me to come to Houston. When we got there, he took us out to a place called Cowboys. It was the newest and hottest disco in Houston.

It was like walking into a New York City version of an old west bar. Everywhere you looked was some kind of western motif, but tragically it was more art deco than reality; rhinestone studded cactus and blue flashing neon wagon wheels.

"What do you think?" Ron yelled over the blaring disco speakers playing country music.

"About what?" I yelled back.

"We need to do this in Jackson. Look around." He yelled. "This place is packed like this every night."

He was right, it was packed and everyone in the place was wearing brand new cowboy boots, designer jeans, huge belt buckles, cowboy hats and some New York designers idea of western attire.

I smiled and yelled. "Looks like a bunch of Coca-Cola cowboys to me!"

""What?" He yelled back.

"They're all hat and no cattle! This is just a short lived fad. They're not real country fans and it won't work in Jackson. I don't care what you say, I'm not turning Marney's into a disco, even a country one."

At his house later he explained his idea more. "I'm not suggesting we turn Marney's into a disco, but I think you need to at least consider doing something other than what you're doing now, because it's not working that well."

He grinned and raised up his hands. "You don't have to say it, I know I forced you to make those changes and I realize now, you were right all along. I'll admit I was wrong and think you need to go back to what has always worked for you the best in Jackson: your country music shows and Home Cookin'."

I was excited and couldn't wait to get back to Jackson to make the change, but Ron and I both agreed it probably wasn't a good idea to do it overnight. We decided to do it slowly, starting with one special all country night a week. We bought a few newspaper ads telling everyone to put on their jeans, boots, cowboy hats and come back to Marney's.

"Order some of Ben's Bar-BQ and kick up your heels, cause Ben

Marney and Home Cookin' are back!"

After we did some quick countryfied decorating, we had the first Cowboy night at Marney's on a Tuesday night.

On that first Cowboy night, the lines were back and the joint was packed. We added a new Cowboy night each week for the next few months until we were doing it every night.

I'm not sure who came up with these words of wisdom first, but whoever it was, knew what they were talking about. Those wise words are: Timing is everything.

I must admit that I didn't recognize the trend at first, even though I had actually seen John Travolta's movie Urban Cowboy. I was under the mistaken impression that the new regained long lines and packed seats at Marney's was due to us returning to our country roots (and that did play a big part in our success), but what I finally realized was that the true draw was because the entire country had gone nuts with a cowboy craze.

On that trip to Houston, when Ron took us out to see Cowboys, to prove his point he took us to a western store called Cutter Bill's. The place was absolutely packed with people lined up to spend an insane amount of money on their new western outfits. The prices in that store would have embarrassed Neiman Marcus. Hundred dollar hats were selling for five, two hundred dollar boots were selling for over a thousand. It was nuts, but every cash register was ringing and had a long line.

While Ron was paying for his new five thousand dollar ostrich leather western jacket, Dana and I were checking out the thirty dollar feather hat bands. Those hat bands were the only thing that I thought was actually kind of cool that all those Coca-Cola Cowboys were wearing--so we bought two.

The cowboy nights at Marney's were doing so well, we decided to have a new grand opening and on that night we officially change the name to Marney's Cowboy.

That was the first night that Dana and I wore our new fancy feather hat bands. Everybody in the place that night wanted to know where we got them. The next day, I called Ron and told him to find out where Cutter Bill's bought those headbands.

We got our first shipment a few weeks later. I had a carpenter build a 10 foot wide glass display case and made a deal with my friend Barry Quinn, who owned the local western wear store, to buy a few cowboy hats to display them on. We sold out of the feather hat bands within a week. But the biggest surprise was, we sold every single cowboy hat as well.

The next week, we ordered a couple hundred more feather hat bands, made another deal with Barry and stocked that case with feather hat bands, cowboy hats, belts, buckles and silver bolo ties.

I think we sold more merchandise out of that 10 foot display case than Barry did in his store.

Dana found a lady in Muleshoe, Texas that made us custom jeans with the Marney's logo stitched in gold on the back pockets and we couldn't keep them in stock.

Due to the enormous success of the Urban Cowboy movie, Mickey Gilley and Johnny Lee, whose songs were featured in the movie, zoomed to the top of the charts. To cash in on their hit records, Mickey and Johnny went on tour together and one of their scheduled stops was in Jackson, at the Coliseum.

I was sitting behind my desk when Pat Vivier opened my door and told me the news. He had just gotten off the phone with the promoters of the Mickey Gilley/Johnny Lee concert and they wanted us to be the opening act.

As well as selling a lot of cowboy hats and feather hat bands, our T-shirt sales were at an all time high. Our most popular ones were black with white lettering, with the Marney's cowboy logo on the front and funny sayings on the back. Sayings like: "If you don't like country music, you can kiss my ass." We couldn't keep that one in stock.

When we walked on stage the night we opened for Jonny Lee and Mickey Gilley at the Jackson Coliseum, the crowd went wild. It was completely sold out and of the 11,000 people there, it looked like at least 10,000 of them were wearing a Marney's Cowboy T-shirt. The crowd was a sea of black with our white shimmering logo glowing in the reflection from the stage lights. The concert promoters had made a wise choice. Although everyone was there to see Mickey Gilley and Johnny Lee, they were also there to see us, and boy did they let us know it. We blew the roof off the joint that night.

On our very first job in Jackson at the Holiday Inn downtown, I started something that had become a tradition. I thought since Jackson was in the heart of Dixie, we needed to end our last show each night with the American Trilogy. What could be better than singing Dixie, in Dixie. They loved it and ever since that night, for our encore we performed the American Trilogy. When we did it, the audience would form a circle around Dana and me on the dance floor, and arm and arm, they would sway with the music and sing along. We had ended our show like that every night for three years.

When we came to the end of our 40 minute set at the Jackson Coliseum, we all bowed and left the stage. You need to understand, it is not normal for an opening act to get a standing ovation in a concert like this, but when we left the stage, the building began to vibrate as the crowd stomped their feet and yelled, "More! More! More!"

If you've read my short story about Home Cookin' and remember what happened when we opened for Mickey Gilley in that venue in Marina Del Rey, you'll understand what happened next.

All 11,000 people in that Coliseum were stomping their feet and screaming for us to come back, but because it was so unusual, I wasn't sure if it was kosher for us to do it.

The band wasn't sure either, so I walked up to our stage manager, Bobbie Bellapini to ask him what he thought about it.

He was talking to Mickey Gilley's road manager when I walked up. He grinned at me, looked over at Gilley's road manager and said, "Well, do you want me to tell them to go back, or just let the crowd tear this place to pieces?"

Extremely pissed, he shrugged and said, "Let em' go back." Then stormed off.

I don't think any one in the band actually thought we'd get an ovation that night, but just in case we had planned for it.

When we walked back on to the stage, the crowd roared, but when we dropped the 25 by 15 foot Dixie flag behind us and started playing the American Trilogy, they went absolutely nuts.

Mickey Gilley Concert - Jackson Coliseum

When we finally got off the stage Mickey Gilley was furious, but Johnny Lee was great about it.

"How the hell am I supposed to follow that?" Johnny said to me laughing.

"You're the one with the hit record." I said smiling back. "I think you'll do Ok."

At that moment in my life, performing in that concert and getting a standing ovation was the absolute pinnacle of my music career. It was something I had dreamed about and worked for since I was 13 years old. I was floating on air, but my euphoria was short-lived.

What happen next is something that I have regretted and cried about more times than I can count.

It would be impossible to put into words the feelings I had racing inside of me after that concert. My ego was inflated way too much and my body was charged with electricity and excitement.

Because this concert was such a big deal, my parents, Dana's parents and her sister and brother-in-law Terry had come to Jackson to see the concert. They were all sitting in the front row next to my brother Ron and his wife Suzanne.

After the concert, Ron came backstage. When I saw him, I screamed and hugged him. "Wasn't that amazing!" I yelled.

His demeanor wasn't what I expected. He didn't seem to be that happy. As weird as it was, he actually seemed a little perturbed that I was jumping around and so excited. He wasn't smiling and was giving me the same look he used to give me when I was a little kid acting stupid.

"It was Ok, but I've heard you sing better." He said coldly. "Come on, let's go watch Johnny Lee."

"Ok," I said, baffled and disappointed with his criticism. "We can see him great over here." I started walking to the backstage wing.

"I don't want to watch him back here. We've got great seats down front––come on let's go" He grabbed my arm and began pulling me.

I jerked my arm away. "I'm not going out there."

"And why not?"

I shook my head and held up my arms. "Because I'll get mobbed and that'll mess up Johnny's show."

He stopped and glared at me, "You've got to be kidding. You're not a star little brother. They probably won't even notice you."

I couldn't believe he was doing this, especially then. All I wanted to do was celebrate with Dana and my band, the last thing I wanted to do was walk out into that crowd.

"Dammit Ron, can't you let me enjoy this one moment. You know I'm not a star. And I know I'm not either, but there's about 11,000 people out there who just might think different."

"For your information, I thought your show sucked!" He yelled. "I was just trying to help you. I thought you might learn something by watching a real star."

"Go fuck yourself big brother!" I screamed. In full rage, I left him standing there and ran to my bus.

I had lost my temper many times before, but never quite like that. I was completely out of control, screaming at the top of my lungs, throwing things around the bus and cussing my brothers name. I said some horrible, unspeakable things that night, ranting on for almost thirty minutes. Unfortunately, Ron's wife Suzanne, who had come to the bus hoping to smooth things out, heard it all.

There was a planned after party celebration, but I didn't go. Instead, I went home and literally cried myself to sleep. What should have been the highest point in my life, turned out to be the lowest.

Ron and Suzanne didn't go to the party either. They took a cab to the airport, boarded their private plane and flew home to Houston. After that night, Ron and I didn't talk much for almost two years. Suzanne took over the business management of Marney's and Ron stayed out of it.

Although he sent me a telegram a week later that said: "I was wrong, you were great and I was proud." I couldn't forgive him.

I've thought about that night for over 30 years trying to come up with a logical reason for Ron acting the way he did. And for all of those years, I've regretted my egotistical, unforgivable and foolish reaction. What could it have hurt for me to just go with him that night?

Some of my friends believe that Ron was just jealous, because up to that point he had always been the most successful. His negative actions were just his way of trying to regain his superiority over me. I guess that could have been part of it, but I'd rather believe what Dana thinks. Of course, she always sees the positive side of things. She believes that what Ron was really trying to do was get me out into the crowd, so everyone would see us together and know that I was his brother. She thinks that would have made him feel proud, but he couldn't tell me that, and when I wouldn't go, he reacted with anger and his sharp tongue. I will always regret not going with him that night.

We eventually patched things up between us, but he never explained that night to me.

Ron was right, I wasn't a star. Ben Marney and Home Cookin' were not world famous or even nationally known, but in parts of

Louisiana, Tennessee, Georgia and Mississippi, we were pretty big stuff.

At that time, we all believed that we had what it took and were close to breaking nationally, so to help make that happen I spent most of what I was earning at Marney's cutting records and promoting them. We got lucky on one called, "Where Cheaters Go" that actually made it onto Billboard Magazine's Top 100. If I had had a little more money I think that song might've made it into the top 40, but I just couldn't afford it. Of course, Ron had plenty, but our relationship was still sort of strained and I wasn't about to ask him for a dime.

Marney's stayed packed until it's fifth year. Although we were paying the bills and making some profit, several other clubs had opened, giving us some stiff competition.

At that time we were still desperately searching for a hit record and in one of our studio sessions, our piano player, Knight Bruce started playing an interesting riff. "What's that?" I asked.

He shook his head. "Nothing really, I was just messing around."

"Play it again." When he finished I asked him. "What is going through your head when you're playing it? Any lyrics?"

He looked up at me and said, "Yeah, but it's sort of weird."

"I don't care, what are you thinking?"

Knight grinned and began playing the riff and singing. "Shoot you now or shoot you later. That's all I've got so far. I think there may be something wrong with me." He said laughing.

I told him to keep working on the music and I would try to come up with some more lyrics. I went to the lobby of the studio and these words just began to flow out of my head.

*Hung my old man late one evening*
*Strung him up in a big oak tree*
*I knew one day that I'd get even*
*That made a gun slinger out of me*
*Sold my soul for some money*
*Spent it on a 45*
*At twelve I killed my first bottle*

*At fourteen, wanted dead or alive*
*Shoot you now or shoot you later*
*Do you really want to die this soon*
*So you're hot to pull your trigger*
*Meet me on the street at high noon*
*They come from miles to see who's faster*
*Kids with guns in a grownup game*
*They want to draw against the master*
*But young or old, I take deadly aim*

WHEN KNIGHT PLAYED me the music he'd come up with, almost like magic, my words fit perfectly. It was almost like we had written it side-by-side, but I swear we didn't.

Five minutes later, we started cutting that song. When we finished and played it back, I felt that something was missing. "I think we need Mickey on this."

Shocked, Knight said. "You hear a fiddle on this? Ben, this is more of a rock song."

"Exactly." I said.

During the first year of Marney's, one night this older guy came up to me and asked if he could sit in with the band. He was actually only in his mid 40's. His name was Mickey Davis and he said he played fiddle. That turned out to be the understatement of the century. Actually, he was a classically trained violinist and was the string section leader of the Jackson Symphony Orchestra. When he started playing that first night, he blew us all away. He was unbelievable, as good as any country fiddle player I've ever heard to this day. When he and Larry joined up and played the Orange Blossom Special, it was truly a world class performance.

Larry, being a born and bred New Yorker couldn't take the slow pace of Jackson. So unfortunately, he left us after a year and moved back to the big city. After he left, about two or three nights a week, Mickey would show up and play.

When we played Mickey our recording of Gun Slinger, he frowned at us. "You're hearing a fiddle? What 'cha boys been smoking in here. That's a rock song."

"Yeah, that's what everybody keeps telling me, but I think your fiddle is what's missing."

He smiled and walked into the studio. We played the song a few times as he listened with his headphones. "Ok." He yelled. "Hit re-cord this time, I'm not sure what to play, but I'll think of something."

The second he started playing everyone in the control room started smiling. When he finished his lead, we started yelling. He absolutely killed it.

In those days, you could still shop a song in Nashville by knocking on the doors on Music Row. I had been there knocking on those doors almost every year I lived in Jackson, and trust me, it is a very humiliating and humbling experience.

If you could actually get in, they would take your cassette, put it in their machine and while staring you in the eyes, hit play. After about 15 seconds, they would hit fast-forward and give the next song about 15, before hitting fast forward once again on to the next one. All the while staring you down. It was gut wrenching and no fun at all.

I normally did this alone, but when we shopped Gunslinger, Pat Vivier went with me.

Honestly I don't remember many details about that day. I'm not even sure where we shopped it. What I do remember vividly is knocking on Capitol Records door and getting in to see the Vice President.

Pat and I took a seat across from him and as usual he took the cassette, stuck it in the machine, hit play and started staring. When he looked away and didn't hit fast forward, I looked over at Pat and raised my eyebrows. When he hit rewind and started listening to it again, my heart started pounding and my hands got sweaty.

"I'll be right back." He said and walked out of the room.

A few minutes later he came back with another guy and played

Gun Slinger for him. They listen to it two times, then exchanged glances.

"You guys have anymore like this?" He asked smiling.

Pat and I looked at each other and grinned. "Well, we wrote and produced that one, I think we can come up with a few more like it." I said.

"Well Ben, if you can do that, I think we can cut a deal. When you get a few more, bring it to me. I'll be waiting."

I'm pretty sure Pat and I didn't walk out of Capitol Records that day, but floated out on a cloud. Finally, we had hit pay dirt!

We hurried back to Jackson and I started writing. I came up with six new songs and we booked some time in a studio to start the recording process.

In the middle of those last Home Cookin' sessions, we got lucky when Jimmy Buffett's harmonica player, Fingers Taylor sat in with us one night at Marney's. After the show we talked him into coming to the studio the next day to lay down a few tracks on one of our new songs.

Because we wanted to make the new songs for Capitol as good as possible, we were taking extra time to record them; spending long hours in the studio with the final mix.

It was on a Sunday and I had been in the studio since 10 am mixing. I had a bad habit of playing the mix too loud and when you do this for hours, you can develop something called ear fatigue. It can actually affect your equilibrium and make you a little goofy.

"That's enough for today." I'm not sure who said that, but I agreed.

"Let's get out of here and go play some golf. If we hurry, we can still get 9 in before it gets dark."

We all decided that we needed to walk the course to get some exercise, but my pull cart was broken. I told them I was going to run by K-Mart, get a new one and meet them at Castlewoods Golf Course in an hour.

Castlewoods was just across the highway from my house, but by the time I made it home to get my clubs and put my new cart together,

I was running late. I could feel my ears burning, imagining Pat Vivier and Jimmy Wilkerson cussing me, standing on the first tee waiting.

I have lived through several major events in my life that have resulted in great change. These events changed the way I think, changed the way I act, change the life I was living and changed the path I was going down. I have purposely left out some gory details of my life in this book, because honestly, I'm not proud of them and believe they are best forgotten. Suffice it to say, I was not heading down the right path and my ego was out of control. But God has a way of getting your attention and putting you back on the path where you belong. I think Job said it best in the Bible when he said:

*The Lord Gave, and the Lord has taken away; blessed be the name of the Lord.*
*Job 1:21*

In a blink of an eye, God definitely got my attention and took it all away, but at the same time, he revealed himself to me, erasing any and all doubts, solidifying my faith and absolute belief in his existence.

I'm sure some of you reading this may think this next part belongs in one of my fiction novels, but I promise you, everything I'm about to tell you is true.

I yelled goodbye to Dana, threw my cart and clubs in the car and zoomed off. At the stop sign, I looked to the right, then to the left. There were two cars coming on my right. When they passed, I hit the accelerator and took off. I didn't see the car until it was a few feet from my door.

I found out later, the girl that hit me was driving about 65 miles per hour and didn't have time to apply her brakes. It was not her fault, I pulled right out in front of her and she hit me in the door. My only excuse was the ear fatigue and how rushed I was. I was probably too goofy to be driving safely. Simply, I forgot to look back to my left.

I was driving a brand new Cadillac Seville with bucket seats. It had a large console between the driver and passenger seat. I can't explain how, but in a split second, I was not sitting behind the wheel. I was knocked into the passenger seat, the console was gone and the car began to flip in the air. I was not wearing a seatbelt and felt the centrifugal force pulling me. Somehow I was able to bend over and reach the steering wheel. The moment I did, the car smashed back to the ground landing on its roof, collapsing the area where my head had been only seconds before. The car slid on its roof over 100 feet before it finally stopped. I was upside down and the car was smoking. I immediately started crawling out the shattered passenger window, between the shards of glass. Somehow I did this without cutting myself. When I made it out and stood up, I saw my beautiful new car upside down and smashed.

"Look at my car!" I said... and then tried to take a breath, but no air would come.

In my football days, I had the breath knocked out of me seven or eight times, and although it was almost impossible to breathe when this happened, through my gasping, I could always suck in a small stream of air. I tried to breathe again, but I couldn't. I knew then I was in serious trouble and began to panic, gasping for air. I honestly started thinking I was going to die.

"Ben." The soft female voice came from behind me. "Turn around Ben."

When I did, I saw a woman I had never seen before standing there, backlit, by the sun. It was shining behind her head and her curly bright red hair was phosphorescent, ablaze in the sunlight, like a halo. I tried to speak to her, but nothing came out.

She reached out her right hand, touched her fingers to my forehead and said, "Jesus is with you."

The second she took her hand away, I took a deep breath and my lungs filled with air.

In a calming voice, with tones I will never forget, she said, "You will be alright, but you are hurt. You need to lay down."

I remember hearing sirens blasting in the distance as I carefully lowered myself to the ground and laid down on the pavement.

She squatted next to me and said, "Would you like me to go

get Dana?"

I was beginning to feel pain growing inside. I shook my head yes and she immediately stood and walked away as the first police car pulled up.

A few minutes later the doorbell rang at my house and Dana answered.

"Dana," The woman said calmly. "Ben has been in a little accident, but he is going to be Ok. Would you like me to take you to him?"

In shock and panicked, Dana said, "No thanks, I can drive there," and closed the door.

She had been in the pool and was in her bathing suit, so she ran to the bedroom and threw on some shorts and a shirt. When she grabbed her purse in the kitchen, she remembered I had taken the car, so she ran back to the front door hoping to catch the lady before she drove off.

When she opened the door, the lady was still standing there. "You don't have a car, let me take you."

When they pulled up to the stop sign, she turned to Dana and said, "I need to tell you, the car is upside down, but don't worry, Ben is going to be ok.

When Dana walked up I was laying on the ground wiggling my feet and hands, making sure everything was still working, surrounded by two of my highway patrol friends.

"I'm Ok." I said.

She smiled and said. "I know."

I can still remember the incredibly painful ride in the ambulance on the way to the hospital. When they finally got me there and ran the tests, they discovered that I had seven broken ribs, my right lung was completely collapsed, my spleen was in three pieces and my liver was bruised and swollen.

Another absolutely amazing part of this story is that in the entire state of Mississippi there was one doctor, a surgeon, that specialized in liver and spleen repair. When they rolled me into the hospital, he was finishing up a surgery one floor above.

A few years earlier I'd had my appendix removed and in the process they had shaved my chest. I am very hairy and that growing back process was a real pain.

When the doctor came in, he pointed to a screen above my head. "Can you see those three blobs? That's supposed to be only one big blob! If I can, I'm going to go in there and sew it back together."

I was more worried about getting my body shaved than all my busted parts. "Where are you going to shave me?"

He took his finger and drew a line from my nose to my legs and grinned. "Only from there to there."

Dana told me later, that the mysterious red headed lady wasn't alone. When she drove her to me, there was another lady and a young girl in the backseat.

The word spread fast and the hospital lobby and waiting room soon filled with my friends and fans. The woman with the bright red curly hair was there along with her friend and the little girl as well, but according to Dana, none of my friends or fans knew who she was either. No one had ever seen her before.

The surgery lasted for several hours and when the doctor came out to tell Dana that I was going to be OK, she immediately began searching for the redheaded woman so she could tell her how thankful she was for what she had done, but she was gone.

To this day, I don't know who that redheaded woman was, and although I tried my best to track her down, no one knew her or had a clue how to find her.

I guess there is an argument to be made, that because I was pretty famous in Jackson in those days, it is possible that that woman instantly knew who I was, knew about Dana and also knew exactly where I lived. I guess it's also possible that she just happened to be standing there seconds after I crawled out of my wreck, but I don't think so.

You can believe what you want, but I choose to believe that that woman was an angel sent there to help me, because the facts are, I should have died that day.

I was on the phone in my hospital room when my doctor came in to check on me.

When I hung up, he frowned at me. "I didn't mean to eavesdrop, but I couldn't help but overhear what you were saying on the phone. Do you really believe that this wreck was no big deal?"

I smiled and shook my head. "I know I was hurt pretty bad, but here I am, doing great."

The doctor sat on the edge of my bed and looked down at me. "Ben, you took a car driving 65 miles an hour in your chest. Honestly, I don't know why it didn't kill you instantly. It should have, because the human body isn't designed to take that kind of force. When they called and told me about you, I wasn't sure you would make it through the surgery, but somehow you did. Trust me when I say this. It was a very big deal and you are lucky to be alive."

It took almost 3 weeks before they let me out of the hospital, but I was still pretty busted up and had a long recovery ahead.

Unfortunately, the local news had actually reported that I had been killed in that car wreck. To quote Mark Twain, the reports of my death had been greatly exaggerated.

Of course they recanted that later, but it was too late. Marney's quickly turned into a tomb and we had no choice but to close the doors. Home Cookin' started performing at the Holiday Inn downtown, but for whatever reason (I never really found out), that didn't last and a few weeks later they broke up.


THREE MONTHS later we put Marney's up for sale, Home Cookin' scattered and that was that...

# 14

# RON

Due to the severity of my internal injuries from my car wreck, it took me several long months to recover. When I was finally back on my feet, the reality I had to face was: Marney's had been sold, Home Cookin' had broken up and my music career was basically non existent. In the blink of an eye, I had lost everything.

The only thing I still had was a little money in the bank and the connection with the Vice President of Capitol Records. Fortunately, I was very close to finishing the new songs we were recording for them before my car wreck. So a move from Jackson to Nashville seemed to make the most sense.

I had booked some studio time to finish mixing the last songs Capitol was waiting on and was just about to walk out, when my doorbell rang. When I opened the door, my brother Ron was standing there with a suitcase in his hand.

Since our big blowup at the Mickey Gilley, Johnny Lee concert, Ron and I had not talked much. Ever since that fateful night, all of the Marney's business transactions had gone through Suzanne. When we did see each other on Thanksgiving and Christmas, we were cordial, but didn't have much to say to each other.

I was so shocked to see him standing in my doorway, I was speech-less. "You gonna let me in little brother, or just stand there staring?" He said.

"Sure, come on in." I said opening the door wide. "Sorry, I'm just kinda surprised to see you here."

"I'm here on a mission. You care if I crash here tonight? We've got a lot to talk about. I think it's about time we bury this hatchet between us."

"Sure, I would like that a lot," I said, "but I can't talk now, I've got to be at the studio in thirty minutes."

"Would it be Ok if I go with you?"

After he put his suitcase in the guest bedroom, we drove to the studio together. For almost two hours he sat there quietly, not saying a word watching every move I made.

On the drive back to my house, he smiled and said. "When did you learn how to do that? How the hell do you know what knobs to turn and what buttons to push?"

I shook my head and grinned. "By watching other engineers. And a lot of trial and error."

"Well, I have to tell you, I'm impressed little brother. I guess you aren't as dumb as I thought you were." He said laughing.

That night Ron took Dana and me out to dinner and the drinking started. Because I didn't keep any booze at my house, he had me stop at a liquor store on our way home and he bought another damn bottle of Remi Martin.

When we got home, knowing we needed to talk, Dana pour two snifters full of the Remi, excused herself and left us alone in the living room.

Grinning, Ron lifted his snifter and clanged it against mine. "The last time we did this, it cost me a shit load of money."

We both laughed. "But you got it back and then some." I said.

This was the second and last time I ever got drunk with my brother, but no new night clubs developed that evening. Instead, we had a conversation that I will cherish for the rest of my life. With the courage I gained from the Remi Martin, I was able to actually tell Ron what was in my heart, and for the first time in our lives, Ron actually told me what was in his.

It was a talk we should have had years earlier--one of those "Mom liked you best" conversations, and the first time in our adult lives, we opened up and talked honest about everything that had been building up inside of us for years.

"I'll never get it Ron. Since I was a little kid, I've never been able to please you. No matter what I did, it never seemed to be good enough for you. Even now. You put up a half million dollars to open Marney's, so I know you have to think I must be pretty good, but never, not one time, have you ever told me. You've seen me get a thousand standing ovations, but instead of saying "Good show Ben", you only tell me what you didn't like about it.

You can tell Dana how great you thought she was, but to me it's always, "Why did you sing that song, or wasn't that one a little too high for your kind of voice? Why can't you just one time say, "You did good.""

He thought about what I had said for a long time. "Do you believe in reincarnation?"

I shook my head, "No, I don't."

He smiled, "I think I do. I'm pretty sure I must have been a General or something in a past life, because I thrive on the battle, not on the victory. When I win something I'm never really interested in celebrating that victory, I'm more interested in finding another battle. I forget how different we really are. When I criticize you I'm just doing it because I want you to be the best you can be. I thought you sort of knew the rest. I'm sorry if I've hurt you," He took another sip. "But you know kid, your ego is big enough."

He still couldn't say it. Feeling brave from my buzz, I confessed to how jealous I'd always been of him; of his intelligence, his straight A's, his amazing success and his wealth. I even confessed how much of a fool and failure I believed I was, because I couldn't seem to stop chasing my dreams.

When I said that, he started laughing hard. "Are you serious? You are jealous of me?"

He shook his head laughing, picked up his snifter and took a long sip of his Remi. "Listen to me you little shit. I always wanted to run track, but I was too slow. You ran like a friggin' deer. I always wanted to be in the backfield and run a touchdown, but I was too clumsy and awkward, so they put me in the line. But of course, you were the star half back running all those friggin' touchdowns. Yeah, I made straight A's, but I worked my ass off for those grades, but you... you never even cracked a book. And to top it all off, you asshole, you can sing like a fucking canary and I can't carry a tune in a bucket. Ben, all my money doesn't mean shit. I'd give everything I have, to be able to stand on that stage and hear that applause. You don't get much applause in my business."

I'm sure the Remi Martin had a lot to do with it, but that night we both laughed and cried and confessed our deepest darkest secrets.

About a month later, Dana and I moved away from Jackson, but we didn't move to Nashville. My big connection with Capitol had disappeared when he had been replaced by a new VP. So instead of Nashville, we moved to Houston and I went to work with my brother.

He had convinced me to (as he put it) "stop betting my life on a magic trick," take a break from my music career, go to work with him and make some serious money for the first time in my life.

If you've read my first novel, Sing Roses, this next part will be familiar. Although that book is a work of fiction, it's based on a true story that involved Ron. So rather than try to re-write what I worked so hard on in that book, I've decided to just change the fictional names I used in Sing Roses back to the real ones, and include... those very painful words here.

∼

THE YEARS HAVE HEALED my wounds and the bleeding has stopped, but the scars on my life will never go away. It happened on September 1, 1983, and it was the worst day of my life. It is a memory so haunting, so horrible it's hard to believe it really happened, but it did. Even now, thirty plus years later, the pain comes rushing back and still makes me cry every time I think about it.

It was an unusual day for Houston, especially for that time of year. A glorious morning, cool, around 70 degrees with very little humidity and not a cloud in the sky. I'd stopped in Memorial Park on my drive to work that morning to finish my coffee, eat my doughnut and admire the splendor of the day. As I sat there listening to music, watching the ducks swim in the pond, I had a feeling of euphoria running through me.

The planets had aligned, my life for the first time in a long time had some form of true direction, but most importantly, I was finally, after thirty years, bonding with my older brother. For the first time in our adult lives, Ron was treating me with respect. We were actually working together, had become friends and had somehow overcome our silly childhood sibling rivalries.

When I finished my coffee in the park, I cranked up my truck and headed to North Point Central: my office and Ron's newest office tower under development. The traffic was horrible, as usual, backed up for miles, so it was almost 9:30 am before I walked into my office. Taped to my phone was a message: Call Ron. He wants you to fly to Louisiana with him this morning. I tried to call him but he was on the phone, so I left a message with Peggy, his personal assistant, for him to call me back.

Things had picked up around the office and I'd honestly forgotten about Ron until the phone rang on my desk. It was almost 1 P.M.

"How fast can you get to Androngh Airport?" Ron asked.

"I don't know. The traffic was hell this morning, maybe an hour or so I guess. Why?"

"I've got to go to Lafayette to take this dumb ass coon ass cash money to close the deal on a new quarter horse. Hey! What do you think about that? A dumb ass coon ass! Sounds like a country song to me. Write that down little brother it might be a hit."

"You know," I said. "It's a damn good thing you've got a shit load of money, because if you're considering a career change to show business, you're gonna need it; otherwise you'd starve your ass off."

"Little brother you always were jealous of my singing voice. Seriously, can you make it to Androough by two? I've got to take off by then to make it back in time."

"Are we flying in the new one, the Merlin?" I asked.

"Nah, the damn nose gear is still out on the Merlin. My pilot's coming to get me in a Beach Baron. I hate those damn planes, but he says this is a good one. He flies it all the time. It's got six seats, so why don't you leave now and head that way? If you make it, we'll take a cab downtown and get some crawfish ettoufee' or some gumbo while we're there."

"I'll do my best to get there by 2, but it's going to be close."

"Ah, one more thing little brother." He said before he hung up.

"What's that?"

"I know your heart's not in this construction business, but stick with me on this for a while. As soon as we've got your pockets lined with a little gold, we just might ship your ass back to Nashville and see what you can do. Hell, we might even start our own record company one of these days. I figure you got a hit or two in you."

I was so taken aback I didn't know how to respond. That was the first time he'd ever said anything positive about my music. He'd always been my worst critic, but now out of nowhere he was talking like this?

"Be careful what you're suggesting big brother, I just may hold you to it one day."

"I think it's something we need to talk about. " Ron said. "Look, get your ass to the airport and we'll talk about it on the plane. See you there. Hurry up."

I rushed out of the office and started working my way to southwest Houston through the bumper-to-bumper traffic. I looked at my watch. It was 1:45 and I wasn't even close, so I took the next exit and tried to call his car phone. There was no answer. Back on the freeway, it was obvious that I'd never make it in time, so I gave up, took the next exit and began driving down the side streets to Ron's office complex near Gessner and Westheimer. His office suite took up most of a floor of a beautiful, three-story, mostly glass building he'd built a few years earlier. I had a small office there, so I figured I'd finish out the day there, rather than fighting the traffic back to North Point Central.

At 2:15, I heard a special announcement over my truck radio. A local businessman and his pilot had been killed in a crash at Androuph Airport. The reporter said the crash happened as they were taking off at 2:05 pm. Both were killed instantly. A wave of fear came over my entire body as I wondered if it could be Ron. I began pondering all the horrible consequences of his death. How could I tell Mom and Dad? What would happen to his company? His kids? How could I go on without him; without his wisdom and guidance? His love? If this was true, and it was his plane, suddenly I'd be working for Suzanne, his wife. Oh, God! What a horrible thought.

Suzanne was Ron's second wife, not the mother of his children. Their relationship was a real life cliché, the same old story: married boss, hot secretary... you know the rest. Suzanne was an absolute knock out. She had a beautiful face, a tiny waist, huge tits, but definitely was not a dumb blonde. She was smart, real smart, but a conniving kind of smart that was obvious to everyone who knew her, except Ron.

For whatever reason, she didn't think much of me, so I did my best to just stay out of her way. I assumed that she'd heard one too many dumb little kid stories about me from Ron, because she always treated me with aloofness; not rude, just a total lack of respect for my intelligence and complete disregard for anything I had to say.

The thought that it might have been Ron's plane was so horrible and preposterous I quickly put it out of my mind. After all, Androuph was a very busy airport with private planes taking off every few minutes; it could have been anyone. No way could it have been Ron's plane. No possible way!

It took me another thirty minutes to reach the office, so the thought of the plane crash was far from my mind. I was in a great mood, winked and said "Hey there," to the receptionist as I walked past her desk, but she didn't respond to me: nothing. She just sat there staring forward. It was a bit strange, but I didn't think much of it and walked on by her down the hall to my office.

When I sat down behind my desk, I overheard Peggy, my brother's personal assistant, talking to Suzanne. "I don't think Ben knows," she said. "Someone's got to tell him."

The moment Suzanne and Peggy walked into my office, I knew. They didn't have to say a word. My brother, my idol, my mentor... was dead.

A Houston motorcycle cop told me that it was the longest line of cars he'd ever led. The parade stretched for almost two miles and created a major traffic problem on the Katy Freeway, backing traffic up all the way to the 610 Loop, as we crept along working our way to the gravesite. Soon the nightmare I'd been living the last three days would be over. Ron would be in the ground and the rest of us would have to figure out how to go on with our lives without him. We all knew that wasn't going to be easy, but we had no choice.

I'd been quiet, not saying much to anyone since it had happened. The last person I'd talked to was my father and I'm not sure those were actual words. My dad and I have always been very close and as long as I can remember, we've had a slight telepathic communication between us. I never really had to go into deep detail about anything with my father. He just always seemed to know what I needed or wanted. When I knocked on his door, only hours after Ron's plane crash, my father took one look at me and instantly knew.

At the gravesite, I sat on one of the small green chairs reserved for the family and listened to the preacher pray for my brother's soul. It seemed like an eternity, but it actually only took a few minutes. When it was finally over and everyone moved out from under the small canopy cover, I just stood there with my hand on his casket. To this day, I can still see it clearly. It was made out of beautiful dark mahogany wood and was so highly polished I could see my reflection.

As I stood there with my hand on that cold wood, the memory of the last time I'd seen him alive flashed through my mind. It was only a few days earlier at a party at his ranch.

Ron loved throwing big Texas size parties and this was one of his best. One of Ron's side businesses was racing and breeding quarter horses. The purpose of this party was to celebrate the success of one of his horses that had just been named the Aged Champion Stallion of 1983. It was a big deal and lots of people, dressed up in all of their finest boots and hats, showed up. Ron had asked me to put my old band back together for the entertainment, so I did and we were a big hit with his friends. It was one of those magical musical nights for me; things had gone especially well. During my breaks, everyone was coming up slapping Ron on the back talking about what a great singer his little brother was. Although he never said it, I know he was proud of me that night.

When the party was over and most of the guests had left, he came up to me, backstage, as I was packing up my guitar. "Would you do one more song for me little brother?" he asked.

"Sure." I said, "What would you like to hear?"

"Sing Roses for me again," he said, smiling. "I love that song."

He was talking about a song called Run For The Roses, by Dan Fogleberg. I'd already sung it three times during the night, always at his request. "Hang on a second, I'll round up the band."

"You don't need the band. Sing it for me here at the table. Just you and your guitar."

I pulled up a chair and sang it for him one last time. Every time I'd come to the chorus, he'd lean back in his chair and join in, singing at the top of his lungs. I didn't realize it at the time, but that was a monumental three minutes in my life––a performance forever imprinted in my brain.

When the gravesite service was over, I went back to Ron's house. Within an hour, the place was packed with some of Ron's closest friends and everyone had a story to tell about him. Some were about his generosity, some were about his intelligence, but all were from the heart. After listening to one story after another, I soon realized that I didn't really know Ron at all. He had so many dimensions, so many layers, and I only knew what he chose to expose to me. The more I learned about him, the more I felt a little cheated. I'd missed out on so much of his life. I didn't really know him at all––not the real Ron.

The biggest surprise of the day came when four of his closest friends came to me and said, "Come with us, there's something we have to do." I had no idea what they were up to, but I could tell it was important, so I went with them without hesitation.

They took me upstairs to Ron's library and sat me down in his favorite chair. Bob Hugley opened the bar and poured five tall scotches, neat. Randy Woodham opened the doors to the stereo and began searching through the albums. To my surprise, he pulled out one of mine and put it on the record player. Before I could protest, my voice was blaring out of the speakers. It was almost as if they'd rehearsed what to do next. Bob handed me a scotch and sat in the chair next to me. Randy, Howard and Sidney sat on the couch. For the next hour, no one said a word; we just sipped our scotch and listened to my music, all three albums.

I was very confused at all of this, but didn't question it, because for whatever reason, his friends were enjoying it. Each one of them lost in deep thought, no doubt memories of Ron. It was all very bizarre and surreal.

When it was over and my music had finally been turned off, I asked them, "What was that all about?"

The four of them looked at me with shocked expressions. "You're kidding right?" Howard Stone said.

"No, I'm not kidding. Why did you guys want to listen to my music?"

"Because that's what Ron loved to do," Bob said. "That's what we always did up here, drank scotch and listened to your albums."

"My albums? You listened to my music?" I asked.

"Of course, your albums. Ben, he loved your music," Randy said.

I had to sit down. My legs felt like rubber and my head was spinning. I tried not to cry, but I couldn't hold it in. "I didn't know," I said, wiping my eyes. "He never told me."

Sid sat down next to me and put his arm around me. "He knew every word of every song. He thought you were brilliant. It was all he ever talked about."

"Yeah, he drove us all nuts with it." Randy added. "I can't tell you how many times he made us sit here with him and listen to your damn albums. To be honest, I'm a little sick of hearing you sing." He broke into a loud belly laugh. Soon everyone was laughing, even me.

That experience was a true revelation in my life, an epiphany that changed me forever. It made me realize something I'd hidden away from myself for over thirty years; I'd been living my life not for me, but for Ron. Everything I'd ever done I did hoping that it would garner his acceptance and somehow meet his standard of excellence. Until that day, I thought I'd always missed the mark somehow. I was sure that everything I'd ever accomplished was not quite good enough, just slightly sub-standard. That day I found out that I had done something Ron approved of... my music. He loved my music.

I GUESS if Ron had not died, I would have never known what he thought and would have continued living my life not believing in my talents and myself. Why he couldn't tell me, I'll never understand. I guess he had his reasons. However, from that day forward, I changed. From then on, I lived my life for me and no one else. It had taken my brother's death and 32 years, but I'd finally grown up.

Ronald Dean Marney 1945 - 1983

# 15

# NASHVILLE

Everyone has their own process of grieving. Some people lose absolute control and just can't stop crying. Some just sort of disappear for a while, lost in their grief. I don't lose control. I do cry when I lose someone that I love, but not much. I cried the most when I lost John Sivil. Of course, I cried when I lost Ron, but my crying quickly turned to anger and that anger lasted almost a year. I was angry at God, but it didn't make me lose my faith. However, I did let him know what I thought about it often.

I was not a pleasant person to be around, because my anger evolved into cynicism. For several months after Ron's death, I got up every day, went to work and criticized everyone and everything around me. I became a real jerk, no matter what anyone did to try to cheer me up, I didn't react well. At that time, nothing seemed important to me. I honestly didn't care whether I lived or died, I just wanted everyone to leave me alone and the day to be over, so I could go home and be by myself.

It was especially hard on Dana, because she didn't know what to do to help me. She kept encouraging me to get back into my music, call a few of our agent friends to book some gigs, and maybe even write again. At that time, I couldn't see music being part of my life anymore, but that changed soon.

When I had agreed to become the president of Marney construction, Ron and I had struck that deal over dinner and had signed it with a handshake.

He made it very clear that night, that if I didn't do the job, brother or no brother, he would fire my ass, but if I did do good, we would split the profits 50-50. Dana and Suzanne were there that night as well and both had heard the conversation and saw us shake on it.

Unfortunately, a few months after Ron's death, Suzanne made it very clear that things had changed and she wasn't about to honor that deal. Angry and frustrated, I began making plans to move on and do something else, but had no idea what that "something else" was going to be.

A few weeks later, Dana and I went out to dinner with one of Ron's dearest friends, Bob Hugley and his wife Rosie.

I told Bob that I was planning on quitting my job with Marney Construction and explained why.

"Are you going to sing again?" He asked.

Reluctantly I nodded my head yes. "I think I have to, at least for a while, but there's not much of a future for Dana and me there."

"I don't understand," He said. "You guys are great, what's the problem? All you need is a hit record and you'd have a great future."

I started laughing. "Yeah, that would do it alright, but like Ron always said, 'we'd be betting our life on a magic trick.' And besides, I don't have the money to even try."

Bob smiled. "What would it cost?"

I sighed and set back in my chair. "To have any real chance, I'd have to do it in Nashville, with a Nashville producer. The way things work these days, if you're not part of the good old boy network, cut in Nashville with Nashville musicians and hire one of those good old boy producers, they won't even talk to you. And that, is very expensive."

"You didn't answer my question." Bob said. "How much would it cost."

"With studio time, Nashville studio musicians and a Nashville producer, maybe five grand a song or more."

He thought for a moment. "So, ten songs at five each... think you could do it for fifty grand? I could raise that in a heartbeat."

I shook my head and smiled. "Bob, that would be the riskiest investment anyone ever made. Just because I get them cut doesn't guarantee a label will sign me. Bob, I appreciate the thought, but that's way too much of a risk."

Exactly 7 days later, Bob showed up at my house with a cashier's check made out for $50,000 to Ben Marney. Somehow he'd found several investors who wanted to roll the dice with me and didn't care if we won or lost.

I met Jimmy James Stroud the first year I lived in Jackson. He was the drummer in the rhythm section at the Malaco Records Studio there and had played on more hit records than I can count. "Old Time Rock and Roll" by Bob Seger to name one.

In 1984, he was one of the top studio drummers in Nashville and was also a recognized up and coming Nashville producer, with a few hits under his belt.

James was also a world renowned studio musician. When Elton John's drummer, Nigel Olson, cut his first solo album, he flew him to England to play the drums on it.

James Stroud was the first person I called when I arrived in Nashville. As soon as Dana and I settled into our new house there, James came over and after dinner, I played him all of my original songs that I had written to that point.

He loved five of them and set a time for me to come to his office the next day to listen to a few songs from his writers. He had formed a new publishing company called "The Writer's Group" and had signed up four or five struggling unknown songwriters.

The next day, we selected five songs from two of his writers and started making plans to record them, as well as the five he liked of mine. I had projected the price correctly: Five Thousand a song.

To pay our bills, I had called Mike Ford. Mike owned a large entertainment booking agency out of Cape Gerardo, Missouri. I had met him at Marney's years earlier. He was booking a few of the other rooms there in Jackson and always dropped by to see our shows and say hello when he was in town.

On every visit, as he walked out he would say. "If you ever need an agent, give me a call."

When I called him, within a few weeks, he had our Duo booked solid. On our breaks, we would drive back to Nashville, go in the studio with James and cut a couple of the songs. It was a slow process.

We had only finished 7 of the 10, when James called me and told me that he thought we may have a deal with Warner Bros.

Ironically, Warner Bros. was dropping their deal with Johnny Lee. His record sales had fallen off, and as a result, their traditional male country artist slot had opened up.

He told me that he'd played my songs for Jim Ed Norman, the President of Warner's country division and said he loved them. He was bouncing off the walls excited.

To get the deal, all that was left was a required unanimous vote from all 7 of the Artist Representatives. They were having that meeting in a few weeks and supposedly, after that vote we were home free.

"I've already played the songs to all of the A & R girls, "He was actually yelling this in my ear over the phone, "and they loved them! I'm telling you Ben, we are there!"

We worked our road gig schedule, so we could be back home the week of the A & R meeting. Dana's mother, Elaine had flown in for a visit and after we arrived back from the airport picking her up, the message light on my answering device was flashing.

Dana and her mother were standing in the kitchen when I hit the playback button on the answering device.

"Hello Ben, this is Jim Ed Norman from Warner Brothers. I know this is a little premature, since we haven't had the A & R meeting yet, but from what I hear that's just gonna be a formality, so I wanted to call to welcome you to our label and to tell you how excited we all are to have you in the Warner family. I love your voice and am looking forward to the future."

Dana and Elaine screamed and hugged, jumping up and down like two little girls. I just stood there smiling, not believing what I had just heard. I had just received the phone call every singer on the planet dreamed of.

My mind was whirling already conjuring up fantasies of my future. Immediately, I started thinking about Home Cookin'. I wasn't sure if they would be interested or not, but I had planned to call every member that I could track down and let them know that I wanted them to be part of whatever happened next. As it turned out, I'm glad I didn't make those calls.

There is no way to verify the next part of this story, it's not written down anywhere and to be honest with you, I'm not absolutely sure it's the truth. At the time, I believed it to be absolute fact, but since then I have learned to question anything James Stroud ever told me. All I can do here, is to tell you exactly what I was told and what went down.

The A & R meeting was held on a Thursday. I waited all day long to get the call, but it never came. I tried to call James, but only got his answering device. He never called me that day.

My guts were telling me something was wrong, but Dana, being the ultimate optimist, kept reminding me of Jim Ed Norman's phone call.

"Why would the President of Warner Bros. call if this wasn't a firm deal? Stop worrying, everything is going to be alright."

James finally called me the next morning. Sadly he said. "I don't know why yet, but they passed. As soon as I can find out something I'll let you know. I'm really pissed over this."

After I hung up and told Dana and Elaine the news, I walked into my backyard and lost it. I cried like a baby for a long time.

About a week later, James came to my house and told me what he'd found out.

Once a month, Jim Ed Norman and the seven A & R (Artist Representatives) met to talk about business and to cast their votes on any new artist presented. To be considered, each new artist had to be presented to the group by one of the seven Artist Representatives.

James had decided to have me be represented by Kinney Wearmer.

Although he knew all seven of them, he chose Kinny, because she had once worked for him at The Writer's Group and wanted her to get the industry kudos for getting me signed to the label.

Apparently, James had given the impression to another Artist Rep by the name of Martha Sharp (no relation to the famous lawyer), that she would be my A & R person.

Over the past year and a half, Martha Sharp had presented two projects to the group from an artist named Randy Ray and on both of those projects, Kinny Wearmer had voted no. To get an artist through, the vote had to be unanimous from Jim Ed and all seven of the Artist Reps. So two times in the past, Kinny had shot down Martha's guy, claiming she just couldn't stand his nasally sounding voice and because of this, there was some bad blood between them.

Although James had gotten thumbs-up from all seven of the A & R women the day before the meeting, when Martha realized that Kinney was my representative, she voted no.

Unknowingly, James had put me in the middle of a catfight that we lost.

Supposedly, Kinney and the other five Artist reps had pleaded with Jim Ed after the meeting in his office to make an exception and sign me anyway, but he wouldn't do it. He firmly believed that everyone in the company had to be on-board. It had to be unanimous, those were the rules.

Kinney was so upset that she resigned the following week and moved to a new label. With her gone, at the very next A & R meeting, Martha Sharp presented Randy Ray for the third time and he finally got the deal. As it turned out, Martha was a very close friend of Randy's manager. Oh yeah, I guess I should mention this, once he got the deal, for whatever reason, he decided to change his name to Randy Travis.

There's one last thing I need to tell you about this and I swear it's true.

Since Randy had the new record deal and I didn't, James called and asked if I would be willing to give up two of the songs I had on hold from his writers. He said Randy wanted to cut them and it would be a big break for his writers.

Of course, I agreed and those songs were "Digging Up Bones" and "On The Other Hand". Two of his biggest hits. What can I say...

By that time the money was getting pretty thin, we had spent most of the 50,000 producing the first seven songs, but James didn't want to give up. With what I had left and some of his, we went back into the studio and recorded a new project, two of the songs were duets with Dana and me. James even brought in the same producer who had produced Kenny and Dolly's "Islands In the Stream" hit.

With the new finished project, James and I began knocking on the doors in Nashville, looking for a new deal, but to no avail.

Fortunately, Mike Ford had booked us solid for almost a year, so Dana and I headed back on the road. Before we left, James had come to our house for dinner and that night he actually broke down and cried blaming himself for not being a good enough producer to land us a deal.

During that next road tour, I woke up early one morning, looked in the mirror and saw my father's face. That was the inspiration for my song called "The Mirror."

When we finally got back to Nashville, James came over for dinner and I played him "The Mirror."

A week later, with James Stroud's money, we recorded it. When we finished, we all gathered in the control booth and listen to the first rough mix coming out of the big speakers.

When the song finished playing, William Lee Golden (of the Oak Ridge Boys), stood up from behind the board and said, "That's your hit son. It's gonna be a smash!"

He had been there listening throughout the entire session but I didn't know it.

We had to head back on the road the following week, so I left "The Mirror" with James to see what he could do with it.

We were gone on the road for almost 6 months and so far James hadn't had any luck shopping "The Mirror." When we got back, he called and told us that he was now one of the "go to" producers at Capitol records.

"I can't bring you in with me. We need to make it look like they discovered you. When they find an act they're interested in, they give the project to me for my opinion. If I like it, they usually sign them. So, this is what I want you to do."

James had it all arranged. He had me sign a management contract with a company called Praxis International. They were a Nashville entertainment management company who handled the group called the Georgia Satellites, who at that time had a hit record called, "Keep your hands to yourself".

James' plan was for me to create a partial project that he would hopefully finish for Capitol. He wanted me to write a couple new songs, record two new songs from his writers and to produce a music video of "The Mirror". When the new half project was finished, Praxis would walk it over and present it to Capitol, specifically asking for it to be presented to James and he would take it from there.

"Sounds like a great plan James, but how am I gonna pay for all this?"

He laughed, "Don't you worry about that, I'll pay for it. Trust me, I'll get it back later once we get you signed."

Again, because of my road work, earning a living, it took us almost a year to get that project finished. When it was finally ready to be presented, James was no longer just a producer for Capitol, he had just been nominated for Producer Of The Year by the CMA, so he was 'the' producer in Nashville.

When he got nominated, I was in the studio working with the engineer on the final mixes. Don Spicer, my producer at Praxis, ran into the control room and actually started dancing.

Jumping around and laughing he yelled. "Talk about a slam dunk! The guy paying for the session, Mr. James Stroud, has just been nominated for producer of the year. Anything he says is gold and Capitol will do anything he wants!"

∾

I AM NOW in the sixth decade of my life. I've lived through many highs and lows, ups and downs.

Like my dad always said, "You have to have a few bad days to appreciate the good ones." I'm ok with that, because that's what life is all about.

When things have happened to me, good or bad, I usually can look back and put my finger on the cause, but there are two things I have lived through that are completely inexplicable and for the life of me, I can't figure out what happened.

The first one is my incredible popularity in Jackson, Mississippi. Why those people loved me so much, I will never understand, but I'm so thankful that they did. The second one that to this very day is a complete mystery, came in the form of a letter.

I was at home working on a song when Don Spicer called and read me the letter.

*"Mr. Don Spicer*

*Praxis International*

*Dear Don,*

*We regret to inform you that James Stroud and Capitol Records have decided to pass on the Ben Marney project at this time.*

*We wish you much luck and success with your future endeavors with this project. Sincerely."*

It wasn't signed by James. It was the CFO of Capitol Records' signature on the bottom of the page.

"What the fuck?" Don shouted. "Call James and see if you can find out what the hell is going on."

I called him, but they told me that he was in a meeting. I called him an hour later and an hour after that, and every single day for the next week, but he was always in a meeting and never called me back.

Finally, I asked if I could at least leave a message on his answering device.

"James, I've tried for over a week to call you, but you're always in a meeting. It's apparent you don't want to talk to me. I have to say I am totally mystified by that. After all we've been through... I thought we were friends.

"I understand that Capitol Records sent Don Spicer a letter saying that you and Capitol had passed on my project. It wasn't signed by you, so Don and I are wondering if this was actually your decision or perhaps a mistake. Honestly, everyone at Praxis is totally baffled and mystified by the letter, especially since you were the one that set this project up and paid for it out of your own pocket. If this is your decision, we will accept it, but could you at least let me or Don know why?"

"I guess the biggest question I have now, is when I go to RCA., Electra or Warner to shop this project and they ask me who produced "The Mirror," I will have to say James Stroud. They will then say, James produced this? What are you doing here, why aren't you down the street signing up with him? What am I supposed to say?

"James, you and I have worked side by side for years knocking on these doors trying to get a deal. We have actually cried together when we couldn't make that happen. Now, with a snap of your fingers you could do it, but instead you passed. There has to be a reason. All I'm asking is to know what that is. Please call me back."

As unbelievable as it may sound, I never talked to James Stroud again, not one time in all these years. I did find out that I wasn't the only one he did this to. No one really knows why, but James severed ties with almost everyone he had been connected to in the past about that time.

James won Producer Of The Year at the 1989 CMA awards. A year later, he became the president of Giant Records and eventually was the head of Dreamworks Nashville. During his active years as the head of those labels, he signed and produced Clint Black, Toby Keith, Faith Hill and Tim McGraw to name a few. Between 1993 and 1994, he produced 31 records that hit the top of the Billboard charts, 21 of those hit number one. Again, what can I say...

As you can imagine, the guys at Praxis International, were outraged and furious, he wouldn't talk to them either. They still believed in my project, so in an effort to promote me, Don Spicer took "The Mirror" video over to CMT and soon my video became part of the regular aired rotation.

*(If you would like to see that video, search youtube for:)*

**Ben Marney The Mirror**

IT WAS THRILLING to see my video playing in between Garth Brooks and Hank Williams Jr. or Willie and Waylon. About once a week, Don would call CMT and ask how "The Mirror" was doing. After the second week they told him it was one of their most requested videos. In the regular programmed rotation, "The Mirror" aired every three hours for the next three months, then mysteriously one day, was taken out of the rotation.

When Don called to find out why it was suddenly taken off, they told him it no longer fit their format.

"How could it be one of your most requested videos last week and now suddenly does not fit your programming?"

They had no real answer to his question, but it never aired again.

"The Mirror" is a song about a guy who suddenly realizes how much he resembles his father and how similar their lives really are.

One month after "The Mirror" was removed from the CMT playlist, a brand new video, written and performed by Paul Overstreet began airing on their regular rotation.

The name of that song was, "Looking like my father" and was produced by.... James Stroud.

That was the last straw. Nashville you win, I give up. I was 39 years old and knew for my own sanity, I had to stop obsessing about landing a record deal and somehow remove any thoughts of getting a hit record out of my heart and mind. There was no question—-It was time to get the hell out of Nashville.

# 16

## THE FIRST SHIP

Nashville had fractured me, I was broken, angry and depressed. My life long dreams had crumbled before my eyes, my confidence had been erased, and that had ripped a large hole in my soul. I had lived through tragedies and heartbreaks before and I knew somehow I would survive this too. It was not going to be easy and I also knew that I couldn't do it on my own.

In the last few years when we had been off the road and actually home on a Sunday, Dana and I attended the First Methodist church not far from our house. On those rare visits, we usually sat in the back and left as soon as the service was over. I really didn't know the preacher at all, but I wanted to talk to him.

We met in his office and he listened patiently to my story. When I finished, he didn't react for a few minutes and just sat quietly across from me, considering his words.

"That's quite a story Ben. I know this may not be what you want to hear and please forgive me for being blunt, but... welcome to Nashville."

I shook my head and laughed, "Yeah, I know the odds are slim."

"No," he said, "I don't think that's the problem Ben. It sounds to me like you've cut right through those odds. Apparently, you have what it takes or you would've never gotten as far as you did. I don't believe that's what's going on here."

I wrinkled my brow, "Then what do you think it is?"

"Two times in your story you told me that you are a believer, a Christian. Were you just trying to impress me, or is that true?"

"No, I wasn't trying to impress you, way too many things have happen to me in my life not to be a believer, but I will admit there are some things I will never understand. Why would he give me the talent and let me get so close...?"

"Because it's not his plan for you." He smiled. "He has something else in mind. You just have to trust him, because no matter how big the storm may seem, if you truly believe, he will calm the waters and show you the way. Go home and read your Bible. Your answers are in there."

So I did:

And when he got into the boat, his disciples followed him.

And behold, there arose a great storm on the sea, so that the boat was being swamped by the waves; but he was asleep.

And they went and woke him, saying, "Save us, Lord; we are perishing."

And he said to them, "Why are you afraid, O you of little faith?" Then he rose and rebuked the winds and the sea, and there was a great calm.

Matthew 8.23-26

I figured that meant God didn't want me to give up and to keep the faith in my music, so I didn't. After a few weeks, my mind began to clear. It was time for the next chapter in our lives.

I had kept my agent, Mike Ford in the loop of my Nashville adventures, so I don't think he was surprised when I called.

"Mike, one of two things are about to happen." I told him. "Either you get me some new gigs that are fun and challenging or I'm going to hang up my guitar and get a job selling life insurance."

He chuckled on the other end. "Let me think about that a second." He was quiet a few minutes, then finally said, "How about a cruise ship?"

Working through Chuck Irvin, an agent out of Fort Lauderdale, Mike somehow got our duo booked sight unseen on the Royal Viking Sea. The contract was for six months with one caveat: if they didn't like us, they could fire us and send us back home after the first week.

Honestly, Dana and I weren't really sure we were going to like living in a small cabin, singing on a rolling ship in the middle of the ocean for six long months, but we were very excited about the itinerary, and because of that, we were willing to give it a shot. I figured that if we didn't like it, since they wanted the option to fire us after a week, we should have the same option, so I had Mike add that to our contract.

In those days, the ships didn't have much sound equipment, you had to bring your own, so I built a shipping crate and filled it with everything I thought I might need. When it was packed and sealed, it weighed almost 600 pounds.

We boarded the ship in Vancouver, Canada and as soon as we got on board and checked in, I started unpacking the crate and setting up.

The entertainment buyer for that cruise line at the time was Bob Sigler and just as I began setting up my equipment, he walked up, introduced himself and asked me how long it was going to take me to get set. He wanted to hear us play something before the ship left.

I forced a smile. "I've never really timed it, I guess it will take as long as it will take. I've got a lot of stuff to hook up, how long do I have before the ship leaves?"

Not liking my answer, he frowned. "They pull out at 4:00 PM, so hurry up, I really want to hear something before I have to debark the ship.

I glanced at my watch. It was a little past 2:00. I had set that equipment up in less than an hour a thousand times before, but Bob's first impression wasn't exactly friendly, so I immediately shifted into first gear, and at a snail's pace, slowly continued setting up and plugging in my equipment.

The way I figured it, if he didn't like what he heard, he just might kick us off the ship on the spot, so there was no way in hell I was going to sing a note before 4:00 that day.

It didn't take us long to realize that we liked working on that cruise ship and apparently they liked us too, because we performed six nights a week on that ship for the next six months.

Royal Viking Sea -1998

The buyer, Bob Sigler and I have become very close friends over the years, enough that I don't think he'll mind me telling you what a terrible first impression he made that day. He really wasn't very friendly, but I soon discovered that was his way; on the ships he was all business, but on the golf course, now that's another story for another book.

For the first five weeks, we cruised through the breathtakingly beautiful inland passage from Vancouver to Juneau, Alaska, making stops in small Alaskan towns like Sitka, Ketchikan, Seward, and on every cruise we slowly glided through the indescribable magnificence of Glacier Bay. If you've never been to Alaska, you need to go. There are no words that can truly describe it.

Our first of many trips to Glacier Bay

The beauty of Alaska and the ocean was all I needed to heal my broken soul. Each night after our sets, I would sit alone at the back of the ship for hours, watching the wake of the sparkling luminescence trailing behind the ship, talking to myself and God.

To be very honest, finally accepting God's plan and putting those life long dreams behind me was one of the hardest things I've ever done in my life, and it took a long time. But watching that ocean trail each night and talking to God helped open my eyes and made me see how lucky I really was. So I was never gonna be rich and a big star! Who cares! I had Dana, my talent and my health. I had nothing to be depressed about.

In Alaska, one of our favorite stops was Sitka. It was a rare, untouched authentic Alaskan town, free of the T-shirt shops and diamond stores that have erased the culture in so many cruise ship ports . In Sitka, you could still find genuine whale bone scrimshaw and view ancient hand carved totem poles.

A few miles out of town they had the Rapture Rehabilitation Center. It was there where we got to see several American bald eagles only a few feet from where we stood. All of the wild animals were there to be rehabilitated because of an injury, usually caused by irresponsible hunters. Dana and I spent hours there, every time we stopped in Sitka.

From Alaska, we made a nine day ocean crossing to Kyoto, Japan. There, a group of us boarded a bullet train and toured Colby and several other small Japanese villages.

When we got back on the ship that afternoon, the Captain

informed us that there was a typhoon headed our way, but rather than try to fight the high seas in the open ocean, he had decided to take the inland passage to Nagasaki. He told us that although we would still get the typhoon force winds on the ship, by going through the inland passage, the outer islands would block most of the huge waves.

The crew went to work lashing down everything on the ship, including chaining our speakers to the floor. The wind started blowing that evening and lasted throughout the next day, reaching a high of 120 miles per hour. We didn't have to perform long that night, because there was no one there. Every passenger on the ship was seasick and stayed in their cabins next to the head.

I was 38 years old at the time and old enough to know better, but the next day several of us entertainers, including a few of the dancers in the production show, made our way outside so we could experience what 120 mile an hour winds felt like. When you stepped into that kind of wind, it pinned you against the walls, took your breath away and took all your strength to pull yourself back behind the wind blocks. One of the young and very strong male dancers actually climbed up on a chinning bar. As he held on for dear life, the wind flapped his body like a flag.

It was completely insane being out there and very dangerous, but we did it anyway. I have to admit it was a blast! We found out later that that typhoon was the largest storm to hit Japan in 20 years

In Nagasaki, we toured the Peace Museum and walked around the ground zero site where the second atomic bomb was dropped in World War II. It was a sobering experience seeing the devastation.

From Japan we sailed to Hong Kong and that became our home port for the next five months. From Hong Kong, on fourteen day cruises, we cruised to Indonesia, Bally, Thailand, Sri Lanka , India, Madagascar, Africa and back.

Because the Royal Viking Sea was a small ship, we could get into ports that the larger ships of today could never visit. Every morning we would wake up, look out our port window and see a strange new, exotic place. The second the gangway was down, our group, which consisted of a few of the singers and dancers in the production show, the other ship musicians, the magician and the comedian, would meet up and head out together to explore.

The things we did and the places we explored was truly a once in a life time experience. I have so many wonderful memories of those days, way too many for a short story, but I will tell you about a few of my favorites.

The Royal Viking Sea was a 5 star rated ship, and each week they had two formal nights. On those nights, the men were required to wear tuxedos and the women wore fancy, sparkling full length formal gowns. Actually, there were only a few male passengers––most were women. The average age of the passengers was about 75. As you might expect, all the passengers fell in love with Dana and the women especially loved her clothes on formal nights.

If you know my wife Dana, you will not be surprised to hear that she had brought on board two large suitcases and two old-fashion steamer trunks full of gowns and dresses.

One of my favorite memories is when our good friend David Reed, (an older, very British, but funny as hell comedian) would knock on our door on formal nights, and with me following behind, escort Dana to the dinning room. The old ladies would actually ooh, and aah, when Dana entered. She looked like a super model walking in and every head would turn to watch her entrance.

We had met David Reed in Alaska and had instantly become fast friends. He claimed he had done the same shows word for word for over 15 years and even though we saw him do them a thousand times, he always cracked us up. David wore tuxedos in his shows and always looked very debonair. One of his bits was to start talking about the amazing bargains to be found in Hong Kong. He would walk into the audience and let them inspect his shirt, French cuffs and his collar.

"Just look at the quality of this material and the workmanship on these cuffs." He would go on and on about the quality. "I only paid 5 dollars for this shirt and have worn it for years." Then he would move on telling jokes. Toward the end of his act, when no one was expecting it, he would start talking about how hot it was in the room.

Then he would take off his jacket and exposed the rest of his shirt. It was torn to shreds. It always brought down the house.

To keep the passengers entertained on the 9 day ocean crossing, the cruise director decided to have a carnival in the show room.

David, the magician Garin Bader, Dana and I were assigned one of the booths. It was up to us to come up with some kind of game for the passengers to play and to also decorate our booth.

Every other team was running all over the ship in a panic, trying to find decorations, balloons and streamers for their booths, but David told us not to worry about it.

"I've done this a million times." He said. "Relax, let's all go get a drink. I know exactly what to do."

He waited until all the other booths were decorated and the teams left to go get dressed, then walked around and stole a little from each of the other booths and hung them up in ours. Then he took out a deck of cards and put an old hat he had also stolen from one of the booths on a chair.

"We're all set. Throw the cards in the hat. One buck for three tries." He smiled wide, "Don't you agree? I believe we have the best decorated booth in the entire carnival."

Dana and I were both a little embarrassed when we actually won the award for the best decorated booth.

In those five months, other than not seeing the Taj Mahal because we were working that night and couldn't go on that trip, Dana and I got to see all of the amazing sights and wonders in that part of the world you would expect. We still have vague memories of most of what we saw back then, but what we remember best are the things we experienced that were off the beaten path; sights and experiences the passengers didn't get to see or do.

In those days, Dana and I were really into running to keep in shape. We jogged through back alleys, down dirt roads and busy highways all over Hong Kong, Southeast Asia, India and Africa. We created quite a stir as we ran along in our head bands, bright colored running shoes and short shorts.

Accompanied by our entourage of entertainment friends, we took a lot of trips that resulted in amazing experiences: In Sri Lanka, we all took turns riding bare back on Indian elephants. In Cochin, India we split up in groups squeezing three at a time into tiny three-wheel motor scooter taxis to visit a 2,500 year old Buddhist temple. In Zanzabar we all walked together down the tiny winding paths of that ancient island city. In Mombasa, Africa, we visited a thatched roof factory where, using only a machete and knives, the native artist carved beautiful sculptures from wooden logs. But the most memorable experience I've ever had on a cruise ship happened in Antsrianana, Madagascar.

Our crazy group of entertainers/explorers

One of our closest friends on that ship was the magician, Garin Bader. He was an amazing slight of hand artist and could do impossible things right before your eyes that would just blow your mind.

When we landed in Antsiranana, our group walked the two miles together from the ship pier to the small downtown. In the center of town was an open market where the locals came to sell their wares. In one of the stalls Garin noticed a stern faced, older native woman, sitting very erect and stoic behind a large stack of oranges. He always carried a tiny device that he could somehow conceal in his hands that made a loud squeaking sound. Garin walked over to the woman and began inspecting her oranges, picking up a few, smelling them and putting them back down. Finally he picked one up, smelled it, then shook it. When he shook it, it made a loud squeak. We were all about to bust out laughing, but the old woman didn't move a muscle, staring straight ahead, stoned faced. Garin continued inspecting the oranges. He made a few more squeak as he shook them, then paid her for the ones that squeaked and walked away.

We all walked around the corner just far enough that she couldn't see us, but we could see her. She sat there motionless, not moving for a few minutes. Then she looked around to see if anyone was watching. We all lost it laughing when she started picking up and shaking the oranges.

After we walked around that market, there wasn't much else to see, so we walked to the taxi stand and tried to explain where we wanted to go.

"Ocean front hotel?" We asked the drivers.

In very broken English, they said, "Yes, we ride, ocean front hotel!"

In town, we had run into the ship's chef and invited him to join us, so it took two taxis to fit us all in, but eventually we got loaded up and took off.

Forty-five minutes later we pulled up to a beach, lined with small shacks. The tide was out, so the water wasn't even visible. We could only see a few hundred yards of wet sand, where the ocean had been.

I looked at our driver, "Ocean front hotel?" I asked waving my hands in the air.

He smiled. "Yes, Yes." He motioned for us to follow him and started walking down the beach.

After we passed about 20 of the shacks, he stopped, grinned at me and pointed at one of the buildings. "Hotel."

The small shack had a 20 by 20 foot concrete slab in front with a basketball hoop on one end.

Before we could respond, three smiling native women rushed out of the shack. "Food? Beer?" They asked.

We all shrugged and smiled. "Sure, why not."

Within minutes, the women had set up folding tables and chairs out on the concrete slab and started passing out cold beers. The chef was able to explain to the women what we wanted, and soon we were all served some kind of seafood soup and fresh bread. It was delicious.

It was obviously a family run hotel, because one of the servers was about eight years old and cute as a button. Garin called her over and tried to talk to her, but she didn't understand English. He reached over to her and magically pulled a quarter from her right ear and gave it to her. When he did it, she squealed with excitement and ran off. About fifteen minutes later, we were surrounded by excited, laughing children. We all emptied our pockets that day, passing our change to Garin under the tables. We were all having fun, but the children were over the moon. Every time Garin would do his ear trick, they would scream with laughter. I'm sure those children still talk about the day a magic man with long blonde hair came to their village and pulled money out of their ears. I know I'll never forget it either.

A few hours later, the tide came back in and the beach began to fill with small fishing boats.

Apparently, the word had spread throughout the village, because when we walked back to the taxi, we were presented with four of the biggest lobsters you've ever seen in your life. It was their gift to us for entertaining their children. We insisted on paying for them, and after a bit of haggling we finally got them to except a 20 dollar bill. That night after our gig, the chef cooked up the lobsters and we had an amazing midnight feast at the bar.

My memory banks are full of stories like that from that cruise. Like the night off the coast of Bali, the first officer actually let Dana steer the ship. Or the day Garin bribed the room stewart into letting him into our room so he could slip about a million rubber spiders under Dana's sheet. That night, when she pulled back the covers, you could hear her blood curdling scream throughout the entire ship and we could hear Garin laughing behind our door.

On that ship, we were lucky enough to be invited to go on a personal guided tour of Bombay (now called Mumbai) in the back of a Mercedes limousine with one of the passengers who just happened to be the Ex President of Jeep Canada. The highlight of that day was getting to visit Gandhi's home and eating a 5-star traditional Indian meal with no silverware at the Oberie Hotel. We were only allowed to use our right hand fingers and the traditional Indian flatbread called "naan" as a scoop.

Because the ship was so small, we only had one seating for dinner and all the entertainers sat at one long table. I'm not sure why, but one night during dinner I took a bite of the entrée and it was so amazing, I jumped to my feet and started spinning around, squealing like a pig. "Wheee, wheee, wheee."

A few days later, one of the dancers jumped up and did the same thing. A few days after that, Garin did his pig dance as well. Soon, the pig dance became a regular thing at the entertainers table. When one of us would do it, the passengers would laugh and clap. Then one formal night, one of the passengers, a little old lady about 80 years old stood up and did it too. From that night on, without fail, someone would stand up, spin around and squeal like a pig.

On our last week, Dana and I were presented with two Swarovski crystal pigs in honor of starting the pig dance. Those two crystal pigs are sitting on our coffee table as I write this.


DANA and I didn't know it at the time, but that six-month contract on the Royal Viking Sea would turn out to be our favorite ship contract ever. Probably because it was our first, or the fact that we got to spend two full weeks in Hong Kong after we got off, but the things we saw, the things we experienced and the friends we made on that ship, even after all these years, still remain in a very warm and special place in our heart.

17

## THE CARIBBEAN TO COLORADO

A week before our Royal Viking Sea contract ended, the entertainment buyer, Bob Sigler, called and told us we could stay on the ship for another month if we wanted. The ship was sailing to Sydney and he thought we might enjoy seeing Australia. That was a difficult offer to turn down, but it was mid November and we would miss Christmas with our family. We had also made arrangements to stay in Hong Kong two more weeks after we got off the ship to do some serious exploring and Christmas shopping as well, so we passed on his offer. We found out later that that was a good decision, because within that next month, Royal Viking sold that ship and I assumed to save money, rather than docking in Hong Kong, they anchored. All of the musicians on board had to offload their equipment onto a dinghy in those rough waters in the Hong Kong Harbor.

The harpist actually lost her 30,000 dollar harp overboard trying to offload it. It would've been impossible for me to offload that 600 pound shipping crate full of my equipment onto a dinghy.

Dana and I had a blast checking out every inch of Hong Kong for those two weeks and came home with a new suitcase full of silk ties, silk Kimonos and everything else we could find within our budget. Without question, we gave the best Christmas gifts that year.

We were so glad to be home after such a long trip, but we were only there a few weeks before Bob Sigler called, asking us to fly to San Juan, Puerto Rico to board the Norwegian Cruise Line ship called the Skyward.

The duo on that ship had just been fired trying to smuggle drugs on board in their shoes, so Bob was stuck and needed our help.

Three days after Christmas, we flew to San Juan and boarded the MS Skyward. That began a four and a half year adventure working for the Norwegian Cruise line.

On the Skyward, our itinerary rotated each week. One week we would cruise the ABC islands in the Leeward Antilles: Aruba, Bonair, Curacao and then over to the American and British Virgin Islands of St. Thomas and Tortola. The next week we sailed the Lesser Antilles: Barbadoe, Martinique, Antigua, Sint Maarten and back to Tortola and St. Thomas.

During those four and a half years working for the Norwegian Cruise line, Dana and I jogged and explored every square inch of those islands.

Our favorite islands were Antigua, Sint Maarten and Tortola. We especially loved Tortola, because the ship let the crew take one of the tenders over to Virgin Gorda. After Dana and I jogged to the "Baths" and back. We would walk over to Little Dix Bay and spend the afternoon sunbathing under a thatched roof umbrella at the 5-star Rockefeller resort there.

I still have vivid memories of lying there thinking, "My life does not suck!"

You would think living on those ships and eating all that rich food, we would have been fat as pigs, but because we rarely took taxis and walked or jogged everywhere, we were in the best shape of our lives.

The only island where we did take a taxi was in Sint Maarten. Dana loved going over to the French side (St. Martin), to Marigot to browse the new French fashions in the clothing stores. After that, we usually made a stop at Orient Beach, the nude beach.

Believe it or not, we didn't go there to ogle beautiful nude French girls strolling along the beach, because they weren't there. We went there, because that's where the crew hung out, the beach was incredibly beautiful and the food at the restaurants lining the beach was great. It was also a good place to people watch. Unfortunately, the only people brave enough to actually go nude on that beach were the ones who should only take off their clothes to take a shower. It was usually the older, fat, saggy, flabby ones proudly strolling along butt ass naked! Dana and I never joined in.

I've always said, "Little Elvis has never seen the sunshine and he never will!"

On the island of Antigua, Dana and I usually jogged. It was a great place to run, because there were several upscale resorts only a few miles away from the downtown port, and a lot of other interesting places to explore close by.

When we did take a cab, it would be up to Shirley Heights. The view from there was magnificent, overlooking English harbor and Nelson's boatyard.

During those years, we worked on two different ships for the Norwegian Cruise line. In 1991 they sold the Skyward and moved us over to the Starward. When we got to the Starward, our performance schedule was sort of wacky. It was a split shift, starting at 4:00, ending at 1:00am, with two long breaks in the middle. Apparently, the duo we followed never complained about it, but after the first week, I had a meeting with the Cruise Director.

"Who set up this performance schedule? We're playing when there's no one there and not playing when they are. It's nuts."

The cruise director's name was Peter Grant. "I don't know who set that schedule up, probably the last cruise director. Tell you what Ben, make me out a new schedule and we'll go with that."

That was music to my ears. The next day I presented him with our new schedule and for the next two years, with only a few minor adjustments, we followed it and it worked great. I know it may not sound like it, but allowing me to set our own schedule was a very smart move. There's nothing more disheartening to an entertainer than to have to play to an empty room, so I chose the times when there were actually people around and the room was packed for every set. It was rare for that cruise director to trust me and let me make up my own schedule, but because he did, we doubled the revenue.

The unfortunate truth on most cruise ships is that the management, including the ship's officers, believe that entertainers are overpaid and underworked. It's a legendary argument. Because everyone else on the ship has to work long hard hours, it drives them crazy that the entertainers make a lot of money and only work a few sets a night. It doesn't matter to them that what we do is a unique skill that takes actual talent and years of practice. If it were left up to them, they would have the entertainers swabbing the deck during the day, and singing at night.

Unfortunately, this negative attitude toward entertainers has gained momentum in recent years on most cruise lines. This is a result of the change in the qualifications needed to be a cruise director. When Dana and I began our cruise ship career, all of the cruise directors were entertainers or singers and understood and respected what it took to do what we did. Today, most of the cruise director's only experience on a stage is when they introduce the talent. Unfortunately, some cruise directors start believing that when they are doing their introductions of the talent, because people actually laugh at their corny jokes (that usually they have stolen from real comedians) they are talented as well and are entertainment experts. The other unfortunate truth about cruise ships, it that the livelihood of the actual talent on the ships is in the cruise director's hands. It really doesn't matter what the passengers think, even if you get great ratings. If a cruise director doesn't like you, for whatever reason, you're out of there.

Fortunately, Peter Grant did not have that attitude and appreciated what the entertainers did on the ship and because of that rare respect he gave all of us, in return, we gave him back 110% and it was reflected in his ratings.

Peter Grant is now and has been for years a Vice President of

Norwegian Cruise lines, and Director of Entertainment for all their ships.

Because Dana and I had a good cruise director that we didn't have to walk on egg shells around, for the next few years things went great. We did our job well,  kept a low profile and didn't complain, because we had nothing to complain about.

We were working six months on, with one month off for vacation. When we were on the ship, we spent our days in paradise, frolicking in those beautiful islands and spent our nights performing to packed rooms to very enthusiastic passengers who loved our music. Bob Sigler told us, as far as he was concerned, we had an open ended contract and could stay as long as we wanted. Life was sweet.

I know what you're thinking. Why would anybody in their right mind end something like this?

One of the biggest problems I've had in my life is not being able to recognize and appreciate what I had in the moment, I've always wanted something more.

We had been performing on cruise ships for almost five years, I was 44 years old and had a nagging, never ending feeling in my gut that I hadn't really accomplished a damn thing in my life.

So, when my old friend Bob Hugley called and asked, "How would you like to own a piece of a casino?" I jumped at the chance.

Bob was involved with the development of a casino in Cripple Creek, Colorado and wanted Dana and me to not only perform there, but wanted us to be in charge of all of the entertainment.

The company was based in Colorado Springs, so Bob's wife, Rosie found us a house in Woodland Park--about half way between the office and the proposed casino in Cripple Creek.

The house was two stories with a large basement, built on the side of a hill. One side was all glass, exposing an amazing, unobstructed view of Pike's Peak. It was the most beautiful house Dana and I have ever lived in, and one of the biggest regrets of my life that I only rented it and didn't buy it when I had the opportunity.

I had only been to Colorado once before, when we performed at the Denver Marriott, but that was before I had become a runner. A few days after we had unpacked and settled in, I put on my jogging shoes and shorts and ran out the door, but I only lasted a few minutes before I was lying on the ground gasping for air.

Almost every day for the past five years, I had run at least three miles, but that was at sea level. Woodland Park was at 8,500 feet, and as far as I could tell on that first run, the air up there had no oxygen in it. I gasped for air a long time that morning.

It took me a while, but I eventually got my body acclimated, so I could run again.

Dana and I were very excited for the next chapter of our life to begin, but when we got there and realized that Bob had left out one minor detail, we were a little pissed and discouraged. The Casino wasn't actually under construction yet. In fact, they were still raising the money to build it. Although he didn't tell me when I was still on the ship, Bob wanted me involved in the casino development stages, because of my background in running Ron's construction company. He didn't actually lie, we would be in charge of the entertainment, and Dana and I would perform there once it was built. The question for us was, how long would that be.

On our very first cruise ship we had met a great singer and become close friends. Her name was Linda Millikan and not only was she a good singer, she was beautiful and smart as a whip. We had talked to her at length about our opportunity with the Casino, heading up the entertainment and in hopes that in the near future we would be developing some shows, Linda decided to move to Colorado and be part of our team.

Unfortunately, Bob and his partners never raised enough money to actually build that casino, and Dana and I were beginning to think we had made a terrible mistake leaving the ships. But out of nowhere another amazing opportunity for all of us revealed itself.

Linda's mother Jean and her father Blair stopped in Colorado Springs on one of their vacations to visit Linda. Since we'd never met, Linda invited us out to dinner to get to know them.

That night, Blair asked me a million questions. He wanted to know every detail of my life, from how I started my music career, to how I wound up in Colorado and everything in between.

I really liked her parents, but Blair's constant questions made me feel like I was being interrogated by the police.

The next day they left Colorado on their planned drive to California, but after only one day, they called Linda and asked her to set up a meeting with all of us. All he would tell her was that he had an idea he wanted to talk to us about.

Two days later, Blair, Jean and Linda came to our house and we all gathered in the living room to hear what he had to say.

Blair had work for Dupont Chemical for years, had take an early retirement and had made millions investing his retirement package in the stock market.

"After talking to Ben at dinner the other night, I am confident that this Cripple Creek Casino is never going to come to fruition." He began. "My question is, and I'm asking all of you, Ben, Dana and Linda, what do you want to do next?"

We all looked at each other, shook our heads and said, "We don't know."

Blair smiled. "I know you're questioning your decision to get off the ships, but I agree with you Ben––I don't think there is much future for any of you out there, not long-term. My question to you is, if you could do anything you want, what would you want to do -- and I'm talking about the three of you as a team."

Ironically, it had been less than two months since I had received a phone call from one of my old Marney's fans. He was calling to tell me about his recent trip to Branson, Missouri and told me that I should check it out. He thought I should open a music theater there.

"Well Blair, if I had the money," I said. "I would probably head to Branson, Missouri and look into opening up a theater. I understand that place is booming."

The next hour or so, we all discussed the possibility of what we could do with our own theater in Branson and the more we talked, the more all of us liked that idea.

"Ok guys, here is what I am thinking." Blair said. "I don't think I can afford to buy an entire theater, but I am willing to put up $500,000 to get it started."

I don't think I have to tell your how stunned and shocked we all were that night when Blair made that offer, but that was the beginning of the next huge, exciting, challenging and amazing chapter in *all* of our lives.

# 18

# FROM NASHVILLE TO BROADWAY

I f you've read this book from the beginning, you've probably noticed that I had lived my adult life, so far, in five-year increments. I can't explain that, but it just seemed to have worked out that way, so I'm sure you won't be surprised when I tell you my next big adventure lasted exactly five years.

After a few trips to Branson, Missouri and a lot of due diligence, we decided to make an offer to buy the John Davidson Theater. It was an older, smaller theater with only 800 seats. In hindsight, I wish we had closed that deal, but before we wrote the check, someone told us about Myrtle Beach.

Honestly, Dana and I didn't mind the idea of living in Branson, but Linda wasn't that excited about it. Unlike Dana and me, Linda was not into country music at all, and she was afraid for us to be successful in Branson, our show would have to be predominately country. She was probably right. Also, Branson was out in the middle of nowhere and the idea of living there wasn't very appealing to her.

When we heard about the theaters being built in Myrtle Beach, with over 100 golf courses and a 60 mile long beach, it didn't take us long to switch our attention to there.

The problem was, in Branson, with just a little bit more money, we could have bought the John Davidson Theater and opened our show within a few months. If we moved to Myrtle Beach, raising enough money to build a brand new theater from scratch was going to be a major hurdle. However, after our very first trip there, there was no question in any of our minds that Myrtle Beach was the place we all wanted to live, and the place we wanted to build our theater.

I contacted Bob Hugley and got him involved raising the money we needed, but even Bob, Mr. Optimistic, wasn't sure he could raise the five million it would take to do it. But once again, like so many times before in my life, fate stepped in and took over.

To keep our living cost down, Linda, Dana and I rented a large house together. Linda took the downstairs and we took the upstairs. It had a large room where we set up our production office, and one day while we were all in there working, the phone rang.

In our search for theater locations in Myrtle Beach, we had visited the two theater development areas there. One was called Broadway At The Beach and the other was called Fantasy Harbor.

Broadway At The Beach was still in the planning stages and had just broken ground, but Fantasy Harbor had five theaters up and running: The Larry Gatlin Theater, The Ronnie Milsap Theater, Medieval Times, The Savoy Theater and a large tent structure with a pseudo Cirque du Solei show.

The phone call was from the operators of Fantasy Harbor. Rich Little, the impressionist, who was performing at the Gatlin Theater had lost his opening act, and they were wondering if we would like to open for him. That turned out to be a big break for us, because by doing so, we apparently impressed the folks at Fantasy Harbor.

We open for Rich six days a week for the next few months and then opened for him for four weeks at the Golden Nugget in Reno, Nevada. When we got back from Reno, the guys at Fantasy Harbor called and asked to have a meeting.

In that meeting, we learned that Ronnie Milsap did not actually own his theater, they had only hired him to perform there and part of the deal was to be able to use his name on the building. Apparently, his numbers were not that good, so they were looking to make a change.

"Rather than you guys building your own new theater, why don't you buy the Milsap Theater from us? We'll even finance it."

Blair, Linda's father was at that meeting and since he had started this whole thing, had put up most of the money, and he had an MBA, I smiled and turned the meeting over to him to make the deal.

Two months later, we took possession of the previously known Ronnie Milsap Theater. To do that, as the CEO of the company, I had to sign my name as the guarantor on a five million dollar mortgage.

I can still remember feeling the butterflies in my stomach, standing in the window of my new office, overlooking the lobby of the theater thinking, "What in the hell have I gotten myself into now!"

The first thing we did was renamed the theater. We called it "The All American Music Theater." The second was to talk Wayne Cockfield into being our musical director. We had met Wayne when we were opening for Rich Little at the Gatlin Theater. He was a brilliant musician and with him onboard we all knew the band would be fantastic and in good hands.

Next, we contacted Mary Barton to be our lead dancer and choreographer. Like Linda, Dana and I had met Mary onboard the Royal

Viking Sea. She was beautiful, a phenomenal dancer and a huge asset to the show.

The next critical part was to actually write a show. We wanted a show that showcased what Linda, Dana and I did best. I had seen all of the shows in the other theaters in Myrtle Beach and understood the basic big production formula, so I locked myself in my office, went to work and came up with a show called "From Nashville To Broadway."

Wayne Cockfield -Musical Director

With Linda in charge of all of the staging, Mary doing the choreography, Dana organizing all of the costumes and Wayne leading the orchestra, we all went to work producing the show.

From Nashville To Broadway was two acts with a fifteen-minute intermission. The first act was a big variety of songs divided between the three of us, but leaning toward country music, the Nashville part.

Because every show in Myrtle Beach had a comedian, I convinced my good friend Art Updike to come fill that role. He wasn't a professional comedian, just completely nuts and one of the funniest guys I've ever met in my life. In the first act, Art did an impression of an Elvis impersonator. Not an impression of Elvis, but an impression of an Elvis impersonator. I told you he was nuts. Before his act was over, he was usually in the crowd putting his Elvis wig on some poor old man that made the mistake of sitting too close to the stage. He was always a big hit with the audience, because he was a great entertainer and naturally funny.

The second act started with a big band section that showed off our 16 piece orchestra. We ended that section with a song by Frank Sinatra from the Broadway show Guys and Dolls, called "Luck Be A Lady Tonight."

From there we moved to the Broadway part, performing short sections of famous Broadway shows, with full sets and costumes:

Evita, The Music Man, Phantom of the Opera, A Chorus Line and Les Miserables.

In Evita, Dana sang "Don't Cry For Me Argentina" from an 18 foot high balcony, towering 25 feet above the audience.

In The Music Man, Art absolutely nailed "Trouble In River City" and ended the song marching through the audience leading the band down the isles.

Linda, who was an alto, had dreamed for years of playing the part of Christine in the Phantom Of The Opera. That part is normally sung by a soprano, so by dropping it down to the alto range, no one could sing the Phantom's part but a low baritone. Unfortunately, that meant me. The cast and crew used to joke that when I did it, it was more like Phantom of the Opry. Like the Grand Old... I didn't think that was funny at all.We also enlisted the voice of our piano player, Tom Garber. When Wayne hired him he told me, "He can sing too." That was a big understatement, because Tom could sing as well as he played that piano!

He was also a real good looking guy, so he made the perfect Viscount Raoul de Chagny, the Phantom's rival.

When I think about our performance of The Phantom, the huge chandelier our stage crew created always flashes in my mind. I'm not sure where we found him, but we were incredibly lucky to have Kelly Berry as our Stage Manager. He recruited some very dedicated stagehands to work with him, and his team built unbelievable sets. The Phantom chandelier was seven or eight feet tall and ten feet around. It was spectacular to see lit up and glowing.

To MAKE the set change after The Phantom, our dancers, dressed in white tuxedos, leotards, top hats and tails, dazzled the audience with the A Chorus Line finale song, "One."

For the Les Miserables segment, I asked Kelly to do the impossible, but somehow he did it. I wanted to have a clean stage for Dana's performance of Fantine's "I Dreamed A Dream", Linda's performance of Eponine's "On My Own" and my rendition of Jean Valjean's "Bring Him Home." Then, for the finale, I wanted to transform the stage into Paris in 1832 and fill the center stage with a twenty foot wide, ten foot tall barricade, and I wanted to be able to do this in a few seconds.

To accomplish this, Kelly and his team painted a scene of Paris on a backdrop and came up with an unobtrusive black box that was barely visible on stage left. On cue, the backdrop fell into place and the black box folded out to reveal the massive barricade I wanted. With the help of the entire orchestra and the dancers dressed in period costumes, as well as all of the stagehands, they did this transformation in about thirty seconds.

I loved it, but Kelly wasn't satisfied with the backdrop. A few weeks later after one of our shows, I had forgotten something in my office, so I went back to the theater to get it. When I got there at 1:30 am, I found Kelly and the entire stage crew hanging in the rafters painting and decorating the very back wall of the theater. None of them were on the clock, but because they were so dedicated to making our show as good as possible, they worked hours on the actual back wall of the stage to make it look like a city. From the audience, you'd swear you were looking at a view of Paris in 1832 behind the barricade.

We ended From Nashville To Broadway in front of that amazing barricade and backdrop with our entire cast of 26 musicians, dancers and singers, dressed in period costumes singing "One Day More."

Linda had done an incredible job staging the entire show, but what she did with this finale song was her best. Every time we did it, I had chills running down my spine singing that amazing song, and we always got a standing ovation.

We opened The All American Music Theater on July 4, 1997. We performed from Nashville to Broadway six nights a week, plus three matinee performances each Wednesday, Thursday and Friday until mid November. Just before Thanksgiving, we switched to our Christmas show. That show was the best I've ever written and will always be my favorite to perform in ever.

Because I knew my cast so well by the time I began to write that show, I wrote it specifically with them in mind, highlighting their individual talents.

Again, with Linda's brilliant staging ideas, Mary's great choreography, Dana's costume design ideas and Kelly's great sets, the show was spectacular.

The first act started with Linda, Dana and me sitting on stools taking turns singing our favorite Christmas songs. Then, Art and Tom joined us and we did a few more with big five piece harmonies, Manhattan Transfer style. From there we moved onto a variety of traditional and nontraditional Christmas songs featuring Dana, Linda, Art, Tom, the dancers and me. I even got to wear my cowboy hat and sing a George Strait song called "Christmas Time In Texas."

For the second act, I wrote a one act play. It started with a cast Christmas party at Linda's house. Kelly and his crew did their magic and the stage was transformed to look like a cozy living room-- Christmas tree, fireplace and all.

Since it was supposedly a cast Christmas party for a bunch of singers, dancers and musicians, when the curtain opened, several of the musicians were set up in the corner jamming, playing a Christmas song, while the rest of the cast was mingling around the room, decorating the tree, chatting or dancing to the music.

To set up the premise, I had Art walk up to me and asked me if he could talk to me about something. It was the first dialogue in the play.

With a confused look on his face he would ask me. "So this is our cast Christmas party, right?"

"Yes." I answered.

"...and this is supposed to be Linda's house?"

"Right again."

Art would turn and look around at the audience for a while, and with that same confused look on his face, pointing toward them, he would ask. "Then who the hell are all these people in her back yard. She sure has some nosy neighbors!"

In the past months, I had discovered a few hidden gems of talent in our cast and crew. I had discovered that our string, synth, keyboard player, Becca Bongiorno was also a singer, so I featured her at the cast party. Becca was absolutely beautiful, so taking full advantage of my position as the writer of the show, I wrote in a scene where Becca sang "Let It Snow" sitting on the edge of the couch with my arm around her waist. That was always an enjoyable three minutes.

In that show, I also featured Tom Garber playing his dulcimer, all the dancers singing a goofy version of the 12 days of Christmas and I had Bernie Kennerson, our saxophone player, play his rendition of Silent Night, while Mary Barton and Ken Santos danced a beautiful pas de deux.

The synopsis of the play was, during that cast party, Myrtle Beach was hit with a sudden snowstorm and the party broke up early. Not wanting to be alone on Christmas Eve, Linda begged Tom, Dana and me not to leave, to stay over and celebrate Christmas morning with her.

After we all retired for the night up stairs, with only the glow of the fireplace lighting the stage, the statues of the toy soldier and the ballerina on each side of the fireplace magically came to life and performed a ballet to the music of the Nutcracker.

When the dance was over and they transformed back to statues, Santa Cause (played by Art Updike) made his grand entrance through the fireplace, slapping out a fire that had caught, burning on his butt.

With a snap of his fingers he turned on all the lights, but before he left his presents, he noticed the musical instruments the band was playing earlier. He picked up the guitar and did a quick Elvis impression, then put on a pair of shades and did Ray Charles behind the piano. The audience was usually laughing hysterically at that point. Then Santa sat down behind the drums and began to play. Art was actually a great drummer, so his drum solo always received a big round of applause.

Hearing all the noise from the drums, Linda, Tom, Dana and I rushed into the room, dressed in our PJ's, holding baseball bats, brooms and Lamps as weapons to fend off the intruder.

Convinced he was just a burglar dressed in a Santa suit, Linda wanted to call the police, but, one-by-one, he proved to us he was the real Santa Claus.

He did this by giving us presents out of his big red bag we had always asked for in our letters we had written to him when we were children: A BB gun for Tom, a Barbie doll for Dana and a baseball glove for me. Linda, still very skeptical, slowly opened her present. Inside the box, hidden from the audiences view, was supposed to be a book and her line was, "Oh Santa, it's a book!" Then Santa would explain what a book worm she had always been, even as a little girl.

One of the goals of our stage crew was to try to break us up during our performance. When Linda opened her present each night, she never knew what might be inside the box. Her presents ranged each performance from a slice of pizza, a plastic dog turd, nude pornographic pictures, to a vibrating dildo. Somehow, she never lost it and always delivered her lines flawlessly.

Once we were all finally convinced he was the real Santa, I asked him how he could possibly travel all around the world delivering his presents to the children in one night.

"It's my magic Christmas dust." Santa said. "All I have to do is throw it up into the air and it stops time."

Then Tom asked him what 'he' was going to get for Christmas.

Shaking his head, he said, I don't *get* presents, I *give* presents."

We all decided that that was not fair and asked Santa if we could give him a present.

"What would you like for Christmas, Santa?"

He thought hard about it for a few minutes and then said, "What I would really like is a vacation. I have to work all year long to make these toys, so I don't get much time off."

After we sang to Santa, "How'd You Like To Spend Christmas On Christmas Island,"

...using some of his magic Christmas dust to stop time, we took Santa on a vacation and the stage transformed into an island

scene in the Caribbean, with a beautiful full back drop photo-
graph of St. John. With the band playing steel drum island music,
the dancers filled the stage wearing Carmen Miranda-ish
costumes and performed a big choreographed production
number.

During the dancer's performance, including Santa, we all re-
appeared on the stage, dressed in island clothes.

In this Caribbean section, we took turns performing some great
Jimmy Buffett Christmas songs and even got Santa up to sing, "Run
Run Rudolph." From there, we transformed back to Linda's living
room, still excited about the island trip.

Next, Linda asked Santa why he did it, why he worked so hard
every year. Art was not only funny and a great drummer, he could
also sing. So to answer Linda's question, Santa sang the Barry
Manilow song, "Because It's Christmas."

To pay us all back for his Christmas gift, he granted us one wish,
anything we wanted. We all agreed with Linda that we would love to
be able to spend Christmas in Vermont, just like in the movie White
Christmas with Bing Crosby and Danny Kaye.

Throwing his magic Christmas dust into the air, the stage transformed into a replica of the lodge in the movie set of White Christmas.

Linda, Dana, Tom and I had exactly a minute and 30 seconds to change out of our Caribbean island outfits into our winter clothes of long pants and sweaters. To accomplish this, we set up a small dressing area at stage right, ran in, lifted up our hands and the stage crew un-dressed and re-dressed us, with only seconds to spare.

In the White Christmas section, we performed several of the songs from the movie including "Snow" perched around the circle shaped fireplace. We dressed the band in army uniforms and had them march in singing, "We'll Follow The Old Man Wherever He Wants To Go." That was always a challenging number because even though they were great musicians and had perfect timing, they couldn't march worth a damn, especially Junior Mercer, our steel guitar player. In all of our performances, he never once got it right, but it was funny as hell watching him try.

For the General, I recruited my theater manager, Jack Phillips to play that part. Jack was a lawyer and an ex secret service guy, and had never been on stage in his life. I'm pretty sure he never got over his stage fright, but always delivered those famous lines from the movie perfectly.

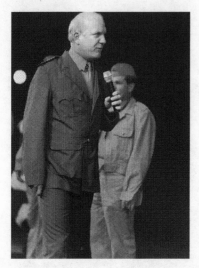

Replicating the movie, the General, pacing in front of the men standing at attention said, "I am not satisfied with the conduct of this division! Some of you men are under the impression that having been at Anzio entitles you not to wear neckties! You are wrong! Neckties will be worn in this area! I have also noticed a deterioration in the quality of saluting! This is to be improved! Private Kenerson, do you still play that horn?"

"Yes sir." Bernie answered.

"Then how about playing us a song?"

That's where Bernie played "Silent Night."

We ended the show with Dana and Linda wearing exact replicas of the long red dresses with the white fur hats and muffs Rosemary Clooney and Vera Ellen wore in the finale of White Christmas. Framed by two large Christmas trees, surrounded by the entire cast and Dana and Linda in those incredible dresses, the finale was spectacular.

Most of the other Christmas shows in Myrtle Beach were basically secular, trying to be politically correct, avoiding the true meaning of Christmas. That made no sense to me, if it was not a religious holiday, then why is it called Christmas?

Although it concerned Linda, not wanting to offend any of our audience members, I personally didn't care. I figured if they came to see a Christmas show in our theater, it was OK for me to remind them about the true meaning of Christmas, so for our grand finale, we performed, "Because We Believe," by Don Moen. I really loved performing that show!

I've always believed that when you run a business, you should run it like a family. That's probably why I'm not what you would consider a great businessman and why the businesses that I have run have not lasted long term. Like my brother Ron always said, "Ben, you're thinking with your heart again and not your head. Of course he was right, but honestly, I'm glad I thought that way and I hope I never stop.

The All American Music Theater was as close to a family business as you could get. I had hired a lot of my close friends to help me run it, and as a bonus, some of their wives went to work there as well.

I hired my old friend Herman Fillingane from Jackson, Mississippi as our PR guy, because Herman has never met a stranger in his life and was perfect for the job. His wife, Brenda was also our secretary.

When I convinced Art Updike to move from Houston to Myrtle Beach, his wife Monika, who had a background in banking and was brilliant, oversaw the gift shop and concessions and helped keep our books in order. Art and Monika's son, Austin, was also one of our stage hands.

Our stage manager, Kelly Barry met and fell in love with Holly, who worked managing the gift shop. They are still together and happily married today.

Our general manager, Jack Phillips and I had graduated from high school together, and Bernie our saxophone player's wife, Susan was Dana's dresser.

Even if I hadn't known them before, our cast and crew of over 60 people soon became our very close friends.

I discovered that our spotlight operator, Kelley Ard could sing well, so I put her in our show and then later cast her in another show we wrote for the Savoy Theatre.

Our building maintenance crew were brothers and our theater cleaning crew were all sisters.

When we bought the theater we had enlisted the brilliance of Mike Cook, Larry Gatlin's sound guy, to help set up our sound. His wife, Pamela was our pre-show entertainment.

The theater truly was like a big family and Dana and I are still close to several of the people that worked with us at the All American Music Theater. Tracey Barker, now Tracey Skidmore, one of our great dancers, is still one of my very close friends. Becca Bongiorno has come out on the ships with Dana and me for several cruises as our musical director and backup singer. Wayne Cockfield has written all of the charts for our cruise ship shows. Charlotte Jones, who was in charge of all of our costumes at the theater, designed and made the clothes that Dana and I wear in our shows today. I've had the chance to work with Junior Mercer, our steel player, several times in my reunion concerts in Jackson. I have spent a few afternoons in Cozumel, Mexico when we accidentally ran into one of our saxophone players, Don Colton, who was working on another ship and I am still in touch with our onstage sound mixer, Matthew Rybinski, or "Sleepy" as I called him.

I called him that because he always look like he was sound asleep, resting his head on his elbow behind the mixing board. However, he's lucky to be alive, because I almost killed him one night when that elbow he was resting on, accidentally pushed the mute button on my in-ear monitors right in the middle of my song "Bring Him Home." I couldn't hear one thing, as I stood there in a sweaty panic on the very tip of the stage in front of the audience.

My name for our front of the house sound mixer, Kevin Meyerland, was "Speedy." He was a great sound guy, but the slowest human I've ever known. He moved like a sloth.

Of course a big part of our family was Linda's father Blair and her mother, Jean. Blair had spent his entire life in corporate America and I sincerely believe, no matter what it cost him, that he loved every minute he was involved with the All American Music Theater, because he told Dana and me that often.

Dana and I are still in touch with Tom, Art, Monica, Austin and Herman. Unfortunately, we have lost contact with a lot of the folks that worked there, but they will always be in our hearts.

Thinking with my heart instead of my head is no doubt one of the causes of the demise of the All-American Music Theater. I was the CEO and made the ultimate final decisions, and because of that I take full responsibility for its failure. But unlike Nashville, I know exactly what happened.

Part of our big family was supposedly our "good friends" at Fantasy Harbor. When we made the deal with them to buy the theater, they were the nicest guys you could ever meet, and I honestly thought they wanted us to be successful. After all, they held our mortgage and I naively assumed that they would want us to have that success to be able to pay it off.

The day when we signed the mortgage papers, they suggested to me that rather than spending the hundred grand it would take to set up and staff our own phone bank and ticket office, we should use theirs instead. It was already up and running successfully and the Fantasy Harbor toll-free number was well known and they could easily add our show to the list. As a bonus, they would include our show as part of their package deals and we would also be part of and receive extra ticket sales from their established bus tour business.

The deal with Fantasy Harbor was, for a single show ticket purchase, we got the full $26 per ticket, minus a small processing fee. If it was a multi-show purchase, with us and The Larry Gatlin Theater we would get $18 per ticket after the processing fee. If it was a three show ticket purchase between us, Gatlin and the Savoy or the Circus show, we would get $14 per ticket.

It all sounded logical to me, a win-win for all concerned. That turned out to be one of the biggest mistakes I ever made.

What I didn't realize at the time was that I was dealing with a pack of crooks in thousand dollar suits, with a diabolical plan up their sleeve, and I was too naïve to the ruthless business world to see it until it was too late. In my defense, they even pulled the wool over our lawyer and Blair's eyes as well.

I believe if you ask anyone who was there at the time who saw our show, they would tell you that without question, we had the best show in Myrtle Beach. We had the best orchestra, the best dancers and in my opinion, the best singers and our production was far superior to any of the other theaters. The audience response was always great and the buzz around Myrtle Beach was incredibly positive, but we were barely getting by.

With our mortgage payment, payroll and expenses, our monthly nut was about $230,000. We were bringing in about 200,000 and staying open by continually raising more and more money selling shares of the ownership.

Our ticket sales were pretty good, around 300 per show, but our ticket price revenue was low, averaging $17.

When I would complain to Fantasy Harbor about my low average of per ticket revenue, they insisted that all the calls they received were for the multiple show package deal and they rarely got calls for a single ticket purchase for our show. Although that seemed unlikely to me, considering the buzz around town about our show, I trusted them and never questioned the validity of that statement.

The months went by, and with Blair's and a few other's additional investments, somehow we managed to keep the doors open, but I will admit it was a very stressful time in my life and it became increasingly more difficult to take off my CEO hat, pick up my microphone and perform those shows with a smile on my face. I had to force myself not to count the audience each show, doing the revenue math in my head.

Somehow, up to this point I'd always been able to sign my name on the bottom of that $48,000 monthly mortgage check, so we were current with our "friendly mortgage holders" at Fantasy Harbor.

Then I made the granddaddy of all mistakes. There I was, thinking with my heart and not my head again, believing I could trust my "Fantasy Harbor partners and friends," when they showed up unexpectedly one day and out of the goodness of their heart, made me an offer I couldn't refuse.

"Ben, we know you guys are struggling each month to pay us the mortgage, so we have decided to give you a break. We don't want you to worry about paying us the mortgage each month. We'll just tack the ones you miss on the end. We want to help you if we can, and without having to make that big mortgage payment each month you guys can relax and just worry about doing great shows. We firmly believe that everything will work out in the end."

Blair, Linda, Dana and I were at that meeting and we all heard what they said. When they left we were excited and happy, because it was a welcomed relief, but little did we know that that would lead to the demise of the theater. Four months later, their diabolical plan was revealed.

For the previous six months our buddies at Fantasy Harbor had been in negotiation with a local businessman (so I don't get sued, we'll call him Mr. H) to buy them out, lock stock and barrel. The deal included all the land, their factory outlet stores, all the theaters, and any mortgages they held on them. Of course they only held one mortgage, and that was ours.

For whatever reason, Mr. H wanted our theater bad. He believed he had found the greatest show on earth and wanted to put it in our theater, but as long as we were current on our mortgage there was nothing legally he could do to get us out. So, in one of their meetings, our "Fantasy Harbor friends" came up with a plan to get me to default on the mortgage. Although we had a signed agreement with Fantasy Harbor allowing us to miss those payments, since the entire complex was now owned by Mr. H, that agreement went out the window. Mr. H gave us 30 days to bring the mortgage current or get out.

We did our final performance on New Year's Eve, 1998 and turned over the keys to the theater February 1999.

I will spare you all the gory details, of which there were many, but I will tell you what I learned later from a very reliable source, someone who was a part of the Fantasy Harbor team, who couldn't live with it on his conscious any longer.

After they originally built the theater complex, they quickly realized that they had miscalculated how much profit they would make and how long it was going to take to regain their investment. So they came up with a plan, starting with the failing Milsap Theater--sell it, collect a minimum of one million as a down-payment, finance the balance, and through their box office system.......manipulate the numbers to make sure the theater was not successful.

They did this by threatening to fire any of the telephone operators in the ticket office if they made a single ticket purchase to our theater. All calls for our show had to be converted to at least a two show theater package or more. Simply, no one could call and just buy a ticket to our show. I know this is true because I heard this directly

from more than one of the telephone bank operators and from several
people who had called trying to buy just a ticket to our show. After we
discovered this, we tested it ourselves, making anonymous phone calls
trying to purchase a single ticket and it couldn't be done.

By doing this, they effectively cut our revenue in half. They
wanted us to fail so they could resell the theater to someone else,
make them fail  as well, and then sell it again collecting a million or
more as down payment on each transaction.

I know this may be hard to believe and sound like another story
that belongs in my fiction novels, but in one of our very heated meetings toward the end, Linda, Blair and Dana heard the owner of
Fantasy Harbor tell me, "There are a lot of Ben Marneys out there
with a million dollars. All we have to do is find three more after you
and that theater will be paid for and we'll still own it."

I'm not sure if the deal with Mr. H was just some kind of a sham to
get us out of the theater, but I do know that he never finalized his deal
buying the Fantasy Harbor complex. I assume it was just another one
of their scams to screw him out of some of his money.

I guess we could have sued them for fraud, but by the time I
learned the true details, we didn't have the money to hire the lawyers
and honestly I didn't have the energy to do it.

The only good news I have to report is that a brand-new modern
factory outlet complex was built just down the road, and the old worn
out, old fashioned factory outlet stores owned by Fantasy Harbor
closed down. Since that time they have tried many different projects
to revive the Fantasy Harbor complex, but they have all failed miser-
ably. And the value of that property has been drastically reduced.

Our theater and the Gatlin Theater are now occupied by churches
and seem to be doing well.

The real tragedy of the story is that Dana and my friendship with
Linda Milliken ended badly. I assume it's because her father, Blair lost
a lot of money and she blames me for it. I do take responsibility for
making a lot of stupid mistakes, but I believe if Linda would be truly
honest with herself, she would see that it wasn't really all my fault, but
so far that hasn't happened. We haven't talked to her in years.

For the last year of the All American Music Theater, because there was no money to spare, Dana and I didn't take a salary and basically lived on our savings and when that ran out, on our credit cards. And, because I was the CEO and had to sign my personal guarantee on things like billboards, advertising and office equipment leases... in the end we were in some serious financial trouble that took years to overcome.

IF IT HADN'T BEEN for Mickey Mouse, I'm pretty sure we would have never made it.

Tracey Barker Skidmore - Candace Atencio - Krissy Ormond

Tommie Gibbons - Stephanie Todd - Scott Earl - Krissy
Ormond - Ken Santos - Candace Atencio

9

## MICKEY MOUSE

Only a few weeks after we had turned over the keys of the All American Music Theater, I got a call from my good friend Elvy Rose. Elvy was a headliner for the Norwegian Cruise Lines and had been invited to perform at the Latin American Music Awards that conflicted with one of her ship dates. She wanted to know if we could fill in for her for that week on an NCL ship. She had already cleared it with Sue Carper, the ship's buyer. I told her we'd be glad to help her out, but immediately regretted that decision. Although we had performed on a ton of ships in the past, Dana and I had never performed as headliners.

We had always wanted to move up to the headliner position and thought that some day we would, but I wasn't sure this was the right time for us to do it. We didn't have a show written that would work on a ship and honestly, we weren't really ready mentally for it. We were both still in a state of depression, grieving the loss of the theater.

But I had given Elvy my word, so we went to work writing a show. We only had a couple of weeks to throw it together but somehow we did. We had Wayne write the charts, caught a plane to San Juan and boarded the ship.

From the moment we walked on board that ship things began to fall apart. On the very first night, I started to feel a tingle in the back of my throat and woke up the next morning with a raging cold. Dana got her's the following day. Our show was scheduled for the third day of the cruise and we were both sick as dogs.

We had thrown the show together so fast we hadn't actually had a chance to rehearse with Wayne's new charts and although we knew the songs, we didn't know the arrangements at all.

The way it works when you are the headliner, you meet the band, give them the charts and run the songs the day of your show. You have about an hour to do this, which is usually enough time it you actually know the show. But if you don't know the show and can't read music like me, that hour of rehearsal is not nearly enough time. Add raging colds from both of the singers to that problem and you have a complete fiasco.

All I can say about our shows that night is that we started them on time. Our second show was a little better than our first, but neither one was what you could call good. Facts are, we were too sick to sing, and too unsure of the music to fake it. So very embarrassingly, we laid two rather large eggs right in the middle of the stage that night. The technical show business term is, WE BOMBED BIG TIME! To this day, Sue Carper, the headline buyer for NCL hates us because of our stellar performances on that ship.

Those colds lasted almost two weeks and we coughed for months after that. When we finally got to feeling better, the reality of that large screw up set in. For the next few months, we laid on the couch in a deep depression watching bad television wondering, what are we going to do now?

In an effort to save money in the last year of the All American Music Theater, I had taken over all of the graphic design work. I did it after I had made a phone call to our graphic designer and asked him if there's someway I can get our color logo converted to black-and-white. The next day he dropped it off with his bill of $700.

I almost fainted when I saw the price and immediately called a graphic designer friend in Houston and ask him what something like that should cost.

"If you were a regular client, I wouldn't have charged you a penny. All you have to do is open it up on Photoshop and convert it from color to grayscale. Takes about a second."

I bought a copy of Photoshop the next day, loaded it onto my Mac and fired our graphic designer. I had no idea what I was doing at first, but it didn't take me long to figure it out and soon I was designing all our brochures, billboards and print ads.

Dana and I were still moping around the house, in our state of funk when our phone rang one day. It was Herman.

"Ben, you know all that graphic design work you used to do at the theater? Do you still know how to do it?"

"Herman, it's only been a couple of months. I'm pretty sure I can remember how to do it. Why?"

"I've got a new job working for this company called the Orion group." He said. "They're having a heck of a time finding a good graphic designer, so I told them about you. My new boss wants to meet you, can you come over here?"

After I took a shower and shaved off my week and a half growth of beard, I jumped into the car and drove over to meet Herman's new boss.

He explained to me what he was looking for, so I went home, fired up my old Mac laptop and started playing around with a few designs.

A few days later, I drove back over to his office and showed him what I had come up with. It was probably because I had never had any real training in graphic design and didn't really have a clue what I was doing, but apparently what I showed him was a completely new look and concept of what he had seen from all the other graphic designers. When he saw my designs, his eyes widened and he started smiling. He picked them up and ran out the door, yelling for all his employees to come see them.

When he came back and sat behind his desk, he opened his drawers and started pulling out folders and stacking them on his desk.

"Ben, The Orion Group is actually a group of several companies." He said. "I want you to re-design all of their graphics. Can you do that?"

The thought of becoming a graphic designer had never crossed my mind, but when I left the Orion Group's office that day, I suddenly 'was' one. I walked out with a signed contract to completely re-design everything for fourteen corporations.

I knew my old Mac laptop wasn't going to be adequate for a graphic design business, but Dana and I were flat broke and our credit had been destroyed from the loss of the theater. With the help of my good friend Art Updike and a little money from my father, I was able to upgrade my computer with a much larger screen and go to work.

Apparently not knowing what the hell I was doing was a good thing. Since I hadn't had any formal graphic design training, I wasn't bound by any rules or thoughts of what is standard or usual. As a result, I guess my designs were sort of unique.

When I took my designs to the printer that had been turning out all the Orion Group's previous work, the guy stood there for a long time not talking, staring at them.

"Did I do something wrong?" I asked. I honestly didn't know.

"Oh no, I'm just admiring your work. What did you use to do this?"

"Photoshop."

He raised his eyebrows. "You did all of this on Photoshop? Really?"

I found out later, most designers used something called Adobe Illustrator. I had no idea what that was, I still don't.

A few days later, I got a call from a guy who owned six cellular phone stores. He told me the printer had told him about me. After that, my phone started ringing and I began adding more and more clients. Before I knew it, I was designing for over twenty businesses and was also hired to design a 100 page magazine, called the Myrtle Beach Guide, and ironically, four music theater tour bus magazines.

I had quickly outgrown my small back bedroom office, so I found some office space a few miles from the house. In a little over a year, I had gone from moping around the house depressed with nothing to do, to working 15 hour days trying to get out all my design work.

Dana had taken a job selling clothes in a small boutique located at the Broadway At The Beach complex called Tango Bay, and soon was moved up to the assistant manager. With my income from my graphic designs and Dana's income from Tango Bay, we were finally able to pay our bills again, but for the first time in our entire marriage, we weren't working together and rarely saw each other.

I actually had to buy a couch for my office to sleep on, because on several of my magazine publications, I literally had to work around the clock to make the deadlines. The worst one was the Myrtle Beach Guide.

That magazine had three publications a year, every four months. The publisher was a blonde bombshell I quickly labeled "the publisher from hell!" She was so good looking, it was easy for her to get in to see the local businessmen and did an amazing job of selling full-page ads at $15,000 per page. Because she made so much money on these full-page ads, she sold them up to the very last second.

She had no appreciation of what I meant when I said. "We have to stop adding new ads by Friday, so I will have time to finish the final layout for the printer."

I was using a layout software called QuarkXPress and every time she walked in with a new full page add, I had to completely recon-figure the magazine. On every issue, with absolutely no time left, she would walk in my office with a new full page ad for me to design and then add to the magazine. She was one of my biggest accounts, so I had to do what she asked, but it was a real nightmare to get through every four months.

Dana had joined a professional choir that did performances a few times a month at special events, but I hadn't sung a note since I had stepped off the stage on our last disastrous ship contract.

My design business was booming, so singing was the last thing on my mind when Mike Cook, Larry Gatlin's sound man, walked in my office unexpectedly one day.

"I've got something you need to buy." He said. It was a JBL Ion sound system and three microphones.

"I don't need that," I said. "I'm not singing anymore."

"I know you don't have any equipment. I got this out of a church I replaced the sound system for. They're practically brand-new, you need to buy these. I know you're going to need them someday and you'll never beat this price."

Mike was so insistent, just to get him out of my office, I wrote him a check and put the system in the corner.

Dana and I were like ships passing in the night. With her schedule at Tango Bay and my ridiculous round-the-clock routine, there was not much time left for us. When we did find time to be together, our lives were so completely different, we had nothing in common to talk about.

Although Dana was proud of the business that I had built, she missed singing together and hated the distance that was obviously growing between us. The truth was, I didn't miss singing like Dana. I loved what I was doing, except for the long hours and was excited and proud of myself for building such a successful business from scratch. When she would bring up the possibility of us singing again and maybe putting together our duo to at least do a few gigs around Myrtle Beach, I would fly off the handle.

"Are you out of your mind, where the hell do you think I'm gonna find the time to do that! Forget it Dana, our singing days are over!" When I would say those things, I could see the hurt in her eyes, but I said those hateful words to her often.

I had just turned 50 years old and for the first time in my adult life, I wasn't earning a living as a musician. I just couldn't seem to get it through her head that we were too damn old for the music business. And every time I tried to explain it to her, I just hurt her more and that pushed us further apart.

When my mother was 39 years old, she had a mole removed from her nose that tested positive for melanoma cancer. Fortunately, they caught it early and she has remained cancer free. Because melanoma was detected in my family, once a year I get a thorough check up from my dermatologist. I had done this every year since I was 20.

A few months after my 51st birthday, I was again in the middle of getting out the Myrtle Beach Guide, working with my publisher from hell, when I went for my annual check up.

Every other year I had done this the doctor would ask, "Has

anything new come up?"

Then I would show him a new mole or strange spot and his usual reaction would be to just glance at it and wave it off. But on this day, when I showed him a tiny spot on my ankle, he didn't wave it off.

Instead, he studied it for a long time. "I think we need to take a biopsy of that."

"Really?" I asked, instantly scared to death. "Is it a melanoma?" He told me he wasn't sure, but I could tell in his eyes he was worried.

He took the biopsy on a Friday, the last day of August, and because Labor Day fell on a Monday that year, all the labs were closed. He told me we probably wouldn't get the results of the biopsy until Thursday or Friday of the next week. I walked out of his office, stunned, numb, and very scared.

When I got back to my office and opened the door, the publisher from hell was standing there with, what a surprise, a brand-new full page ad she had just sold. She wanted me to add it to my layout that had taken me the last 24 hours to finish.

When I told her not only no, but hell no, she stood there in disbelief. I was in no mood for her bullshit that day.

"I stayed up all night long last night finishing the layout, so I could get it to the printer tomorrow. There's no way in hell I'm staying up all night tonight to do it again."

After she stormed out of my office, I sat in silence for the next few hours thinking about my life and what the future may bring. I wanted to call Dana and tell her the news about the biopsy, but I just couldn't do it to her.

That afternoon the publisher from hell called me and told me that she had talked to the printer and moved back the deadline until Monday. That gave me all weekend to design it, and add it to the layout.

"Gee thanks," I told her. "That's exactly how I wanted to spend my weekend."

Although it was almost impossible to focus and concentrate on my design work throughout that week, being so busy kept me from obsessing on thoughts of my impending demise.

I was at lunch when the doctor's office called and left a message on my answering device.

Before I picked up the phone to call and get the news, I had a conversation with God.

"Jesus, If you get me out of this one, I promise you I'll make a drastic change. This is no way to live. There's got to be more to life than just making money."

The biopsy was benign. When I hung up from the doctor, I immediately called my old friend and agent, Mike Ford. "Mike, I think I want to sing again."

He told me to call a woman by the name of Chris Irvin. "You worked for her husband Chuck. He was the agent I went through on your first cruise ship. Unfortunately, Chuck passed away a few years ago, but his wife Chris is running the agency now. Tell her I told you to call."

I immediately called Chris and had a nice conversation with her. She was very nice, but honest with me and said that she wasn't sure she could get us work anytime soon on a cruise ship.

"What I need, "she said. "Is a video of a live performance, so on your next gig, just throw up a camera and record it. It doesn't have to be a professional shoot. I just need to have something showing what you look like and sound like."

Of course I couldn't tell her that we didn't have any gigs to video-tape and that I hadn't sung a lick in over two years, but I promised anyway to get her a video as soon as possible.

That night, I surprised Dana. I had called her boss, talked him into letting her off early and took her out to dinner.

Over dinner, I revealed my melanoma scare to her. After she calmed down and wiped her eyes, I filled her in about my phone calls to Mike Ford and Chris Irvin. She was ecstatic that I was even considering singing again.

That weekend we pulled out our video camera, moved the furniture out of our living room and set up the JBL system Mike Cook had forced me to buy.

We recorded six or seven songs, well, at least parts of them. To be honest, we didn't know the entire songs because it had been too many years since we'd sung them. I edited together the parts we did know, and mailed the tape to Chris Irvin.

She called the day she got it. "I just watched your tape. You guys are really good. So, tell me more about your ship experience."

I told her about the Royal Viking Sea, that we had booked through her husband Chuck and about the years we had spent working for NCL.

"So you know Bob Sigler?" She asked.

"Yes, we worked with him for years."

"I'll call you right back." She said and hung up.

Exactly 30 minutes later she called us back. "I didn't want to tell you this until after I talked to him, but Bob Sigler is now the buyer for the Disney Cruise Lines. Are you sitting down?"

"No." I said.

"Well, I think you need to, because he just offered you and Dana a five month contract starting October 25th on the Disney Magic."

This was the first week of September. "Are you talking about *'this'* October, in less than two months?"

Yes she was. We signed our first Disney contract on September 6, 2011. We had exactly seven weeks to learn enough songs to play four sets, and at the same time, I had seven weeks to dismantle my company. The next day I started calling my clients and recommending new graphic designers.

I only had a few more clients to call, when I woke up on September 11, flipped on my television and saw the first plane fly into that tower. When the second one hit, I knew that nothing in our world would ever be the same again.

I wasn't sure what effects 9-11 may have had on our Disney contract, but Chris assured me everything was still a go.

Fortunately, all of my clients took the news well and wished me luck. Dave, the publisher of the tour bus magazines was the last one to find out.

He and I had become close friends and he called me late one night, while Dana and I were rehearsing.

"Ben, I heard a rumor today that there is a goofy graphic designer in this town, calling up and firing his clients. I couldn't believe that, because that's not how it works; clients fire graphic designers, graphic designers don't fire clients! Do you have any idea who this moron is?"

To work for Disney, you have to attend a three day class they call "Traditions". That's where you find out the Disney way of doing things, and those ways are very specific.

After we finished Traditions, we drove to Port Canaveral and boarded the ship. Working on a cruise ship had changed drastically since 9–11, so for the first several days of that cruise, we took safety classes in the daytime and performed at night.

The first day, when I walked to the stage to set up, we met our music manager and direct supervisor. His name was Peter Marsh, but he told us to call him (I swear this is the truth) Unkl Stinki . It was even on his Disney name tag. He was an older British guy, a great musician and funny as hell. He told me how impressed he and the stage techs were with my equipment. Because it was all new, they had assumed we must be a top notch successful act that stayed on top of the current technology. Of course, I didn't tell him the real reason it was brand new.

Somehow we had learned enough songs to perform four sets, six nights a week, but in two of those sets, our first and last, the room was usually pretty empty. During those empty sets, we tried everything to draw the people in, but nothing seemed to work. After two weeks with no success, I began telling Dana that I wasn't sure we were going to make the five month contract. We both thought we were bombing terribly and assumed that it wouldn't be long before we'd be called to the cruise director's office to be fired.

On our fourth week, Unkl Stinki let us know that Bob Sigler was on board for the week. "Here it comes." I told Dana.

Although we had worked for Bob for years, because I had dragged my feet the day I met him on that first ship and didn't get set up in time, he had never heard us perform live. We assumed he would come see us that night, but prayed that he would come during one of the sets where there were actually people... but of course, when he walked in, the place was empty. We only had two tables of passengers watching us in the entire bar.

He took a seat at the bar and sat there through the entire set, not moving, sipping his drink, with a frown on his face. After we finished the set, Dana and I looked at each other, shrugged and slowly walked over to face the dreaded news.

When we walked up, Bob said. "Great set! I love the variety of your songs. I knew you guys were good, but I didn't know you were this good. And by the way, they love you here."

"Seriously?" I said stunned. "Bob, the place is empty. We've tried everything, but there's never any one here this set. We thought we were bombing big time."

He started laughing. "You're on Disney, remember. The ship is full of kids with worn out parents. Everybody goes to bed early. You have more people here than in the other lounges. Relax, they love you! In fact, they'd love to clone you, so they could have you on both of their ships."

We worked for the Disney Cruise Lines for the next eight years, four months on and two months off, switching between the Disney Magic and the Disney Wonder.

After the first year, we moved out of our house in Myrtle Beach, put our furniture in storage, and brought our 36-foot sailboat to Cape Canaveral. We lived aboard "Lady Love" on our breaks, when we were not visiting our folks in Lubbock, for almost seven years.

Disney earned our never-ending respect and loyalty three months after our first contract when Dana's mother, Elaine, passed away.

It was January 2nd, 2002 when our phone rang at 7 am in our cabin. We'd just docked in Saint Thomas and the phone call was from Unkl Stinkii . He gently told us the bad news about Elaine, then told Dana to start packing. Before he hung up, he told me the Captain of the ship wanted to see me.

When I got to Captain Henry's office, Peter Marsh and Jackie Perry, our cruise director was also there. On my walk up the stairs to the Captain's office, I had already figured out how I could do the job as a solo act a few days, while Dana flew home for her mother's funeral.

When I got there, Captain Henry asked me what I wanted to do. I began telling him my plan of performing a solo act while Dana was gone, but he interrupted me.

"Ben, you didn't answer my question. What do 'you' want to do?"

"Well... I'd love to fly home and be with Dana through this, but I can't afford to lose this job right now."

He told me to go back to my cabin, pack my bag and bring Dana to the gangway in thirty minutes to meet a car that would take us to the airport.

Before we got into the car, Jackie Perry gave me an envelope. Inside was our return air information to fly back to the ship in two weeks.

I was glad I was able to be with Dana during those dark days. She was very close to her mother and it was a difficult time for her.

Elaine was without question Dana's biggest fan. She had discovered Dana's voice when she was only 5 years old. Elaine was a graduate of the University of Texas with a degree in child psychology and music. She was also a classically trained pianist and had taught most of the kids that grew up in Muleshoe, Texas how to play. When she discovered Dana's singing voice, she made arrangements with a local voice teacher, to trade piano lessons with her children, for voice lessons for Dana.

Elaine was a tough cookie, a little controlling, with a strong personality, but at the same time one of those special people that was constantly doing things for the community and her church. She was always the first one to show up with food or flowers for a sick friend. She also played the organ at the First Methodist Church and was responsible for raising the money to build the beautiful pipe organ that is still there today.

Elaine was a beautiful, sophisticated, classy woman with grace and poise. Dana inherited that class and poise and looked a lot like her mother when she grew up. Although she was a couple of inches taller than her mom, they could somehow wear the same clothes and had the very same taste in fashion.

There's no question that Dana got her musical talent, her class and poise, good taste and eye for fashion from her mother, but the one thing she didn't get was Elaine's culinary expertise. She was an amazing cook and loved to throw large dinner parties at their house. Although their home was always beautifully decorated, Christmas time at the Damron's, with her mom's decorative flair, was a sight to behold.

As Dana has gotten older, I recognize more of her mother in her every day. They were like two peas in a pod, and because of that, they were extremely close for Elaine's entire life.

In the last year of her life, Elaine began developing respiratory problems and heart trouble. She was taking a lot of medication, had been ill for some time and for several months had been very confused and out of her head. Fortunately and miraculously, Dana had had a long phone conversation with her two days before she died. In that conversation, she had been very clear, just like her old self and they had talked for almost an hour. I believe having that last great conversation with her mom helped Dana get through her death a little easier.

I must admit, for the entire two weeks we were off during that time, I was calculating the money we had lost and was trying to figure out how we were going to cover our bills.

Elaine Damron 1927 - 2012

A week after we got back on the Magic was payday, and we were absolutely stunned to see that our check was for the full amount. Disney had not only paid for our flights to and from Lubbock, they had paid us for every day we were off the ship. From that day forward, I have always been, and will be until the day I die, a dedicated and devoted fan of Mickey Mouse. Disney has to be one of the greatest companies to work for in the world. Dana and I absolutely loved our time singing on the Disney ships.

In our seventh year there, I began to get the feeling that maybe we were getting a little too old to be performing on a Disney ship.

Driving that feeling in my mind a little further, one day Dana and I were standing in a long line of crew members waiting to get off the ship, when Unkl Stinki , who was ten years older than me yelled. "Hey Ben! Guess who's the oldest crew member on this ship?"

He was standing all the way at the other end, so I yelled back. "I don't know Unkl Stinki , who is it?"

"Me!" He yelled. "Guess who is the second and third oldest." He didn't have to say it, we knew, but he yelled it anyway. "You and Dana! We're older than the friggin' Captain!"

Unkl Stinki - Peter Marsh

SINCE WE WERE NOW in our eighth year of our normal five year life cycle, I knew we were overdue for some kind of change, so I started racking my brain trying to figure out what the hell we were going to do next.

I honestly had no earthly idea what that might be. I know you're probably tired of hearing me say this, but once again... fate took over.

BUT THIS TIME, it came written on a bar napkin...

# 20

# JOHNNY CASH

T he waitress brought me the napkin in the middle of my song. I was singing and playing my guitar, so I couldn't pick it up and read it until I finished. It said: Please play anything by Johnny Cash.

After I read the note, I said over the microphone, "I'm sorry to whoever sent this up, but I don't do any Johnny Cash.

At the far end of the room, a real tall guy stood up, he had to have been six four or five. Towering over the crowd he yelled, "With your voice? Why the hell not!"

Remember, we were on a Disney ship and we didn't hear a lot of hells and damns there, so the entire audience started laughing. On my break I went over to him and introduced myself. His name was Dave Matheson. He owned a sort of time-share with Disney, called Vacation Club and he and his wife, Chris cruised on a Disney ship several times a year.

I explained to him that I wasn't sure that Johnny Cash would be Disney approved music and apologized to him for not knowing any of his songs.

For the next year, I always knew when Dave and Chris were there when a waitress would bring me a napkin that said: "How High's The

Water Mama?" every time they were on board, he would ask for Johnny Cash and I would tell him that I still didn't know any.

One night when we were on a break we got a call from them. They were in town a day early, planning on boarding the Disney Magic the next morning, so we met them for dinner in Cocoa Beach.

After dinner he asked me, "Ben, do you know what I do for a living?"

"No, Dave I don't," I said, "but whatever it is, you must do it pretty damn good to be able to afford to cruise as much as you guys do."

He smiled. "Yeah, I do alright. I own a few businesses and have to travel a lot-- so what I really do is travel. I spend a lot of time by myself out there on the road and what I love to do when I'm out there is go listen to live entertainment. I just love listening to good singers and musicians. Of all the people I've listened to all these years, do you know how many people I've run into that I thought could do justice to a Johnny Cash song?"

I shook my head. "How many?"

"Maybe one or two, but Ben, I know for sure that you could kill it. Why in the hell don't you sing Johnny Cash?"

"Dave, I don't really have an answer to that question. " I said. "I guess it's because I've never been much of a Johnny Cash fan."

He wrinkled his brow and stared at me. "That doesn't make any damn sense, you sound just like him. Will you do me a favor? Just for me, will you learn one Johnny Cash song. We'll be back out on the ship in a few months and you can do it for me then. Will you do that? Just one song, that's all I ask."

A few months later, during our last set, I decided to practice the two Johnny Cash songs I'd learned for Dave in my cabin.

They were getting on the ship the next day and we'd never actually practiced those songs through our system. The room was completely empty, so I hit the Folsom Prison Blues track and started singing.

I promise this is true. People were actually running down the hall jumping into the seats. When we finished Folsom, the room was half full and they were clapping and whistling. I raised my eyebrows and shrugged my shoulders at Dana and started Ring Of Fire. When we finished, the room was almost full and they were clapping even louder.

Since we didn't have any more Johnny Cash, we went back to playing our regular music and within 30 minutes the room was empty again.

Although I wasn't sure, "I shot a man in Reno just to watch him die" was Disney approved lyrics, the next night we dedicated our two new Johnny Cash songs to Dave and Chris. This was our third and most packed set. When I started playing Folsom, the crowd exploded. They absolutely loved it and I'm not just talking about Dave and Chris, the entire room was whistling and clapping.

Dave, grinning from ear to ear pointed at me on the stage and mouthed the words, "I told you so."

After that, it became pretty obvious to us that although the crowd was always very responsive to our music, the response was at least double when we did a Johnny Cash song.

When I told my agent, Chris Irvin about the amazing response, she told me that I should think about doing a Johnny Cash tribute show. "I bet we could book it as a headliner act on RCCL or Princess."

I had worked with a few tribute acts in the past, and had actually hired an Elvis impersonator at Marney's, but honestly I always felt a little sorry for those people. Everyone of them seemed to actually believe they were the star they were impersonating. The Elvis guy was the worst, he even had plastic surgery to look more like him, and remained in the Elvis persona off the stage. I always thought it was pretty sad, so for me to do an impersonation act was gonna be a big step.

I put the thought of a Johnny Cash tribute act in the back of my head and started milling it around. I mentioned it to a few of my friends including our good friend Melissa Mooney.

We had been living on our sailboat, *Lady Love* for a little over six years and Dana had had enough.

Because we had been working so steady with Disney, making good money, and by not having a house and all of its expensive trimmings, like lights, water, gas, cable TV, etc., Dana and I had been able to pull ourselves out of our financial woes and were doing pretty good. She wanted to get off of that damn sailboat, get her furniture, china, crystal and all her pretty knickknacks out of the storeroom and buy a house, so we started looking.

It took us a while but we finally found the perfect place in a sleepy little suburb called Port Saint John. It was located between Cocoa Beach and a place called Titusville and was only about 20 minutes from Port Canaveral, where the Disney ships docked.

I had to sell my beloved *Lady Love*, to be able to afford to buy the house, but Dana was a happy girl and that's really all that mattered. We were doing three and four day cruises at that time and I have to admit, it was awful nice to be able to hang out by my pool and chill at my own house two days a week. And of course, on our breaks, being able to spread out was like living in a mansion compared to living on that sailboat.

During one of our breaks, in our first Christmas season in our new house, we noticed in the paper that the city of Titusville was having a big Christmas celebration in their historic downtown area. We invited our friend, Melissa Mooney to go with us to check it out. When we were walking around that historic downtown, Melissa noticed an old theater. On the marquee they were advertising the current play that was running, but on the bottom it said: Elvis returns December 30.

Melissa pointed up at the Marquis. "If they have an Elvis tribute here, I'd bet they'd love to have a Johnny Cash show too."

"Maybe." I said walking on by. I honestly didn't think much else about it.

The next day Melissa called me, "Write down this number and call them back, they're waiting. I just got off the phone with them."

"Who's waiting?" I asked. "What are you talking about?"

"The woman at the Titusville theater. I called them and they love the idea of a Johnny Cash show."

I dialed the number and when the woman picked up I said, "Hello, I think you just talked to my friend Melissa Mooney."

Before I could get out another word, the woman screamed, "Oh my God, it's Johnny Cash!"

At that time I had only been thinking about doing a Johnny Cash show and had nothing written. I knew that to get booked as a head-liner act, I would need to have a good video of the show, so I asked the lady if I could just rent the theater to do a video shoot.

"Sure," She said, "That would be great, but could we sell tickets too?"

I explained to her that it would not be like a real show and would have a lot of stopping and starting and re-takes, but if she had some people that would like to see something like that, I'd be OK with it, because we would need some audience shots too. I then had to come up with a name for the show for the theater to have something to call it, so I called it Cash and Friends. That way, Dana could be part of the show singing some June Carter and... well, I wasn't real sure yet, but somebody else for sure, because June wasn't a great singer and I knew Dana wouldn't be happy just singing her songs.

I booked the theater for a Saturday night, a few months out and I went to work researching and writing a pseudo-show. I downloaded Johnny's greatest hits album, watched every video I could find on YouTube of his performances and read both of his biographies. Since it wasn't going to be a real show, just a video shoot, I wasn't that worried about it. All I wanted to do was get some footage of six or seven of the songs, some audience footage and a few shots of the band. No pressure.

My thoughts were, once I had the video edited, Chris could start shopping the show. Most ships are booked up months ahead, so I assumed that would take her a while, and if and when she got some-thing booked, I would have plenty of time to work out the dialogue and logistics of the actual show.

In those days our friend Melissa was working as a nanny on the Disney ships for one of our cruise director's, Kara Boyd. When Melissa told Kara about the show, Kara told one of her friends about it too. Her friend, Richard Ambrose had just gotten a new job... as the entertainment director for the Norwegian Cruise Line. He told Kara that he wanted to come see the show.

We were at sea, on our way to some island and I was in the

Internet cafe' checking my e-mail when I read Melissa's letter informing me that the entertainment director for NCL was coming to see the Cash tribute show. The show I hadn't written yet. The show I was supposedly performing in three weeks! I wanted to jump overboard. We had already blown it once with NCL before. I knew if we did it again, we would never get another chance as a headliner on that cruise line.

After I calmed down and thought about it a while, I realized it was actually a great opportunity. I e-mailed Melissa back and asked her to contact the Titusville theater to find out where they advertised their shows. If the entertainment director for a major cruise line was going to be in the audience, I figured that we probably should have an audience for him to be in.

After our sets that night, I went back to the Internet café to see if Melissa had found out anything from the theater. This is exactly what her e-mail said:

Ben, I called the theatre and asked them about advertising the Cash show. They asked me why you would want to waste money advertising a show that's already sold out!

They had already sold over 300 tickets. I couldn't believe it! All I had to do now, in three weeks, was come up with the show, memorize the songs, find the costumes, line up the musicians and come up with some dialogue. No problem...

While reading Johnny Cash's autobiography, I found out that Patsy Cline had been one of June Carter's best friends. I already knew that Waylon Jennings was Johnny Cash's lifelong best friend, so I wrote a two act show opening with Waylon and Patsy, closing with Johnny and June. After a lot of hard work and help from a few of my brilliant musician friends like Chuck Perry and Wayne Cockfield and a ton of rehearsals... Cash and Friends was born.

Because I still had misgivings about being an impersonator, I opened my show by saying:

"Our show tonight is a tribute to Waylon Jennings, Patsy Cline, June Carter and Johnny Cash. And I think it's important for you to know that this is not an impersonation show. I'm not going to be doing an impression of Waylon Jennings or Johnny Cash. And when my wife Dana comes out a little later, she will not be doing an impression of Patsy Cline or June Carter. What that means is, we're not going to look exactly like them, and we're certainly not going to sound exactly like them.

"But what we 'are' going to do tonight, with love and respect, we're going to honor their legacies and do our very best to perform some of the amazing songs they left behind for us."

I said that standing there with a fake beard, a long wig, wearing an exact replica of Waylon's flat brimmed cowboy hat, and holding a clone of his leather covered guitar, but the audience seemed to love and appreciate me saying it, so I've opened every show that way since.

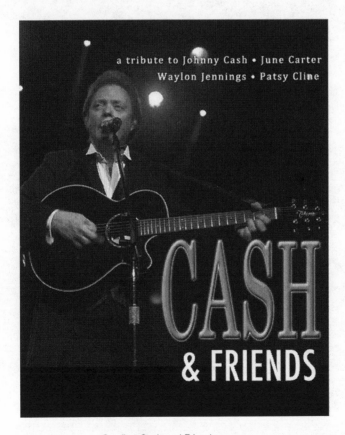

Our first Cash and Friends promo

Dana and Ben singing Jackson

Dana and Ben as Johnny and June

My favorite shot of the show

WE GOT great video footage at that first show at the Titusville theater, because it turned out to be a smash. I had talked Kara Boyd, our cruise director, into being the M. C., and also hired her husband, Tim Boyd as our opening act. I even had my old Home Cookin' friend, Pat Vivier come down to play guitar in the show. It was a very stressful, but amazing night.

And by the way, Dave Matheson was sitting in the middle of the audience and I could hear his very loud laughing and clapping above everyone else from the stage.

Apparently Richard Ambrose liked it too, because he immediately offered us a three week run on the NCL Pearl in Alaska.

From there, Cash and Friends began to get legs and soon we were booked for multiple dates on the Royal Caribbean and Princess cruise lines. We also started picking up dates at local community theaters around Florida.

For the first two Royal Caribbean contracts, they allowed me to bring my entire band, but then things changed and they started cutting the budget and only allowed me to bring a musical director and perform with the onboard ship orchestra.

My first choice for that job was always Chuck Perry. He was a great pianist and singer. We had all met on the Disney ships when he was hired to entertain in the Disney piano bars and also occasionally as the music manager. We hit it off right away, became fast friends and always hung out together on the islands.

One of my favorite Chuck Perry stories happened one night in the crew bar. Chuck and I were sitting at a table when we both noticed one of the very young and beautiful production show dancers smiling at us.

Dana as Patsy Cline

Dana as June Carter

Me as Waylon Jennings

"Ben," Chuck said, tapping me on the shoulder. Check it out, I think she's smiling at me."

Chuck was in his late forties, I was in my mid fifties and this dancer couldn't have been a day over twenty-one.

"I think you're wrong." I said. "She's smiling at me." And she was.

Of course, she was way too young for both of us, but there was no question about it, she was smiling at one of us.

I laughed and told Dana, "I think I'm getting hit on by a 21 year old babe."

She just laughed and rolled her eyes."Yeah, sure you are."

This went on for 30 or 40 more minutes with Chuck and me arguing about which one of us she was interested in. Then she got up and walked over to our table.

I have to tell you that it had been quite some time for Chuck ,and especially me, to catch the eye of a beautiful young girl like that. Chuck was single and liked them young, so he was pretty excited, and I certainly wasn't minding the attention. Both of us had our egos pumped up and our chests stuck out when she sat down at our table.

With her beautiful young smile and twinkling eyes, she looked at both of us and said, "It's just so nice to see you guys in here tonight. I hope you didn't mind me staring, but seeing you in here makes me feel less homesick, because both of you remind me so much of my father."

Dana burst out laughing and both of our pumped up egos instantly melted, like ice cream dripping on the floor.

Chuck and I both felt like a couple of old dinosaurs, as we slowly helped each other limp back to our cabins that night.

With Wayne Cockfield's great musical charts and Chuck Perry as our musical director, performing Cash and Friends on the ships or in the community theaters on land always came off without a hitch. It appeared that our next new five year life cycle had taken off and was going to be great. Then suddenly, things began to go south.

It was 2008 and the stock market took a giant nosedive and almost immediately, all the cruise lines began to cut back. The first place they cut was the expensive music headliner acts, so we lost most of our future bookings.

And although that was bad news, it wasn't even close to the news I got from my father's doctor.

Our phone rang early one morning and I was shocked when I answered. It was their doctor. "Are you aware that both your parents are in the hospital?" .

Of course I wasn't. We had talked to them on the phone just days earlier and had been in Lubbock visiting them for Thanksgiving and Christmas. They seemed happy and healthy, so I had no idea what could be wrong with them.

"Actually, your mother is only here because your father brought her with him when he came to the emergency room. I'm sure you're aware that your mother requires a lot of medication daily and I couldn't administer any medications to her without her being a patient, so I put her in a bed down the hall from your father. I'm calling you because I don't feel comfortable releasing them in your father's current condition. It wouldn't be safe."

"Why not? What's wrong with Dad?"

"His Alzheimer's" he said.

"His what?" It was the first I'd ever heard if it. "Dad has Alzheimer's?"

Things instantly began to fall into place. A year earlier, Dad had called and asked me to come to Lubbock to find a lawyer to draw up some papers putting all of his possessions and his investments into my name. He also gave me medical and legal power of attorney. At the time, I thought it was just his reaction to what had happened with his younger sister, TaJuhanna and her daughter.

Aunt TaJuhanna had tragically developed Alzheimer's at 72, and it quickly took her mind. She became angry and thought that her daughter, Kimberly was trying to steal all her money. Actually, Kimberly needed the money to pay for her 24 hour care, but Aunt TaJuhanna refused to give her access to her accounts. It was a real family nightmare. I just assumed that Dad wanted to make sure that nothing like that ever happened between us. He forgot to mention that he'd just been diagnosed with Alzheimer's.

The reason we didn't see any of the signs on our last visit was because we weren't looking for them, and Dad was also taking medication that helped disguise the symptoms.

When we arrived the next day in Lubbock and I walked into Dad's hospital room, it took him a moment to recognize me. His doctor had taken him off all of his medications to help cure the reason he'd checked himself in, so he was really out there. He had no idea where he was, or why he was there.

Dana and I checked them out of the hospital and took them home. It took several days for his Alzheimer's medication to start working again, but eventually he cleared up enough for us to talk.

Dad was an extremely organized person and had been that way all of his life. His personal records were impeccable, always filed in perfect order. In his house, everything had its place, and his garage was spotless with every tool in its specific spot. He had paid in full, years earlier for his and Mom's grave sites and funeral services. So as you might expect, he had given me very specific orders to follow in case some day he became ill or incapacitated and couldn't take care of my mother. The only thing my father ever really worried about, was my mother. All he ever wanted or cared about was to make sure that she was taken care of.

I knew I wasn't going to be able to say what I had to say without a cigarette, so I set up two lawn chairs in the garage and ask him to join me.

"Dad, you've always told me that when the time came, even if you didn't like it, if you got to where you couldn't take care of Mom, I was supposed to step in and do what I had to do. Unfortunately, I'm afraid that time has come."

Sadly, he shook his head in agreement. "I don't think it's safe for you to be driving anymore, because if you had a wreck and they found out that you have Alzheimer's they would sue you for everything you have. And if you can't drive... you can't take care of Mom here in this big house. I know you've always said you never wanted to go to a nursing home, but I think it's time we look into at least an indepen-dent retirement place. Maybe somewhere like where Dana's father is living. It'll be just like living in your own apartment, but downstairs you'll get three square meals every day and there are nurses there on site to help out in case you need something.

Without any argument, he reached in his pocket, handed me his car keys and said, "Let's go check some out."

We looked at a few places, but settled in the same place that Dana's father, Sam, had been living for a few years called Grand Court.

The timing was perfect. Dana and I didn't have any gigs booked, so we were able to take the next six months getting my parents settled into their new place and packing up their house to sell.

The process of going through all of my parents possessions they had collected throughout their 65 year long marriage, made me realize that material things don't mean a damn thing in life. The only thing that really matters is your family, your friends and your health. There's not much of a life without any one of those things.

My parents adjusted well to their new home and my mother became a social butterfly, attending every event they had. She abso-lutely loved the entertainment, playing bingo and the nightly domino or card games. As Dad deteriorated, he got where he couldn't play the games, but was always there at Mom side.

After those six months, our savings account began to dwindle. The ships were still not calling to book our show, so I began to look around for something else to do. I needed a job and I knew we could probably go back on the ships as a duo, but with my parents' situation I didn't feel comfortable going back out to sea for months at a time. What I needed was a job that I could do in Florida as well as when I was in Texas visiting my parents, but that seemed like an impossible reality. But once again... do I have to say it?

Somehow during all of this I had finished my first fiction novel called "Sing Roses For Me." In my effort to get it published, Dana and I attended a Florida Publisher's Association convention. In one of the meetings at that convention, about 30 writers and publishers were there, sitting around a large table. As a way of introducing ourselves they handed a wireless microphone to one of the writers, told him to introduce himself, tell a little about his book and then pass it down to the next person.

These were all writers and publishers, and apparently had never used a microphone before in their life. Their mic technique was so bad it was difficult to hear what they were saying. When it was my turn, I held the mic to my mouth and started talking. When I did, every head in the room turned, stared at me and smiled. After the meeting, I was swamped with the same questions: Do you do voice-overs, do you do audiobooks? Would you be interested in reading my book?

I had heard the term before, but wasn't really sure exactly what doing voice-overs meant. When I got home, I googled Voice-Over and discovered that it was a thriving business and there were even schools I could attend that would teach me how to do it.

I chose a school in Vermont called, Such A Voice, attended a four-day master class and recorded my first voice-over demo. When I got back from Vermont, I built a sound proof vocal booth in one of our back bedrooms and started doing auditions. I landed my very first job exactly 5 weeks later. After that, my voice-over business took off.

My biggest break happened when one morning Dana and I were sitting out by the pool and the phone rang.

"Is this Ben Marney? Did you do a radio commercial for Home Federal Bank?"

"Yes, that was me." I said.

"Hello Ben. My name is Steven Miller and I am a television producer. I own a company called Super Fine Films in New York City and we are producing a new television show called Secrets Of The Mountain People. I think you are the voice we've been looking for."

"Great," I said excited. "How did you find me?"

He started laughing. "It wasn't easy. Believe it or not I was driving through Knoxville, Tennessee and heard your Home Federal Bank commercial on the radio. I pulled over and called the radio station to find out who voiced that commercial but they didn't know, so I call the bank and talked to the president. He gave me the production company and they gave me your number."

"Wow!" I said. "That was a lot of trouble, but I'm glad you finally found me."

He told me that the show was about two hillbilly MacGyvers that could take just about anything and make something good from it.

"The part we think you're perfect for is the narrator. It's kind of like Uncle Jessie on The Dukes of Hazzard. Do you remember that show?"

"Of course, but the narrator on that show wasn't Uncle Jesse, it was Waylon Jennings." Using my Waylon voice I said. "So, you're looking for something like, 'Those Duke boys sure know how to fly a car, but they damn sure don't know how to land one.'"

I hadn't realized I was on a conference call with him, but when I said that, I heard five or six voices yelling, "That's it. That's the voice!" I didn't mention that I'd been using that voice to make my living with for the past two years.

The actual title of that show was Hillbilly Blood, and it aired in thirty two million homes for five years on the Destination America and Discovery channels. Because of that show, I picked up two more National TV shows, Travelin' Hunter and Guide Fitters that aired on the Sportsman channel for several years. Not long after that, the operations manager of Such A Voice, the school were I had received my training, called and wanted to know if I would be willing to coach some of their students.

Although we weren't singing much, and hoping to get to do our Cash show again on some cruise ships, so far they were not calling. But my parents seem to be happy in their new home at Grand Court. My voice-over business and coaching was doing great. We were paying our bills, life was good and we were happy.

I HAD LOST COUNT, but one more time in my life, God had opened up a hidden door, took me by the hand and walked me through it.

# 21

# THE LAST FOUR YEARS

I t was March of 2013 and Dana and I drove to Lubbock, to celebrate my parents' birthdays. Dad was turning 85 on the 23rd and Mom was turning 86 on the 25th. By this time, Dad was barely there. He had no short-term memory at all, was very frail, and rode around in one of those power chairs. He could walk, but his knees were so bad he could barely stand. Although he wasn't really sure what was going on, he seemed to enjoy the small birthday party we gave them and ate a big piece of cake. That night he became very ill and couldn't seem to stop throwing up. When I got there the next morning, I took one look at him, called for an ambulance, jumped in my car and drove to the emergency room.

The CAT scan showed that dad had a twisted bowel. Because of his Alzheimer's, he hadn't realized how sick he was, and there was no telling how long he had had this condition.

The doctors told me that it was very very serious, his body was full of septic poison and there was a possibility that he would not survive the surgery.

Dad made it through the surgery, but never completely regained consciousness. During the surgery or shortly after, they discovered he had suffered a heart attack. When they brought him back from the surgery, they had him sedated with propofol, and had him hooked up to a breathing machine.

The doctors told me there was little hope. Since I was his medical power of attorney, I had to decide what to do next, but that decision had been made years before. Dad had told me many times, not to let him be kept alive on machines. He made me promise if something like that ever happened, I would unplug him and leave it up to God. He had even taped his signed DNR (Do not resuscitate) document on his refrigerator door.

They turned off the Propofol and removed his breathing tube at noon, Friday, March 28, 2013. My mother, Dana and I were there when they did it. The doctors couldn't tell us exactly what was going to happen, but they suspected that he would slowly stop breathing and pass away, but he didn't. His vital signs stabilized and for the next four hours, Dana and I sat there in his room, watching my mother holding his hand, crying and talking to him at his bedside.

He appeared to be stable and although my mother didn't really want to go, she was completely exhausted and drained, so we drove her back to her apartment at Grand Court to get some rest.

I had turned off my cell phone at the hospital, so when we got back to Mom's apartment, I turned it on. It was flashing, showing that I had two missed calls from the hospital.

Using my headphones, so Mom wouldn't hear, I called the number and talked to the nurse. "Your father's oxygen levels are falling. It won't be long."

I told my mom they said he was not doing well and asked her if she wanted to go back. I don't think she grasped the severity of what I was saying. She was exhausted, very distraught and I was worried about her as well, so Dana and I left her there and rushed back to the hospital.

I knew my father was probably about to die, but I wasn't sure I wanted to be there when he took his last breath. I had never seen anyone die before and wasn't sure what I was going to do when I got there. When we arrived, he was surrounded by four nurses holding his hands and he was gasping for breath.

When I walked in the room, the nurses gave me a sad, but knowing look and left me alone with him. I took his hand in one of mine and began brushing his soft gray hair with the other. "I'm here Dad. It's going to be alright. Just relax. Remember all the times you told me about heaven? It's your time now Dad, time for you to go and meet Jesus, like you've always said you wanted to do."

His breathing immediately calmed and his racing pulse began to slow. "I'm here with you Dad, so just relax. Don't worry about Mother——I promise I'll take care of her. I hope you know how much I love you. You were such a great father and I want you to know how much I appreciate all the things you've had to sacrifice for me. I know how hard you had to work your whole life, and I know you did it all for Ron and me."

As I cried and talked, his pulse rate began to drop and his breathing slowed. "You were the best father any kid would ever want. You were so amazing. I just hope you know how much you mean to me and how much I love you, and I always will."

Dad died at 7:05 pm. I was still holding his hand and brushing his hair when he took his final breath. I am so glad I was there. It was an indescribable experience I will cherish for the rest of my life.

The saddest moment I've ever experienced in my life so far, was when I walked in my mother's apartment that night and told her that Dad had passed. The pain in her eyes and tears is something I will never forget. They had been in love and together for 70 years...

Two days before my father's funeral, I put my laptop on my knee and started talking to my mother, asking her questions about how she and Dad met. I got her to talk about the 70 years they had spent together. She was a little aggravated with me, thinking that I was being more attentive to my computer than listening to her, but actually I was writing down every word she was saying.

That night, I went to their storeroom, grabbed a hand full of old photographs, drove to Kinko's and had them scanned. With the notes I had typed listening to my mother, and all my memories I had of my father, I recorded my voice telling the story and created a video from the old photographs honoring his life and the 70 year love story he had shared with my mother.

Because most of the people that knew my dad in the later years only knew him after his Alzheimer's, and didn't really know the real Truman, I played the video of his life at the funeral. After the service was over, on our way to the grave site, the preacher walked up to me and said. "Ben, I've been doing funerals for over 30 years and I must tell you that's the first one I ever did that had applause." When the video of Dad's life had ended, everyone in the room started clapping.

Mom and Dad at 15 and 16

Mom and Dad at 75 and 85

STATISTICALLY, when a couple are together as long as my parents were, and one of them dies, it's usually not long that the other one follows. I was worried about my mom, and at first she was in a deep state of depression, but when I told her how mad Dad would be if he saw her acting that way, she came out of it and started playing bingo and cards again. As I write this she's about to have her 90th birthday and doing terrific.

Truman Dean Marney 1928- 2013

For the rest of 2013 we continued performing our Cash show in

community theaters around Florida, but the ships were still not calling. It had been almost two years since our last cruise. I was staying
busy with my voice-over work, but because the community theater
performances were sporadic, Dana started itching to sing more and
had joined the choir at our church.

It wasn't actually a real choir, only five or six singers. After almost
a year singing in the back with the choir, the music minister, Robert
Gaulin, eventually recognized Dana's talent and moved her up front
with the praise team.

The front praise team was only Robert, Dana and two other
women. That eventually dwindled down to just Robert, Dana and
Sharon Fletcher.

Sitting in the audience each Sunday, it didn't take me long to
recognize that Sharon was a really good singer, and the drummer was
obviously a pro and absolutely great.

To help satisfy Dana's desire to sing more and to keep our chops
up, I decided to revise our duo and had picked up some bookings in
the country clubs in Naples, Florida and also the LaCita Country Club
in Titusville. One night when we were rehearsing for an upcoming
duo gig at the LaCita Country Club, Sharon came over for a visit. Just
for fun, I handed Sharon a mic and told her to join in. When she did,
her voice blended with ours perfectly. She had an amazing talent for
finding just the right harmony and it was as if we had performed
together for years.

Sharon had never sung professionally before, so she didn't realize
it, but Dana and I knew instantly that the harmony blend the three of
us had together was something unique. That was the beginning of a
new musical group called Marney Fletcher.

It was about that time that we were booked to perform at a
community theater in Eustis, Florida, but my regular drummer wasn't
available, so I asked the drummer at our church if he would like to do
the Cash show with me there. His name was Pete Sarsano. After that
show, Pete and his wife Regina have become two of our best friends
and Pete has been my drummer ever since.

I wasn't really sure what to do with Marney Fletcher, but it was without a doubt the best vocal harmony group we'd ever put together and I knew I needed to do something with it. So I decided to concentrate on some of the new country music that included group harmonies, like Little Big Town, The Band Perry, Lady Antebellum and the Zac Brown band. We also learned some great classic songs from the Eagles.

Marney Fletcher (Ben-Dana-Sharon-Pete)

With Pete on drums, me on guitar and Dana and Sharon singing, we started performing a few nights at the LaCita Country Club, and the crowd absolutely loved us. We performed there several times including New Year's Eve. We also performed at a few other clubs around Florida and we were always a big hit. Performing with Sharon in Marney Fletcher was the most fun we had had in years.

Dana and I were about to board a plane on our way to Vegas to celebrate our 40th wedding anniversary when the phone finally rang again from the ships. The phone call was from the Don Casino agency, one of the largest cruise ship booking agencies in the world. They wanted to book Cash and Friends on the Princess ship that was based out of the Port of Houston. After a little negotiation, I convinced Princess to allow me to bring Sharon and a musical director with us. With Sharon, we could do Cash and Friends in the theater and Marney Fletcher in one of the larger show lounges. Chuck Perry was booked solid and not available, so for our musical director, I called my old friend from The All American Music Theater, Becca Bongiorno to come out with us. Earlier I told you about how beautiful Becca was, but so far I haven't told you about Sharon. She was not only a great singer, she was also a knockout, an absolutely beautiful blonde. When I boarded the Princess ship in Houston, I was trailing behind three blonde bombshells. I guess I don't have to tell you that the three contracts we did together on that Princess ship were successful. Surrounded by the beauty of Becca, Sharon and Dana, it would have been hard to mess those shows up!

Right before the Princess show (Becca-Dana-Sharon)

After our three Princess contracts with Becca and Sharon, Dana and I were booked to do our Cash show on the Holland America ship, The Rotterdam. But on this ship, for the first time, we were not allowed to bring a musical director with us. It was just going to be Dana and me performing with the ship's orchestra. Since I don't read music, I knew it was going to be a challenge getting through the charts and doing the show without a musical director, but we were meeting that ship in Pepeete, Tahiti, so without any hesitation, I took the gig.

We performed the show the second night of the cruise and surprisingly everything went off smoothly. The audience loved the show and gave us two standing ovations.

We were heading to San Diego from Tahiti, sailing through the Polynesian Islands. The next morning after our show, the ship anchored off the tiny South Pacific island of Rangiroa. There wasn't much there to see. The locals had set up a few tables on the pier selling their handmade shell bracelets and necklaces, and a few were displaying their art. There was a small ocean front restaurant and bar, and in the middle of the island, on the main road to the beach was a tiny grocery store.

Dana always wore dark wigs in the Cash and Friend show for her Patsy and June parts, so off the stage with her blonde hair, she was always incognito and rarely recognized, but with my dyed black Johnny Cash hair, I stuck out like a sore thumb.

We were about 100 yards away from the small grocery store, walking toward the beach, when several of the passengers standing in front of the store started waving and yelling at us.

When we got to the store, the comedian on the ship, Marty Brill ran out and yelled, "Hurry, listen to what's playing in this store."

Dana and I rushed inside the store and playing over the sound system was Johnny Cash, singing Ring Of Fire. What were the odds of me being in the middle of the Pacific ocean on a tiny speck of an island at the very moment that store was playing a Johnny Cash song?

Marty pointed at the speaker in the ceiling, then pointed at me and told the young girl running the cash register, "That's him singing! That's Johnny Cash."

Her eyes widen with excitement. "Really, you're Johnny Cash?"

By that time we had a crowd of passengers surrounding us and they all shook their heads and said, "Yes, he's Johnny Cash!"

The young cashier immediately grabbed a piece of paper and pen and asked for my autograph. I looked around at everybody watching. They were all smiling and laughing, egging me on, so I took the pen and signed Johnny Cash. That made her day. She was very excited, but I've often wondered if she ever figured out that I wasn't the real Johnny Cash.

I've had a lot of interesting experiences like that. On a Princess ship one day after my show, I was walking along the pool deck when an older man stopped me and began telling me how excited he was to actually get to meet me, then went on to tell me about the first time he'd seen me perform. Apparently, Johnny Cash had performed in his hometown and he had seen his show. This guy honestly believed that he was standing there talking to the real Johnny Cash. I wasn't exactly sure what to say, so I just talked to him for a little while, told him that it was great to meet a real Johnny Cash fan, shook his hand and went on about my way. I assume he's still telling everybody he knows about the time he met Johnny Cash.

Four days after our show on that first Holland American ship, the cruise director called. We had been offered a new contract for Holland America on the Statendam, cruising from Tokyo, Japan to Alaska. Two weeks later we were offered a third Holland America contract on another ship. Apparently, they loved our Cash and Friends show, and it looked like we had found a new home with that cruise line.

One of my biggest problems I was dealing with performing on those ships, was keeping up with my voice-over business and my teaching. Because the cruise ships were so profitable, and I was traveling so much, I decided I had to give up coaching voice-over students and resigned from my job with Such A Voice, but that didn't solve my problems with my personal voice-over clients.

We were in the middle of our 16 day Stattendam cruise from Tokyo to Alaska when I received an urgent email from Steven Miller at Super Fine Films. The Discovery Channel had just ordered 28 new episodes of Hillbilly Blood. He wanted to know when I was going to be off the ships and available to do the narration for those episodes.

In the past four years, we had only done 12 episodes a year and I had been able to schedule them around our cruises. In fact, I had already completed the 12 episodes for that year. Since my voice was a major part of that show, he told me I needed to be available for at least the 28 weeks it was going to take to film and produce them, plus a few weeks more for any changes, pickups and corrections.

When I informed Holland America and the Don Casino agency that I wasn't going to be available for over six months, I knew it was going to be devastating for my ship career. In the headliner position on the ships, when you're hot, you're hot and when you're not, you're not. Out of sight means out of mind and you are soon forgotten, but there was nothing I could do, I had no choice. I was under contract with Super Fine Films and the Discovery channel for that show.

It took us over eight months to complete those 28 episodes and it was a good thing I was there all those months, because I also had to do 18 episodes of the other two TV shows on the Sportsman Channel. But as I expected, when I was done, the cruise ships were not calling.

Although I was pretty steady doing radio and television commercial voice-over work a few days a week, and we were doing a few community theater concerts and duo gigs, it was not enough to keep me busy. I am not one to sit idle, so I was going crazy with all the spare time I had on my hands. For several years, Pat Vivier, John Hamman, Dana and I had been talking about doing a Ben Marney and Home Cookin' reunion. It had been seventeen years since we had done our last one. My schedule was wide open and I thought it was about time for another one.

I called Pat and got him searching for a venue in Jackson and he found a great one called Duling Hall. It was May, so we booked a Saturday, August 22nd. Happy to have something to do, I went to work putting together a song list for the show. Then I began to think about maybe writing a few new songs to play for our old fans at the concert.

It had been over 20 years since I'd written a song. I had put all that out of my head the day I moved out of Nashville, but our old fans used to love our original music and I thought it would be fun to surprise them with some new ones. So I put on my song writing thinking cap and after all those years, it still fit.

The best word to describe my writing technique is weird. Whether I'm writing a novel or a song, I can't just sit down and start writing, I have to disappear and go off to some little strange place in my head and let it come to me. In my novels, when I go there, it's like watching a movie and just writing down what I see. I can't explain it, but the book sort of writes itself. New characters I've never thought of before walk in to the story and the plot thickens or changes completely... weird, huh?

When I write a song, it's sort of the same way. I have to be inspired by something and that inspiration usually comes out of nowhere. Once I get the inspiration, I drift off to my little weird place and the lyrics just appear. I think Kris Kristofferson explained it best when he said, "It's like you're just holding the pen and the words come out of nowhere." I had been thinking about writing some new songs for a few days, but so far hadn't found that inspiration.

I called my mom in Lubbock a few times a week, so I called her to see how she was doing. My 65th birthday was coming up and I was kidding with her and said, "You know Ma, if I'd known I was gonna live this long, I would have taken better care of myself."

She laughed. "Well you know what you were doing Benny? You weren't thinking about tomorrow, you were just thinking about today."

I was sitting on my patio with Dana and my friend Chuck Perry and Mom was on the speakerphone. When she said that, I looked over at Chuck, he had caught it too. "Write that down." He yelled. "What an amazing line."

When we hung up that night, I drifted off to my little strange place and found these lyrics.

> *I always thought that tomorrow*
> *was a long long time away.*
> *Lots of years to live*
> *nothing to worry about today.*
> *But here I am, with not much to show*
> *Staring in the mirror*
> *at a face that I don't know.*
> *I wasn't thinking about tomorrow*
> *just worrying about today.*
> *With not one thought about my future*
> *because it seems so far away.*
> *But as I look back*
> *at all those years that slipped away.*
> *I wish I could beg or borrow*

*just a few of those yesterdays.*

That was all it took. Once I started writing again, the floodgates opened. I hadn't written a song in 20 years, but over the next four weeks, seven new ones appeared.

It was twelve weeks until our reunion concert and not really thinking it through, I came up with an idea. Instead of just performing my new songs to our old fans at the concert, I wanted to produce a new Ben Marney and Home Cookin' album.

Dana thought I had lost my mind. "Twelve weeks would be plenty of time to record a new album, if we were in Jackson and could rent a studio for a few weeks like we used to in the old days, but we're in Florida! How are you going to do it with John Hamman and Pat Vivier in Mississippi?"

She also reminded me, that my steel guitar player was in Knoxville and my fiddle player was in Nashville.

I grinned at her and said, "I'm not exactly sure, but I think I know how we can do it." In the old days it would've been impossible, but I believed we could pull it off thanks to modern technology.

For my voice-over work, I had built a state-of-the-art recording studio in my house. I was using a recording software called ProTools and had been reading about how it was being used to do virtual recording sessions. If all my musicians had ProTools as well, it would've been a lot easier, but they didn't. However, I still found a solution.

I e-mailed my musicians all the new songs on an MP3 track with the drums, bass, guitar and a scratch vocal. They recorded their parts on a separate track and e-mailed it back to me. They could easily do this using any recording software they had. All I had to do then was add their parts to my ProTools project and poof... they were playing on the new album. It took me a while to figure it all out, but I eventually got it down. I was amazed at the sound we got out of my little studio, especially the background harmonies with Sharon and Dana, and the fat sound we got from Pete's drums was amazing.

We called our new album, Old Outlaws, because that's what we were. I added three unreleased songs I had recorded in Nashville to my seven new ones to fill up the CD. I honestly think it's the best Ben Marney and Home Cookin' album we've ever cut.

(If you'd like to hear the CD, it's available on iTunes.)

*Ben Marney and Home Cookin' Old Outlaws*

The concert sold out completely and it was an absolute smash. To quote Yogi Berra, "It was like déjà vu all over again."

Just like the old days at Marney's, our old fans were standing in their chairs singing along and having a blast. Of course, I had to joke with them about how old we all were now, warning them about falling and breaking their hips.

I think my favorite line I said that night was, "You know when Dana and I found out about this reunion concert we were very excited. We couldn't wait to show up tonight to sing to all those young cowboys and cowgirls who used to come see us at Marney's wearing those tight jeans and cowboy hats. It's a shame that they couldn't make it tonight, but it's awful nice that their grandparents showed up instead."

I warned Pete and Sharon about the response I thought we would get, but I don't think they believed me until Dana and I walked out on the stage that night and the room exploded. Like I've said before, I'll never truly understand why they love us so much in Jackson, but I'm glad they do.

The reunion show was a huge success and our Old Outlaws CD sold like crazy that night. It's also done well on iTunes.

If you'd like to see a live performance from the Home Cookin' reunion concert search Youtube for:

What Am I Doing Wrong (Live at Dulling Hall)

For almost three months, I had been working around-the-clock, recording and mixing the new album, as well as rehearsing for the show, so when it was all over, I was spent and looking forward to some much-needed downtime. All we had on the books was one night in September at the La Cita Country Club and a Cash and Friends concert at the Wellington Ampitheater in Boca Raton in October. I had planned to go to Lubbock in November to spend the Thanksgiving and Christmas holidays visiting Dana's Dad, her sister, Druscilla, our brother-in-law, Terry and my mom.

But that didn't happen, because the ships called once again. They wanted us to fly to Dubai, then on to the Seychelle Islands to board a Princess ship for 10 days sailing back to Dubai.

Once I accepted that contract, we were back on their radar and from October 2015 to March 2016, Dana and I flew over 50,000 air miles performing our Cash and Friends shows on ten different ships. We traveled to Nicaragua, Cabo San Lucas, Houston, back to Dubai and the Seychelles Islands twice, Cape Town, South Africa, Frankfurt, Germany, Hong Kong, Singapore, Myanmar, Burma, Shanghai, Beijing and Kyoto, Japan.

Also during those six months in between the ship shows, Dana and I performed our Cash show in four community theaters, and our duo act for New Year's Eve in a country club in Naples, Florida. It was an incredibly busy six months.

I know it may sound like an amazing and exciting experience to be able to travel to all of those exotic places and it was, but to be honest, when we got off the last 22 hour flight back from Kyoto, Japan, Dana and I had to admit to each other that kind of traveling was becoming way too much for our old bodies to handle.

When you are a headliner on a ship and fly, you have to have whatever it will take to perform your show in your carry-on luggage. That way if your luggage doesn't make it, you can still perform your show. In our carry-ons we had all the charts for the entire show for seven musicians, that's over two reams of paper, our in-ear monitor system, my wireless guitar system and an emergency show outfit for Dana and a pair of black jeans, a black shirt and boots  for me. I also had to carry on my guitar. Each carry-on bag weighed a ton and with my guitar on my shoulder, we had to pull those bags behind us as we walked for literally miles through those international airports making the connections. As you can imagine, getting through security was a nightmare and once we finally made it onboard the planes, most of the flights were in the 20 hour range.

On one of those trips, (I'm pretty sure it was when we flew into Singapore, making a connection to Shanghai), Dana damaged something in her left shoulder dragging her way-too-heavy carry-on. When we got off the last flight from Japan, her shoulder was killing her. That eventually developed into a frozen shoulder that took surgery and a lot of rehab to repair.

Also, for the first time in my life, my knees began hurting and got progressively worse during those six months having to walk through all those airports and all the stairs on the ships. Unfortunately, the doctors told me that all my years of sports, running and traveling had taken their toll and I needed knee replacement surgery, but I'm gonna put that off as long as I possibly can.

Dana and I had boarded our first ship in 1988, twenty-eight years earlier. And as much as we loved performing on those ships, traveling literally around the world, we had to face the unfortunate truth that we were getting too damn old to do it any longer.

That reality became clear, when after finishing a Princess contract in Houston, we had to immediately fly to Dubai, and after a four hour layover there, fly on to the Seychelle Islands. That trip took 27 hours. The next day we boarded the ship, still completely exhausted with our body clocks turned upside down to discover that we had to perform our show that night. Although the comedian that boarded the ship with us had been in the Seychelle Islands staying at that same hotel for two full days and was completely rested, the cruise director had scheduled us, and there was nothing we could do about it. It was all part of the cruise ship game, dealing with idiot cruise directors. I'm not sure, but I believe if I had been a little younger, it probably wouldn't have mattered as much, but I have to tell you the two shows we did that night were not good.

So, it wasn't just the physical stress, we were also tired of all the increasing bullshit like that we had to deal with. I was way too old and way too grumpy mentally to deal with all the ridiculous politics any longer.

It was not an easy decision, but we knew it was time, so we took our name out of the hat and decided to no longer perform on the ships, even if they called again.

There was another reason I decided to stop singing on the ships. I had just turned 65 when I started writing those new songs for the reunion concert, then we started our marathon of traveling around the world, and it seemed like in the blink of an eye, the year had flown by and I was about to turn 66.

Not to be morbid, but I realized I was running out of time and there were a few things left on my bucket list.

The one part of my talents I had not really pursued fully was my novel writing. Although I had somehow completed my first novel, "Sing Roses For Me" a few years earlier, life had been too busy for me to write a second one.

The problem with writing books, is there's no money in it. The chance of an unknown author writing a bestseller, is similar to the odds of getting a hit record, and as you should know by now from reading this book, those are long odds. Of course, I do dream of writing that best-selling novel and I'm damn sure going to try my best to do it, but that's not my true inspiration to write. I write because I'm good at it and I love it.

Since we weren't singing on ships anymore, I had to come up with another way of earning money to pay my bills. I called my friends at Such A Voice and worked out a deal to teach their students how to set up and run their home studios Monday thru Thursday in the evening via SKYPE. Then I called up my voice-over clients, let them know I was off the ships and available and started doing some auditions to get that business going again. In my free time, I started writing my next novel. I just got my first draft of that novel back from the editor and I'm working on the final draft now. I plan on publishing it soon. I'll let you know when it's out.

When I first started doing the Johnny Cash show and started dying my hair, I was 58 years old. My hair at that time was salt and pepper, with slightly more pepper than salt. I haven't mentioned it before, but having to dye my hair black was something I absolutely despised about that show. Of course, I had to do it, because until the day Johnny died, he never walked on stage without black hair. With my hair dyed black and my dark stage make up, it looked great and helped to emulate his image on stage. The problem was when I was off that stage. I am very light complected and with that dyed black hair in the daytime I resembled a vampire.

I guess it was karma paying me back from the days I used to make fun of all the older guys that would come into the bars with dyed hair, trying to hide their age from the young girls. They didn't fool anybody and looked ridiculous.

I would always laugh and say, "Hey dude, you can't dye the wrinkles."

Now *I* was the old man with all the wrinkles and the fake dyed hair. I just hated it, so the moment I got off that last ship from Japan, I stopped dying my hair and let it go back to its natural color.

In one of my earlier chapters of this book I talked about when I was born my hair was white--not blonde--white. I also told you that until I was five years old, my father's nickname for me was Cotton.

Apparently I am reverting back to my childhood, because once all the dye was cut off my hair...

WELL, if you want to... you can call me Cotton.

# EPILOGUE

Before I wrote this epilogue, I went back and read everything I had written so far to see if I'd left out anything important. The first thing I realized was that I started this book writing short stories and ended up writing rather long ones. I apologize for that, but I have always been a little long-winded.

Writing this book has been an emotional roller coaster for me, because a few things I've lived through still make me angry, but most of it just makes me laugh, even if it wasn't so funny at the time. After reading this book again, I realized that I had left out a few important things. Although, I'd mentioned them in the book several times, I haven't really told you much about Dana's father Sam, her sister Druscilla and our brother-in-law Terry.

I've known Dana's father, Sam Damron, now for almost 45 years. He just turned 92 and although he may look a little older and move a little slower, he hasn't changed one damn bit since the day I met him.

In World War II, Sam served in the United States Navy as a medic, and this past year was honored in Washington DC as one of the few remaining veterans of that war. When Sam got back from the war, he graduated from the University of Texas, became a pharmacist and went to work with his father in their drugstore in Muleshoe. When his beloved Elaine passed away 15 years ago, Sam finally retired and sold the drugstore.

It was about that time that we discovered Sam was suffering from hydrocephalus. Before we discovered it, Sam began to deteriorate, losing some of his memory and wasn't able to take care of himself. So Dana and her sister Druscilla decided to sell Sam's home and put him into Grand Court, an independent living facility in Lubbock. It was a heart wrenching time for all of us, because Sam had always been so full of life and very active. But when his doctors discovered his hydrocephalus, which is excessive fluid on the brain, and put in a shunt to drain that off, it was like someone had flipped a switch. Within two weeks, the old Sam was back.

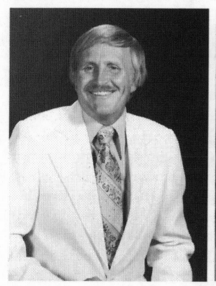

Sam in 1979 and 2016

I tell my friends that Sam is a freak of nature. At 92, he is still a licensed pharmacist and to this day keeps up with his continuing education. Sam is one of the smartest men I've ever known and is still sharp as a tack.

Our only problem with Sam is that he has discovered the Internet, and has found out that there are young girls on there. My brother-in-law, Terry Hutton, who oversees all of Sam's money and investments, has his hands full trying to prevent Sam from buying some young babe a house. There will never be another one like him.

Dana's sister and husband Terry were farmers. While Dana and I were traveling the world living it up, Druscilla and Terry were raising three children in a small farm house in the country, and Terry was busting his ass every day driving a combine or tractor, working long hard hours daylight to dark. All that hard work has paid off, because today they are enjoying the fruits of all those years of labor.

I've always said that the best way to judge someone is to look at their children. Druscilla and Terry are devout Christians and have lived their life as examples to others, especially to their kids. All three of their children, Heather, Holly and Corley are devout Christians, graduated from college, are very successful, happily married and have given Druscilla and Terry ten grandchildren that they are doing their best to spoil rotten.

Because our lives were so completely different, Dana, Druscilla, Terry and I were never really very close. Because we were rarely around, they didn't know us at all, especially me. And because of that, they had developed the wrong impression of us. But in the 15 years since their mom Elaine's death, Dana and Druscilla have grown very close. Terry and I, although he beats me by 20 strokes every time we play golf, have also become good friends. In fact, this past November, Dana and I were lucky enough to be included in their family Thanksgiving feast at their beautiful lake front condo in Horseshoe Bay. Since Dana and I have no children, we always relish the time we get to spend around our nieces and nephews and their ten beautiful kids.

I am also proud to report that my brother Ron's two boys are successful in their lives as well. Tony is a successful businessman in Houston and happily married to Kris, who just received her MBA from Rice University. Ronald, who goes by Ron like his father, is a very successful attorney in Kansas City. He is a full partner in his firm and has a beautiful daughter named Olivia.

I chose the stories I wrote about in this book, because they all affected and changed my life. But the one thing I haven't expounded on that has had the greatest effect on my life, is my wife Dana. I've talked about her many times throughout this book, but I haven't explained who Dana really is. I know you've heard people claim that their wive or husband is their best friend. The facts is, Dana was my best friend before we had our first kiss.

My first wife, Gail, was conniving and selfish. Dana is the exact opposite. She is without question the nicest person I have ever met in my life. If you think I'm just being prejudice because I love her, just ask anyone that knows her and they'll tell you the exact same thing.

Dana doesn't have a selfish bone in her body, has no hidden agendas and has woken up beside me every morning for the last 44 years, smiling with a positive attitude.

It honestly took me years to believe she wasn't putting up some kind of a front. She was just too good to be true. The first year of our marriage, I expected that any day the real Dana, the selfish, conniving, arrogant Dana would appear. This is our 45th year to be together and so far that hasn't happened.

As an adult, Dana has always been stunningly beautiful, but as a child, she was an ugly duckling that developed late. She actually wore braces for nine years of her childhood. Nine years! She was skinny as a rail and didn't start developing curves until her senior year of high school. As a result, Dana didn't get the arrogance that usually comes with beauty.

Throughout our marriage, Dana has always carefully watched her diet and maintained her figure. And although she's in her sixties now, she is still incredibly beautiful and looks closer to forty. If you ask anyone that knows her well, they will tell you that although she's a beautiful woman, her outward beauty isn't even close to how beautiful she is inside.

To her own detriment, Dana too often selfless and giving. She always, always finds the positive side of any situation, no matter how dark it may appear. Her genuine main goal in life has always been to make everyone around her happy. I still fight daily with my character flaws, but I sincerely believe that I am a much better person because of Dana.

Don't get me wrong, we've had our ups and downs like most married couples, but it's impossible to stay mad at someone like her. To tell the truth, the only problems we've ever had between us were caused by my arrogance, insensitivity and stupidity. Dana is so much of a nicer person than me, it took me years to learn how to watch my mouth and not say things that hurt her. It's something I still work on today.

We will be celebrating our 44th year of marriage this August, and when I talk to God, which I try to do every day to thank him for all the blessings he continually bestows upon me, the first thing I always thank him for is blessing me with Dana and allowing me to share my life with her.

Dana at 11 years old

The one thing I haven't included in this book that I'm sure some of you would like to hear, is the romantic story of how I asked her to marry me.

Dana had been performing with me for about six months before we started dating. She had lived through the horror of my divorce from Gail and had become my sounding board and shoulder to lean on. We had become very close friends and honestly I wasn't sure getting involved with her was a good idea, because I didn't want to take a chance on losing that close friendship. She was so damn beautiful and working so close to her every night, I just couldn't help myself.

When we started dating, I made it clear that it was not going to be exclusive. I had just gotten out of a nine year long relationship with Gail and wanted to sow some wild oats. I was single for the first time in my adult life and was going after anything wearing a skirt. Off and on during that time, Dana and I would go out to dinner and get together, but being the insensitive fool I was, I hadn't realized that she was falling for me and that I was falling for her.

On our second booking at the port of Georgetown in Washington DC, the Marriott had rented us a large house in Alexandria, Virginia. It was a huge six bedroom house, so everyone had their own bedroom. One night after our performance, we went to an after hours bar to listen to a rock band.

At that time, we had added another girl to the group, Dana's good friend and sorority sister, Beth Ryan, and as we watched the band play the two of them were going gaga over the musicians. Dana found one especially cute, but for some reason I didn't like that much. I told her I didn't think it would be a good idea for her to date someone like that––a long-haired musician. After their set, of course, the musicians flocked toward our table, because of Beth and Dana, and the one Dana was interested in asked her out. I was not happy about it, but she reminded me that I had insisted that we were not dating exclusively and went out with him anyway.

They went out on a few dates and every time he brought her home, I made a few snide remarks about how I thought she was making a big mistake dating that guy. When I would say that, she would just smile and ask me who 'I' had gone out with that night. Of course, in those days I couldn't remember their names.

It all came to a head one night when I got back home from one of my unforgettable dates and found Dana and the long haired musician sitting on the couch in the living room by the fireplace. I went nuts and started slamming things around in the kitchen and glared at them as I stormed passed, walking to my bedroom.

The guy got the hint quickly and immediately left. Dana tapped on my door and said, "you can relax now, he's gone."

For some stupid reason that infuriated me more. I jerked open my door and told her we needed to talk. She followed me to the living room and took a seat on the couch and I sat in a chair across from her.

Glaring at her I said, "This is not working."

"What's not working?" She asked.

"You and me! Us dating. It was a giant mistake. We should've never gotten together." Speaking from my anger and not my head, I said. "I have to end this, so I'm going to send you back to Muleshoe. It's time for you to go back home. To go back to college and be with your sorority friends."

Her eyes filled with tears and her hands began trembling. "You can't send me back. You can't do that!"

"Oh yes I can, and that's exactly what I'm going to do in the morning."

She was crying hard. "But I love you." She said through her tears. "Please don't make me go home. Don't you understand, I'm in love with you."

Her words hit me like a ton of bricks. I had no idea she felt that way, but being the macho, egomaniac idiot that I was at that time, I didn't back down.

"You love me, really? Sorry Dana, but I'm not a guy to fall in love with. I just can't take this anymore, you're going home tomorrow." I left her crying on the couch, went to my room and closed the door.

It was about 3 o'clock in the morning and no matter how hard I tried, I couldn't fall asleep. I got out of bed, walked outside to the patio, sat down and smoked a cigarette. I sat there until daylight, talking to myself, trying to figure out why it bothered me so much that Dana had dated that musician. I was chasing women like crazy and had no right to tell her who she could go out with. Then why did it bother me so much that she did? I kept asking myself that question over and over. Then like a sledgehammer, it finally hit me. It was because I was in love with her too. What an idiot. How could I not have realized it before.

I waited until I heard noises inside Dana's room, open the door and walked in. She was in the bathroom putting on her make up still crying.

I leaned against the chest of drawers next to the doorway and said, "What are you crying about?"

She turned and looked at me with wide eyes. "What am I crying about, are you kidding? You're sending me back to Muleshoe. That's what I'm crying about!" She yelled.

I grinned, "Oh yeah, that. You can stop crying, I've changed my mind. I'm not sending you anywhere, but I do have one very important question to ask you."

Wiping the tears from her eyes she looked at me. "What question?"

I took her hand and smiled, "Do you want to get married in June

or July?" She screamed and jumped into my arms. We got married
four months later, August 3, 1973.

Our Wedding

I told you in the beginning of this book that I've lived a life that
most people could only dream of. It has been quite a ride. I have had
more than my share of amazing opportunities and have come right to
the edge, but just couldn't seem to cross over and make it to the
big time.

Apparently, being famous and wealthy was not in God's plan for
me, but I certainly have nothing to complain about in my life.

When I was young, I used to think that success was measured by how much money you had and how famous you were, but I was so wrong. Now I know that success is really measured by how many friends you have and how you've lived your life.

To make my point further, I'd like to add some words I didn't write. Supposedly, these words were written by Steve Jobs on his death bed. I'm not absolutely sure it's true, but even if they are not his words, they are profound and worth reading.

〜

*I HAVE REACHED the pinnacle of success in the business world. In others' eyes, my life is an epitome of success. However, aside from work, I have little joy. In the end, wealth is only a fact of life that I am accustomed to.*

*At this moment, lying on the sick bed and recalling my whole life, I realize that all the recognition and wealth that I took so much pride in, have paled and become meaningless in the face of impending death.*

*In the darkness, I look at the green lights from the life supporting machines and hear the humming mechanical sounds, I can feel the breath of God and death drawing closer...*

*Now I know, when we have accumulated sufficient wealth to last our lifetime, we should pursue other matters that are unrelated to wealth... It should be something that is more important: Perhaps relationships, perhaps art, perhaps a dream from younger days. Non-stop pursuing of wealth will only turn a person into a twisted being, just like me. God gave us the senses to let us feel the love in everyone's heart, not the illusions brought about by wealth. The wealth I have won in my life I cannot bring with me. What I can bring is only the memories precipitated by love.*

*That's the true riches which will follow you, accompany you, giving you strength and light to go on. Love can travel a thousand miles. Life has no limit. Go where you want to go. Reach the height you want to reach. It is all in your heart and in your hands. What is the most expensive bed in the world? Sick bed...*

*You can employ someone to drive the car for you, make money for you but you cannot have someone to bear the sickness for you. Material things lost can be found. But there is one thing that can never be found when it is lost – Life.*

*When a person goes into the operating room, he will realize that there is one book that he has yet to finish reading – The Book of Healthy Life. Whichever stage in life we are at right now, with time, we will face the day when the curtain comes down.*

*Treasure Love for your family, love for your spouse, love for your friends. Treat yourself well. Cherish others.*

*Steve Jobs*

MY DAD TOLD me that if I could fill up one of my hands by counting my close friends that I was the lucky man. I must be the luckiest man to have ever lived, because I've run out of fingers counting those close friends.

To be honest with you I'm never going to stop trying to be rich and famous, because I'm gonna do my very best to write one of those bestsellers. I've got about four new novel ideas churning in my brain as I write this.

I'm also going to savor every day I have left, spending time with my friends and family and sharing the next big adventure with my beautiful wife Dana.

So... what is our next big adventure? I have no idea. But I DO know more fiction novels will be part of it. When it comes to my music, I'm getting a bit too old to compete with all these young folks, but I do have an idea or two. What do you think about a new group called "Hot Flash and The Viagra Boys?"

Like I said, I'm not sure what that next big adventure might be, but after I live it, I'll write it down and let you know.

TO BE CONTINUED...

When we first met

Our 44th wedding anniversary

# ABOUT THE AUTHOR

Normally in this section I tell you a little about me and my writing career, but I'm pretty sure you know everything you need to know by now.

Several times in this book I mentioned my first novel, Sing Roses For Me. I love this book. I guess it's because it was my first, but I'm really proud of it and would love for you to read it.

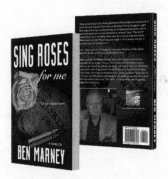

If you would like a FREE copy of *Sing Roses For Me* and a FREE *"color picture"* ebook version of *Lyrics Of My Life* go to:

www.benmarneybooks.com

Made in the USA
Columbia, SC
05 February 2022

55482796R00169